T0305152

Local Resources, Territorial Development and Well-being

Local Resources, Territorial Development and Well-being

Edited by

Jean-Christophe Dissart

Université Grenoble Alpes, France

Natacha Seigneuret

Université Grenoble Alpes, France

Cheltenham, UK • Northampton, MA, USA

© Jean-Christophe Dissart and Natacha Seigneuret 2020

© Cover image: Jean-Philippe Amblard

All rights reserved. No part of this publication may be reproduced, stored in a retrieval system or transmitted in any form or by any means, electronic, mechanical or photocopying, recording, or otherwise without the prior permission of the publisher.

Published by
Edward Elgar Publishing Limited
The Lypiatts
15 Lansdown Road
Cheltenham
Glos GL50 2JA
UK

Edward Elgar Publishing, Inc.
William Pratt House
9 Dewey Court
Northampton
Massachusetts 01060
USA

A catalogue record for this book
is available from the British Library

Library of Congress Control Number: 2019951925

This book is available electronically in the **Elgar**online
Social and Political Science subject collection
DOI 10.4337/9781789908619

ISBN 978 1 78990 860 2 (cased)
ISBN 978 1 78990 861 9 (eBook)

Typeset by Servis Filmsetting Ltd, Stockport, Cheshire

Printed and bound by CPI Group (UK) Ltd, Croydon, CR0 4YY

Contents

PART II MULTIFACETED WELL-BEING

Figures

Tables

Contributors

Coralie Achin has a PhD in territorial sciences and works at the Mountain Ecosystems and Societies Laboratory (Université Grenoble Alpes, INRAE, UR LESSEM), Grenoble, France. She works on issues of tourism diversification in mountain resorts. This work has helped her to characterize the changes in tourism governance at the resorts concerned and to explore the impact that public policy measures related to this issue have on the beneficiary territories.

Karine Basset is an Assistant Professor at the Institute of Urban Planning and Alpine Geography and a member of the Rhône-Alpes Historical Research Laboratory (LARHRA), France. Her research focuses on processes of symbolic construction of contemporary territories and their relations with otherness, time and memory. She studies the heritage making of mountain territories and the utopian dimension of urban and territorial projects. She currently leads a research programme on this subject funded by the National Research Agency (ANR-LabEX ITEM).

Caroline Darroux is an ethnologist, an associate member of the Georges Chevrier Centre at the University of Burgundy and the Scientific Director of the Maison du Patrimoine Oral de Bourgogne, France. Her work concerns contemporary oral narratives and how their dissemination has transformed the social-political context of life in Burgundy's Morvan region and other parts of rural France. She studies collective narratives and the ways in which orality can lead to social emancipation. She develops research/action and research/creation designed to reinforce local capacities.

Cecilia Di Marco studied architecture at the University of Naples Federico II, Italy. She has a PhD in planning and urban design, and her dissertation focused on the urban recycling of contemporary cities through an analysis of waste landscapes. She is currently a post-doctoral researcher at the Grenoble School of Architecture and works on a multidisciplinary project aimed at optimizing health trajectories by understanding and integrating the impact of lifestyle, urban architecture design and the socio-economic environment.

Jean-Christophe Dissart is a Professor at the Université Grenoble Alpes (UGA), France. A former director of the SFR Territoires en Réseaux (Networked Territories), he now heads the Institute of Urban Planning and Alpine Geography, an academic department of the UGA. As a member of the PACTE research centre, he works on local development issues and explores various topics, including quality of life and planning, socio-spatial inequalities, the role of amenities and tourism and applying the capability approach in the context of advanced economies.

Jérôme Gensel is Professor of Computer Science at the Université Grenoble Alpes (UGA), France. His research focuses on spatial and temporal information systems and geomatics against a background of artificial intelligence, knowledge representation and constraint programming. He has supervised 16 PhD and a dozen European and international research projects and authored over 200 publications. He was the director of the CNRS Research Group MAGIS on spatial information and geomatics from 2013 to 2016.

Emmanuelle George is a researcher at the Mountain Ecosystems and Societies Laboratory (Université Grenoble Alpes, INRAE, UR LESSEM), Grenoble, France. She has a PhD in territorial economics. Her research activity includes the governance and evolution trajectories of mountain tourist destinations. By analysing factors of evolution, such as real estate in ski resorts and the implementation of tourism diversification, the goal is to understand ski resorts' modes of governance and to develop the characterization and analysis of resorts' strategies to adapt to climate change.

Pierre Judet is an Associate Lecturer with accreditation to supervise research (HDR) in history at the Université Grenoble Alpes (UGA), France. His work is in the fields of industrial history, mountain societies and the history of the environment. In 2004, he published *Horlogeries et Horlogers du Faucigny (1849–1934)*, Presses Universitaires de Grenoble. In 2016, for his work on alpine metallurgy, he received the 'Techniques, entreprises et société industrielle' history prize awarded by the François-Bourdon Academy and the Arts et Métiers Foundation.

Kirsten Koop is a geographer and an Associate Professor at the Université Grenoble Alpes (UGA), France. She was the director of the 'International Development Studies: Sustainability, Participation, Innovation' master's degree programme at the Institute of Urban Planning and Alpine Geography from 2012 to 2018. Her research focuses on globalization, inequality and local/territorial development theories and models across the North–South divide. She is currently working on transition initiatives and their potential for social and spatial transformation.

Pierre Le Quéau is an Associate Professor of Sociology at the Université Grenoble Alpes (UGA), France and a member of the PACTE Social Sciences Research Centre. He has worked on the study programme to define new indicators of well-being for the Grenoble Metropolis (2010–16), and his research focuses on new forms of solidarity.

Anne Le Roy is an Assistant Professor of Economics at the Université Grenoble Alpes (UGA), France and a member of the Grenoble University's Research Centre for Economics (CREG). As a member of the French Evaluation Society (SFE), she works mainly on evaluating public actions and policies and, more specifically, on the role and place of numbers in analytical practices. She regularly participates in the design, implementation and monitoring of evaluations dedicated to public actions or community activities.

David W. Marcouiller is a Professor of Regional Development Economics at the University of Wisconsin–Madison, USA. He is a resource economist by training, and his work focuses on the linkages between natural resources and community economic development with interests in multifunctional rural landscapes, amenity-driven migration and the compatibility of alternative land uses. He has published over 200 texts in a variety of outlets spanning tourism and forest economics, outdoor recreation planning, regional science, landscape and urban planning and rural development.

David Noël received a master's degree in computer science from the Université Pierre Mendès France (now Université Grenoble Alpes), Grenoble, France in 2013. His PhD, which he defended in June 2019, was funded by France's Auvergne–Rhône Alpes region and deals with the modelling and analysis of life trajectories.

Gilles Novarina is a Professor of Planning at the Université Grenoble Alpes (UGA), France, a researcher at the Centre in Excellence for Architecture, Environment & Building Cultures, School of Architecture of Grenoble and a visiting professor at Politecnico di Torino. A specialist in territorial planning, urban projects and sustainable mobility in Europe, he wrote *Plan et Projet. L'urbanisme en France et en Italie* (2003), *Société Urbaine et Nouvelle Economie* (2010) and co-authored *De la Technopole à la Métropole? L'exemple de Grenoble* (2015) with Natacha Seigneuret.

Fiona Ottaviani is an Assistant Professor of Economics at the Grenoble Ecole de Management (Université Grenoble Alpes, France). She is a member of the Alternative Forms of Markets and Organizations Research Team, the Chair on Economic Peace, Mindfulness and Well-being at Work and the Chair on Inclusive Sustainability: Territorial Ecosystems in

Transition. She works mainly on the conception and implementation of indicators that call into question the goals of 'development' (well-being, sustainability, common good, economic peace).

Benoît Parent is the Director of the *Agence d'Urbanisme de la Région Grenobloise* in France. He has a Master's degree (DESS) in planning, urban planning and local development and is an OPQU urban planner and an IHEDATE 2014 auditor. In addition, he seeks to help elected officials to breathe life into public engineering so that it can be more responsive, efficient and innovative and a recognized ally of tomorrow's territories.

Bernard Pecqueur is an economist, an emeritus professor at the Université Grenoble Alpes (UGA), France and the former president of the French-Speaking Association for Regional Science (ASRDLF). His research focuses on development processes and models in developing countries and is mainly geared towards the study of clusters, industrial districts and territorial development. He recently published *Dynamiques Territoriales et Mutations Économiques: Transition, Intermédiation, Innovation* (2018, co-edited by Fabien Nadou), L'Harmattan.

Jean-François Ruault has a PhD and is a researcher at the Mountain Ecosystems and Societies Laboratory (Université Grenoble Alpes, INRAE, UR LESSEM), Grenoble, France. He is also an associate researcher at the Laboratory City Mobility Transport Mobility (Université Paris-Est). His primary research interests lie in ecological and regional economics, with a focus on regional development disparities, territorial rights and socio-ecological transitions.

Stéphane Sadoux holds planning degrees from the University of Newcastle-upon-Tyne, UK and a PhD in urban and regional planning from the Université Grenoble Alpes in France. He is currently Deputy Director of the Centre of Excellence in Architecture, Environment & Building Cultures (LabEx AE&CC) at the Grenoble School of Architecture. His research concerns planning theory and practice in Britain and, more specifically, master-planned communities and the relationship between health and the urban environment.

Yves Schaeffer has a PhD and is a researcher at the Mountain Ecosystems and Societies Laboratory (Université Grenoble Alpes, INRAE, UR LESSEM), Grenoble, France. He works in the fields of spatial and ecological economics, particularly on topics related to socio-spatial and environmental inequalities, and has published several articles in high-impact journals.

Natacha Seigneuret is an architect, an urban planner and the head of the

Territories federative research structure (SFR Territoires), Université Grenoble Alpes (UGA), France. Her research and professional work primarily focuses on the relationship between territorial planning, architectural and urban projects. She has co-edited two books on these themes: *De la Technopole à la Métropole? L'exemple de Grenoble* (2015), Le Moniteur and *La Construction Métropolitaine* (2016), Berger-Levrault.

Charline Sowa is an Urban Designer and member of the History of Architecture Research Centre (MHAevt) at the Grenoble School of Architecture, France. In 2017, she defended her dissertation, entitled *To Think the Shrinking City: Towards a New Urban Making in the 21st Century*. Her research focuses on the urban project in shrinking cities and on the evolution of practices in architecture and urban planning. At the same time, she works for two architecture and urban planning collectives: CAUE-Allier and OVMH.

Magali Talandier is a Professor of Urban and Regional Studies at the Université Grenoble Alpes (UGA), France. She heads the 'Cities and Territories' team at the PACTE research centre. She studies local economic development and local capabilities to improve the resilience of urban and regional systems.

Rachel Thomas is a sociologist with accreditation to supervise research in architecture and planning. She is a research director at the CNRS, Grenoble, France and member of the Ambiences, Architectures, Urbanities (CRESSON – Ambiances, Architectures, Urbanités) team. She is the coordinator of a research group entitled 'Urban Ambiences, Criticism, Politics', part of whose work is to bring social and political criticism to the field of ambience and pay attention to the societal challenges posed by the changes that frameworks and sensitive forms of urban life are undergoing.

Marlène Villanova-Oliver is an Associate Professor of Computer Science at the Université Grenoble Alpes (UGA), France. She received her PhD in 2002 and accreditation to supervise research in 2018. Since 2017, she has led the Steamer Group at the Grenoble Computer Science Laboratory (LIG), where she carries out research on models, methods and tools to improve spatiotemporal data and knowledge representation, reasoning and visualization in decision support systems with a special emphasis on human cognition.

Foreword: well-being and local resources as the basis for territorial attractiveness

Benoît Parent

The chapters in this book, which presents a state of the art of knowledge about well-being and territorial resources, will stimulate the reader's curiosity by using a transdisciplinary approach.

Well-being. Being well. On the face of it, what could be more subjective, more personal, more immediate? According to the *Oxford English Dictionary*, well-being is the "state of being or doing well in life; happy, healthy, or prosperous condition; moral or physical welfare (of a person or community)". How does such a topic, in connection with territorial resources, relate to an urban planning agency?

The obvious first reason is the purpose of the multidisciplinary studies that the Agency conducts with regard to issues of mobility, housing, environment, health and economy, among others, that are backed by observations and prospective analyses of lifestyles and whose goal is to enhance public policies. These public policies are aimed at improving the living conditions for everyone, reducing economic and social inequalities and ensuring the greater well-being of those who inhabit and use the territory.

Considered from this perspective and provided that it be "objectified", well-being is a central and even the foundational inter-thematic feature of territories in transition, of the renewal of development models and of a metropolitan and territorial dynamic of solidarity. It is tied to the enhancement of its resources and the cooperation of the actors.

It is a common yardstick, as well as a multidimensional and perfectly cross-cutting regulator, that puts the individual at its centre. And it is as much a key to understanding the territory as it is the first criterion of its attractiveness (we know how important it is to choices regarding both residential and economic settlement, just as it is to the creation of socio-spatial inequalities). Along with others, the Urban Planning Agency is particularly justified in making use of it to shed new light on its territory of study: the greater Grenoble, an area rich in its own tangible and intangible resources, which are its common heritage and the cornerstone of its development.

In this work, the diversity of cases shows how the mobilisation of particular local resources can foster sustainable territorial development while improving well-being and social justice. Using this territorial dimension, we can clearly see that both the individualistic dimension of well-being and the classical measurement of development by economic performance alone are overtaken. As a coherent space offering answers to challenges, the territory is also a place of proximity, a space for diagnosis and public debate that makes it possible to elaborate the idea of collective well-being in a shared way and to make it a guide to action. We get to the heart of the matter. To life and societal choices. To political will. To the things to which we attach value. That which cements our living together. That which makes sense and that we have in common: our resources and shared (non-monetary) wealth. Studying and assessing territorial well-being and local resources means being part of a temporal dimension that pre-empts the future and comparing technical expertise with citizen expertise.

The Development Council encourages the greater Grenoble's Territorial Coherence Scheme (SCoT) to take up these issues. The Agency, which plays a pivotal role, is an essential link between the brainstorming partners, by teaming up with the SFR or by mobilising its multidisciplinary scientific council. Since the beginning, it has been involved in Grenoble's IBEST[1] project to reflect on and create participatory approaches that have led to the development of an indicator of sustainable territorial well-being. The goal? To start with individual well-being and develop a shared vision of the common good. With political and technical actors and researchers, this vision builds a case for this indicator to produce a paradigm shift that mobilises local resources to put economies on track towards an ecological and social transition.

Benoît Parent
Director, Agence d'Urbanisme de la Région Grenobloise

[1] IBEST: Indicateurs de Bien-Être Soutenable Territorial (*Sustainable Territorial Well-being Indicators*)

1. Introduction: shifting resources, multifaceted well-being

Jean-Christophe Dissart and Natacha Seigneuret

1.1 THE BOOK: SHORT TAKE

Issues related to well-being and quality of life, as well as the factors that foster them, are central to debates about regional attractiveness and dynamics, residential location choices (from moving to a different neighbourhood within the same city to migrating between regions), firm location, segregation and socio-spatial inequalities.

The view that growth is the sole determinant of quality of life has been challenged so much that analysts now focus on the multidimensional character of well-being, its constitutive components and the methods used to assess it (for comparative or benchmarking purposes; at a single point in time or over time; based on quantitative and qualitative approaches).

Against this background, local resources and amenities (locally specific features that enhance the attractiveness of a given location) are receiving particular attention. From a public policy perspective, their diversity (built or intangible heritage, natural or cultural resources, among others), their generally lasting and systematically local character and their often public use make them especially interesting. Elected officials can seize upon these concepts and adjust local action according to various objectives that range from making living together easier to promoting their district, for example.

This book presents empirical evidence of both the diversity of local resources and the interrelated issues surrounding the concept of well-being. The chapters are based on diverse research settings and methods and have both empirical and theoretical perspectives. Moreover, the chapters pay particular attention to policy recommendations that will help public or collective action on these issues. Furthermore, findings are drawn from cases located in different regions of France, Britain, Germany and the United States of America, which brings an international perspective to the central topic of the book. Lastly, the book uses a multidisciplinary perspective by associating spatial planners, economists, sociologists, architects, historians, geographers and computer scientists, which makes the case for a more comprehensive view of local resources and well-being from a territory perspective.

1.2 POSITIONING WITHIN THE LITERATURE

This book is rooted in multidisciplinary work on the same topic of interest: territories (in short: regions shaped by their relations with sets of actors). Definitions of territories abound – see Paquot (2011) for different perspectives according to various disciplines (geography, ethology, law and urban planning, among others). A simple definition that fits our purpose in this book is the following: a portion of physical space that has been appropriated, not in the sense of legal ownership by an individual or an organisation but because shared history, acknowledged ways of functioning, privileged relations among actors, collective heritage recognised by its residents and so forth make that portion of space specific and different from other territories. As such, it is not necessarily aligned with political or administrative borders. From an empirical perspective, it is a multi-scalar concept and, in France in particular, it ranges from portions of communes (the lowest level of administrative division, totalling over 36 000, more than the rest of the European Union combined) to groupings of communes based on different criteria.

Research on territories has greatly expanded over the past three decades as scholars and practitioners alike have put into question the importance – or even the relevance – of focusing on nation-states in the era of globalisation (Agnew, 2013). Faced with the limits of state sovereignty and national-level austerity budgets, territories have taken centre stage as the adequate level at which an array of social, economic and governance problems could be addressed and potential solutions found.

More specifically, this book focuses on two timely and important topics from a theoretical, empirical and policy perspective: local resources and well-being. There is no lack of publications on these topics, and literature reviews or empirical pieces providing introductions to and overviews of the concepts include work by Blair and Premus (1987), Colletis-Wahl and Pecqueur (2001), Gottlieb (1994), Schaeffer and Dissart (2018) and Wong (1998) on local resources and shifting factors of local development; and Diener and Suh (1997), Dissart and Deller (2000), Romney et al. (1994) and Szalai (1980) on well-being and quality of life.

Basically, these references describe a shift in the processes and objectives of territorial development. Historically, local and regional development was perceived as based on extracting a raw material (e.g. farming produce or iron ore) or transforming it (e.g. canned food or steel) to ship it to a market (typically a city, where demand was concentrated), while trying to minimise costs for the firms involved in the process whose ultimate goal was growth (traditionally in population, employment or income). However, this has changed over the years, with communities shifting from a commodity- to a service-based economy, as illustrated by the famous FIRE (Finance, Insurance, Real Estate) acronym. Also, as growth has not delivered on its promise of happiness for everyone but has been accompanied by rising inequality among households (illustrated spatially for example by gentrification), and its materialistic stance is increasingly at odds with a growing host of environmental issues (e.g. resource depletion or biodiversity loss), there has also been a shift in what should be pursued and how to measure it. This is where well-being or quality-of-life issues come into play, as multidimensional aspects of development are considered.

Therefore, the notion of what constitutes a resource and how it could be used by local stakeholders has evolved, just as the notion of why territorial development is sought and how it should be assessed has changed. As described below in section 1.3, the chapters included in this book explore these changes and shed light on a few examples of such changes.

1.3 STRUCTURE AND CONTENT

In addition to a foreword by Benoît Parent, Director of the Grenoble Regional Planning Agency (*Agence d'Urbanisme de la Région Grenobloise*), this introduction and a general conclusion, the book consists of two parts.

In Part I, 'Diversity of local resources', six chapters address the issue of the contrasting nature of local resources. This means considering resources that are not commonly identified as such: territorial resources in relation to concepts of proximity and urban governance, the ground (in shrinking cities), the past (in tangible and intangible forms in rural areas), outstanding cultural heritage sites (as drivers of community development), the snow (in a changing relation with mountain regions) and energy (from a transition perspective).

More specifically, in Chapter 2, Pecqueur and Koop conduct a critical review of the concept of a territorial resource and its application to the city of Grenoble, France. As the authors explain, the use of the term "resource" in relation to territory not only refers to material resources but also includes immaterial ones (e.g. know-how). They further explain that territorial resources may exist in the actual or potential state and be either generic or specific. The authors discuss the process of revealing and constructing territory-specific resources. They apply it to Grenoble, a medium-sized European city that is clearly part of globalisation as it has developed a strategy of resource specification in the field of technologies (e.g. nano-technologies). Overall, a territory should be seen as the result of a particular form of coordination between various (territorial) actors, whereby specific resources and assets are created out of latent (i.e. not yet revealed) resources. Far from being a static network of actors, territorial coordination is actually a discriminating process that takes place over time, thus providing a method to reconstruct the development paths of territories around the world. Likewise, the case of Grenoble is indicative of the situation of many medium-sized cities in the world economy that are situated below the metropolis in the urban hierarchy and whose position and prosperity are constantly being questioned.

In Chapter 3, Sowa posits that, since the 2000s, research on urban shrinkage has tended to focus on defining the concept, understanding the process and analysing the economic, political and urban strategies that address the situation. Her chapter presents the issue of the urban fabric in the early 21st century by exploring urban remodelling practices in particular and focusing on the ground as a territorial resource. She hypothesises that neglected urban spaces offer fresh perspectives to restructure the city, a reassessment of open spaces in the urban setting and a definition of new ecosystems to improve the urban environment for the remaining population. To test her hypothesis, Sowa analyses two urban projects in Germany – in Halle and Dessau – and a combination of data including urban planning documents and development plans, aerial views of the cities before and after their transformation, photographs and interviews with actors. Two major results are found: on the one hand, abandoned areas should be seen no longer as land reserves but as a territorial resource with a high social and ecological value; on the other hand, we need to think about urban space in its entirety and return to a ground project. In this way, an updated view of the city emerges, as inscribed in multiple urban cycles, having to adapt to the dynamics of both shrinkage and growth, each of which has advantages, potentials, constraints and threats.

Chapter 4 addresses the issue of heritagisation and enhancing resources from the past by focusing on the case of mountain areas. As historians, Basset, Darroux and Judet take account of the dual nature of a territorial resource, that is, as both a symbolic entity and an objectifiable (tangible or intangible) entity that may generate economic value. Drawing on a diverse array of data (oral and written archives, historical monographs, press articles, institutional documents, scholarly speeches etc.), the analysis shows the narratives, the events and the context that enable a reconstitution of the historical trajectory of heritagisation for the two cases at hand: industrial activity (steel cutting) in an urbanised alpine valley (the Arve Valley), and the archaeological and landscape history (Gallic vestiges) of a depopulated rural area in Burgundy (Bibracte/Mount Beuvray). In particular, the authors find a case of "permanent heritagisation" in the Arve Valley, whereas in the case of Bibracte/Mount Beuvray, the question of heritagisation is more open, with tensions surrounding the issue of defining and exploiting the heritage value of the place, drawing an alternative path to considering the local resource as exogenous or a source of enrichment. By using methods based on history and anthropology, the chapter reconstitutes historical paths of heritagisation for the two cases, each of which has its own specificity, to challenge the classical analysis of enhancing the past and, thereby, call into question the economy of enrichment.

The key issue addressed in Chapter 5 is the capacity of outstanding heritage sites to serve as a local resource and drive a territorial development dynamic. Indeed, territories that have remarkable heritage sites are both highly specific (due to the presence of that attraction) and subject to significant regulatory frameworks, including the mandatory protection of their sites. Ruault and Talandier use a mixed methodology approach: quantitative (socio-economic, fiscal and environmental variables to create typologies and evaluate site impacts) for all the sites, and qualitative (survey of local managers and field research) for targeted study sites. The results show that heritage sites can boost the local economy. However, this is not always the case: their positive impact on local jobs, attractiveness and income differs according to the local context. Indeed, a remarkable heritage site entails multiple development constraints but also has huge potential for leveraging cooperation and greater profits usable for site protection. Thus, the findings question the concept of a territorial resource: its mere presence does not ensure local development, and it is necessary to rethink its role as part of a more dynamic model to extend it to the medium to long term so as to accommodate successive interactions between the asset and development. Ultimately, the aim is to turn the territory into a resource for heritage sites and vice versa by striking a balance that benefits both.

Focusing on the case of the French Alps and its ski resorts, Chapter 6 presents how a local resource – snow – has been at the centre of diversification processes over the years. Using the notion of a local resource developed in the 2000s in the field of territorial economics, George and Achin show how the diversification processes succeeded in valorising snow and snow-related resources. Winter sports first exploited the local snow resource before they needed to respond to clienteles' new expectations by widening the range of local resources used. Over time, the environmental and landscape heritage, as well as the cultural (whether agricultural or industrial) heritage linked to the history of the area, have become the local resources to develop. This notion of a local tourism resource has clearly changed over the past few decades and raises corollary questions: at what scale should this diversification be developed, and who should be the actors? Answers to these questions are provided by focusing on the situation of the French Alps and the array of public policies of the Valley Areas (*Espaces Valléens*) conventions. The authors highlight how the diversification processes unfolded, raising questions about the type of activities promoted and the area(s) concerned in a renewed local context and, finally, the leaders of this new tourism.

Since the beginning of the 2000s, in several European cities, territorial planning strategies have included climate change adaptation objectives to bring about an economic, social and ecological transition. In Chapter 7, focusing on energy as a local resource, Novarina and Seigneuret examine the new local strategies of energy transition and the modes of governance that underpin them. The initial comparative analysis of 20 European cities leads them to focus on three cases: Bristol (England), Freiburg im Breisgau (Germany) and Grenoble (France). The in-depth study, based on document analysis and *in situ* investigations, enables them to understand the drivers of urban ecosystems that foster the emergence of social and technological innovations in order to manage energy at the local level. In particular, the analysis shows a process of cooperation aimed at reducing technological uncertainty and increasing the stakeholders' innovation skills, but with local specificities: an integrated and inclusive strategy in Freiburg; an objective-based, pragmatic approach in Bristol; and an incremental strategy, based on demonstration projects, in Grenoble. Overall, the analysis shows that the differences between territorial energy strategies do not stem primarily from a differentiated endowment of resources but rather from the diversity of actors, their degree of mobilisation and the extent to which they share the same vision of the qualities of the territory they inhabit and the potential to transform it.

In Part II, "Multifaceted well-being", the concept of well-being is addressed from multiple perspectives in five chapters that shed light on little-explored topics such as sociabilities vs. income level, accessibility for disabled and able-bodied pedestrians, health via urban design, life course trajectories as indicators of local quality of life, and the connection between amenities and social justice.

In Chapter 8, Le Roy and Ottaviani report on a collaborative project involving professionals and academics to generate local, sustainable and alternative indicators of well-being: the IBEST project. The purpose is to reveal the complexity of the various connections between monetary resources and sociabilities. Even though social relations are a central topic of Grenoble's urban policies and are considered essential to the well-being of the city's inhabitants, they have never before been quantified. To assess the different sociabilities and the role they play in well-being, the IBEST project is based on several principles, including an approach founded on Sen's capabilities. The main data collection instrument is a questionnaire comprising 86 questions. Several variables related to people's actions, aspirations and appreciation of their situation are used to assess relational and institutional sociabilities. The authors show that while monetary wealth does not necessarily go hand in hand with a dense social network and personal satisfaction, it does influence the existence of relationships based on trust and the possibility to reach for help. Therefore, the analysis of social bonds cautions against a simplistic approach to sociabilities and the relationships between monetary and non-monetary resources. The analysis also shows the complexity of the relations between variables included in the notion of well-being, which limits the identification of clear cause-and-effect relationships between interpersonal and institutional sociability.

In Chapter 9, Thomas argues that, over the past 30 years in France, access to urban public space has become a major challenge for city planning and for improving city-dwellers' quality of life. However, the current approach continues to promote a technical approach to accessibility by providing isolated technical devices for disabled individuals. The chapter presents the background and a review of assistive devices to conceptualise those urban public places that have been adapted. Developed from the field of architectural and urban ambience research, which promotes a sensitive approach to the built environment, the critical perspective in Chapter 9 adopts the opposite stance by defending two ideas: first, pedestrian access to the city is the result of a practical and perceptual process of taking root that is constructed during the walk; and secondly, urban accessibility should be conceptualised in terms of the help provided by the city's environment. Drawing on ethnomethodology, urban sociology and *in situ* examples, the chapter introduces the idea of "sensory configuration": visual, bright, sound, tactile and thermal resources afforded by the environment. In so doing, the study casts doubt on the normalisation of design rules and points to a matrix for reading space perceived in motion; it also highlights the practical dimension of situated perception, which goes beyond the mere notion of urban mobility and shapes people's relationships with others.

Chapter 10 focuses on the link between quality of life, as seen through the lenses of public health, and urban planning. In Great Britain, the National Health Service has drawn attention to the impacts of urban and housing design on lifestyles and health, pointing out the promotion of health and well-being through "place-shaping". This context has led Britain to take several actions regarding the environmental determinants of health. Drawing on a cross-disciplinary literature review (mainly planning, architecture and social policy), Sadoux and Di Marco reflect on the return of health to public policy. This chapter also makes use of major government publications to show some of the ways in which health-promotion objectives have been translated into urban policy (the Healthy Towns Programme, 2008; the Healthy New Towns Programme, 2015). The aims and the process underpinning these initiatives are summarised, and a case study of one of the pilot projects (Barton in Oxford) is provided. Although this programme is too recent to be evaluated, Sadoux and Di Marco argue that, regardless of the outcome of the ongoing projects, there is a reuniting of health and planning. They point to the current focus on building strong links at the local level to facilitate the pursuit of these actions once the programmes end. As the selected pilot projects are, if not all, mostly new settlements, the difficulty of retrofitting existing urban areas is also underlined.

The objective of Chapter 11 is to contribute to a finer knowledge of the reasons why households make residential choices whose sequence generates a residential trajectory. Via a study of residential trajectories, it aims to make sense of urban migration processes and to understand the underlying reasons that cause people to move, at what time in their life and to what places: family- and job-related reasons, as well as factors related to leisure or other aspects of people's lives. Describing and understanding migrations is a major tool for urban planning to make more informed decisions regarding housing supply, among others. This multidisciplinary research makes a contribution in terms of methods and tools to observe urban and/or peri-urban migration and understand metropolitan dynamics. The preliminary findings show that this generic approach may be used to model multidimensional life course trajectories since individuals are observed from several perspectives: spatial, temporal and thematic. The other major feature of this approach is its integration of the capacity to explain the reasons behind a given choice. Villanova-Oliver, Noël, Gensel and Le Quéau also argue that this framework, which is rooted in the semantic web, is well equipped from the perspectives of methodology and software, which guarantees its relatively easy implementation. Finally, the authors discuss data collection issues in order to feed data to the model and as a precondition to analyse life course trajectories.

In Chapter 12, Dissart, Marcouiller and Schaeffer define natural amenities as place-based natural attributes that provide local benefits to people or firms. As such, they have often been central to quality-of-life debates over the past few decades. As access to amenities and, thus, to an enhanced quality of life may be unequal among socio-economic groups and across space, this chapter addresses the question of the extent to which natural amenities and social justice are related. First, a theoretical connection is made between the two concepts. Most of the chapter, though, empirically addresses the amenity–justice relation by focusing on two different cases: rural lakefront property in the Lake States (USA), and amenity-driven migration in the metropolitan areas of Marseille and Grenoble (France). In the US case, qualitative experience-based and interview methods triangulated with parcel-level tax information show that the presence of water furthers inequality between long-time residents and relative newcomers. In the French case, a statistical analysis of individual migration data is used in combination with the amenity preferences of household types to demonstrate the heterogeneity of preferences between social groups for different amenities. Therefore, in the US and French cases, natural amenities are associated with economic inequalities, environmental gentrification and socio-spatial segregation processes, that is, social justice issues. These results suggest the need for greater consideration of the connection between amenity and justice in urban and regional plans.

1.4 CONTRIBUTIONS AND GENERAL FINDINGS

In a highly diverse and changing context, the general contributions of this book include the following:

- Bringing together experts from a wide range of social science disciplines: urban and regional planning, economics, sociology, geography, architecture, history and computing science.
- Addressing in a single volume the two concepts of local resources and well-being. Moreover, although other contributions have been published about classic location and growth factors (access to markets, raw materials, etc.), few have addressed the ground or energy as territorial resources. Similarly, other publications have explored quality-of-life issues (objective and subjective measures, etc.), but few have tackled them from the perspective of geomatics, disability or social justice.
- Little research has been published in English about the cases (France, Germany, Great Britain, the USA) presented in this book, all of which feature different contexts and settings. Throughout the book, these international and diverse perspectives broaden the interest beyond local or regional specificities, especially since issues of the

enhancement of local resources and quality of life are not specific to a single country or region but also because the topics addressed across the chapters (sustainable development, stakeholders and governance, regional factors and impacts, culture and heritage, characterisation/identification, ambiences in urban settings, local and regional dynamics etc.) are both cross-cutting and international in nature.

- Putting much-needed emphasis on policy recommendations. Therefore, the primary audience for this book includes researchers, academics, upper-level students and senior public servants. Professionals, practitioners and policymakers involved in the design and implementation of urban and regional development strategies, who wish to get a broader understanding of current local resource and well-being issues, are also likely to find chapters of interest to them.

More specifically, the chapters included in this book invite us to revisit the notions of resources and well-being by addressing two main questions:

1. What makes a resource a resource (what are the factors that qualify as "local resources")?
2. What contributes to well-being (how can we characterise well-being)?

The answer to the first question is basically: time and stakeholders. The answer to the second question varies by chapter to produce a more comprehensive view of well-being. To reassess their significance, let us consider the chapters in the two parts in turn.

In Part I, Pecqueur and Koop show that, over time and with a changing set of actors, the metropolitan area of Grenoble has chosen an evolving path of technology-centred growth. Sowa demonstrates that, as cities grow and shrink, the ground is viewed from different – if not contradictory – perspectives, first as a land reserve for built use, then as an opportunity for (social and environmental) creative use given its "void" property. Basset, Darroux and Judet show the extent to which tangible and intangible entities become part of diverse heritagisation processes, depending on the local contexts and stakeholders. The findings by Ruault and Talandier demonstrate that, even in the presence of unique heritage sites, a territorial development dynamic is not guaranteed but is heavily related to stakeholder cooperation and the medium- to long-term site development vs. protection strategy. George and Achin show how snow, a local resource, has been viewed differently over time, from being key to snow-centred development to being part of a more diversified set of resources, including environmental and landscape heritage with an evolving set of public policies and development stakeholders. Lastly, Novarina and Seigneuret show how energy transition strategies vary more on the basis of the local set of actors and their vision and degree of mobilisation than on the basis of resource endowment.

Therefore, across these chapters, one understands that the notion of a local resource is neither fixed over time nor a given because of its mere presence: it is a set of stakeholders, depending on their level of coordination or proximity, that gives it different meaning, hence potential, for growth and development over time. Also, there is an ever-increasing tendency to consider resources to be in constant interaction with their local (environmental, socio-cultural, economic) context, yielding a dynamic, dependent upon development paths and cycles, character to local resources.

In Part II, the question of what contributes to well-being varies chapter by chapter, but it does expand the range of classic factors associated with well-being. Indeed, well-being or quality of life is usually considered from a multidimensional perspective, along with fostering factors such as income level, health status, satisfaction with one's professional occupation or living in a pollution-free environment. Thus, Le Roy and Ottaviani work on classic indicators associated with well-being, that is, monetary resources and social relations, but address the complexity of their interrelation. Thomas focuses on the urban environment as it affords (visual, sound, tactile etc.) resources that enhance accessibility for different social groups (notably, the disabled). Sadoux and Di Marco also focus on the environment but from a city design and planning perspective to impact people's lifestyles and, consequently, their health. In Chapter 11, the impact of the local environment or quality of place on well-being is indirectly assessed via people's residential choices, which outline life course trajectories over time. Finally, Dissart, Marcouiller and Schaeffer explore the connection between access to the (natural) environment, hence an enhanced quality of life, and social justice.

In this way, the chapters that comprise Part II contribute to expanding the range of factors associated with well-being (various types of environments, institutional and personal sociabilities, accessibility) and to presenting alternative methods to evaluate it, such as hybrid approaches (the IBEST project) or the semantic web (Villanova-Oliver et al.).

Overall, we hope the readers understand that, from a territorial development perspective, the two concepts of resources and well-being are subject to change regarding both identification/characterisation and measurement/assessment. Also, the variety and complementary entries and cases show how the mobilisation of specific local resources can feed sustained territorial development while potentially improving well-being.

REFERENCES

Agnew, J.A. (2013), "Territory, politics, governance", *Territory, Politics, Governance*, **1** (1), 1–4.

Blair, J.P. and Premus, R. (1987), "Major factors in industrial location: A review", *Economic Development Quarterly*, **1** (1), 72–85.

Colletis-Wahl, K. and Pecqueur, B. (2001), "Territories, development and specific resources: What analytical framework?", *Regional Studies*, **35** (5), 449–59.

Diener, E. and Suh, E. (1997), "Measuring quality of life: Economic, social, and subjective indicators", *Social Indicators Research*, **40**, 189–216.

Dissart, J.-C. and Deller, S.C. (2000), "Quality of life in the planning literature", *Journal of Planning Literature*, **15** (1), 135–61.

Gottlieb, P.D. (1994), "Amenities as an economic development tool: Is there enough evidence?", *Economic Development Quarterly*, **8** (3), 270–85.

Paquot, T. (2011), "Qu'est-ce qu'un 'territoire'?", *Vie Sociale*, **2**, 23–32.

Romney, D.M., Brown, R.I. and Fry, P.S. (1994), "Improving the quality of life: Prescriptions for change", *Social Indicators Research*, **33**, 237–72.

Schaeffer, Y. and Dissart, J.-C. (2018), "Natural and environmental amenities: A review of definitions, measures and issues", *Ecological Economics*, **146**, 475–96.

Szalai, A. (1980), "The meaning of comparative research on the quality of life", in Szalai, A. and Andrews, F.M. (eds), *The quality of life: Comparative studies*, London: Sage.

Wong, C. (1998), "Determining factors for local economic development: The perception of practitioners in the northwest and eastern regions of the UK", *Regional Studies*, **32** (8), 707–20.

PART I

Diversity of local resources

2. Territorial resources, proximity economics and new urban dynamics: the case of the city of Grenoble

Bernard Pecqueur and Kirsten Koop

2.1 INTRODUCTION

In the context of globalisation, the urban phenomenon is a type of organisation that currently structures most of the global population. Cities are seen as the spatial concentration of global production and consumption processes and the nodal points of global exchanges. Regional economic studies explain such (economic) concentration processes by analysing the potential effects of economic agglomeration and proximity, as well as their endogenous dynamics. Since the early 1990s, we have witnessed an extraordinary explosion of analytical concepts, including Marshall's revised industrial districts clusters (Becattini 2004), local production systems, innovative networks and "milieu" (Camagni and Capello, 2013), the innovative environment (Aydalot and Keeble, 2018), creative cities (Florida, 2002) and, more recently, smart cities (Kitchin, 2014). These concepts make it possible to focus on innovation and/or the positive externalities of cities or city-regions and are highly useful for urban planning in order to maintain or increase (economic) competitiveness in a globalised world. These concepts, however, do not specifically address the high dependency of cities and regions on the great *nomadic* and transnational firms that continue to dominate the commercial exchanges and, thus, the economic prosperity of cities and regions.

The French school of territorial sciences and, more specifically, the Grenoble school of territorial development,[1] which is still relatively unknown in English-speaking academia, have developed an original approach towards conceiving of an endogenous form of regional develop-

[1] See, among others, Bernardy de Sigoyer and Debarbieux (2003), Colletis et al. (1990), Courlet and Pecqueur (2013), Dissart and Vollet (2011), Gumuchian and Pecqueur (2007) and Judet (1980).

ment. This conception points to ways of lowering the dependency on such nomadic global firms that continually expose cities and regions to excessive competition and the danger that has to be supplanted. First of all, it operates with the concept of "territory" rather than "region". Contrary to its use in the English-speaking academic world, the notion of "territory" has definitively been taken out of its political realm in French social sciences and has been transformed into a holistic concept that equally embraces social, historical, economic and political dimensions, while also replacing the term "region" (Koop, 2014).[2] Territory is considered a "socially produced and appropriated space, to the point where it constitutes, at the same time, an identity referent, a framework for regulations, and an area for public action" (Vanier, 2008). In French regional economy, *territorial development* is understood as the product of coalitions of actors set up to solve unprecedented problems of production, therefore intervening in the constitution of relational local economic processes (Courlet and Pecqueur, 2013). This interpretation leads to a consideration of territory as a complex social construct rather than a surface onto which local action is projected.

This might not yet constitute a major difference with the global spectrum of related concepts, as almost none of them considers the region as a passive receptacle for the globalised economy any more. A more fundamental difference seems to lie in the much more profound conceptualisation of the (possibly) endogenous character of economic development, by focusing on the revelation and construction of *territorial resources*. Again, the use of the term *resource* (in relation to *territory*) needs further explanation for the English-speaking reader. Contrary to the common assumption that the term refers only to natural (or material) resources, it also includes immaterial ones, such as skills and specific know-how. As the following section will show, such territorial resources can already exist or be potential, generic (e.g. mining resources) or specific. It is the process of specifying resources, in the sense of making them so specifically linked to their territory that they are irreproducible elsewhere, that makes it possible to escape international competition (Koop, 2014).

In this chapter, we present and discuss this process of revealing and constructing territory-specific resources/assets and illustrate our purposes through the case of the city of Grenoble. The choice of this city is related to its being a medium-sized European city that is clearly part of the globalisation movement, thanks to its having developed a strategy of resource specification in the field of new technologies (nanotechnologies and

---

[2] For more insight into the differences between the uses of the terms *region* and *territory* among English- and French-speaking academics, see Del Biaggio (2015) and Elden (2010).

semi-conductors). The Grenoble example will be used essentially by way of indicating the numerous medium-sized cities in the world economy that fall below this metropolis in the urban hierarchy and whose position, wealth and prosperity are constantly under stress (Charbonneau et al., 2003). Our methodological approach consists in the theoretical presentation of the territorial specification approach, which has been developed on the basis of numerous empirical case studies in France over the past two decades (Pecqueur, 1999). The Grenoble case study is based on a critical literature review. Section 2.2 presents a typology of site resources and assets and explains the process of creating specific resources and assets. We subsequently present the emergence of specific resources in Grenoble. Section 2.3 discusses the specific characteristics and modes of governance on which such territorial specification processes are based. As in section 2.2, the theoretical consideration is then illustrated by using the Grenoble case study.

2.2 CITIES AND PRODUCTIVE RESOURCES

2.2.1 Externalities, an Insufficient Concept to Analyse the Productivity of Cities

The city is traditionally thought of as a producer of externalities without any real distinction between the different sorts of externalities. In 1966, Remy even spoke of "the large city as an incubator of new products", taking the example of the North American electronics industry. For Remy, "the city is a basic structural condition for ensuring the good organisation and growth of the economic system, both to increase its productive capacity and to maximise the well-being of the end user" (Remy, 1966, p. 117). The question has been addressed in the work of GREMI (*Groupement de Recherche Européen sur les Milieux Innovateurs*), a European research group on innovative environments. Its work focuses on analysing cities as vectors of technological innovation and on the conditions required for this. Reference may be made to a number of its studies that are already well-known, and particularly the publication concerning urban environments and innovation (Crevoisier and Camagni, 2000), where the question of the city as a producer of goods and services is developed through an analysis of the urban expression of the principle of the innovative environment.

Faced with these perspectives, which were new in the 1970s but have received little attention since, the issue that interests us here is that of *the city that produces*. In the beginning, there was the idea of *a city that creates externalities*. These may be seized on by the producers, which are not, a priori, constituent elements of the city, since they exist both in themselves and for themselves but would be the sole beneficiaries since they are the sole producers on the scene of economic activity. This representation is well within what we feel is going to be the process at work from the strict point of view of the production of goods and services. For us, cities produce not only economic value but also more than the total output of all the firms that are located there. Furthermore, cities' interest does not necessarily correspond to that of the firms located there.

The advantage of the city as a form of organisation is its ability to produce *externalities*. Numerous authors agree on this point and on the fact that the word is not precise enough, since it may refer to economies of different sorts (agglomeration, location, urbanisation etc.) More than 50 years ago, Remy (1966) drew attention to the city as an "economic phenomenon" that could not be reduced to a simple juxtaposition of firms and their customers in a dense spatial concentration:

> Therefore, the global utility of the city cannot be completely understood by the simple addition of pre-existing individual demands. (. . .) The city is an economic form whose dimensions are related to the juxtaposition of firms and population. However, any juxtaposition, even one that is relatively marked, does not automatically give rise to this dimensional economy. This only occurs if the spatial concentration generated by a process leads to a certain number of new advantages (p. 6).

For all that, the understanding of externalities remains at the heart of the mystery of urban dynamics. Lacour (1998) makes the same observation in the context of the metropolisation debate in France. For him, the metropolitan issue and the attention paid to the future of the metropolis demand a return to the very foundations of cities and of urban analysis. An examination of these foundations leads us to rethink externalities and agglomeration economies from new perspectives: those of endogenous growth and of the analyses of city/job relations, namely by examining social polarisation and the *spatial mismatch* hypothesis.

In an attempt to identify these urban externalities, we propose to show that the *productive resources of cities* are revealed by the institutional processes specific to each place and to each history. Therefore, it is not sufficient simply to take into consideration the contribution of the factors that the urban system has at its disposal. Consideration must also be given to the hidden resources, particularly those of the cognitive or relational type. Beyond the dilemma between specialisation and activity diversification, we find *specification*, seen as the essential process in the territorialisation of economic dynamics/economic processes (section 2.2). Identifying cities' productive resources is part of the process of *urban governance*.

Governance varies not only from one city to another but also within each city, according to the objects being governed (section 2.3).

It has been shown that recent debate, at least as far as French economic geography is concerned, has abandoned the special approach of the industrial districts for an analysis of the city as a complex productive organisation. The resources (the production inputs of the city) cannot be assimilated with the classical factors of production (raw materials, labour and capital) but result from a specific process in which the institutions, in the sense used by North (1991), play a central role. Thus, the institutional process of resource emergence constitutes a movement of territorial governance peculiar to each site.

2.2.2 The Productive Resources of Cities: are they Given or Constructed?[3]

In the competition between cities, the provision of services for potential firms is crucial. In the most trivial case, a site will attract activity by offering services based on the most abundant factors available: low-cost unskilled labour, natural resources and so on. Often the situation regarding these resources – or their rarity – will condition the type of development that takes place onsite, as can be seen in those areas where development remained dependent on the availability of coal or steel, or even the proximity of the sea or the presence of fertile land.

However, the offer may depend on resources that are not given *a priori* but result either from a long process of know-how accumulation or from the production of collective goods financed by the local authorities and appropriated by the users alone. For example, a supply of qualified and specialised labour would represent part of a site's public offer that incoming firms on the site could benefit from. For each of these types of supply, there is a corresponding strategic approach.

Therefore, the nature of resources differs depending on whether they are *given* or *created*. A typology of resources will help to reveal the strategic issues at stake for cities as service providers. Cities become producers of value and no longer simply areas of consumption or outlets for goods and services, where only the firms are creators of value. To clarify the nature of these resources, a two-fold distinction is used in the proposed typology: on the one hand, between *assets* and *resources*, and on the other hand, between the *generic* and the *specific*.[4]

---

[3] This section discusses concepts and terms that have been developed in articles published in French over the past 10 years. Large parts have been translated from Pecqueur (1999).

[4] This distinction between generic and specific, based on the dichotomy proposed by Williamson, was redefined and finalised in Colletis and Pecqueur (1993).

Resources represent a potential for the territory in that they are not "active". Two distinct cases may be identified to illustrate this point. The first concerns resources that exist but are not exploitable because the costs of exploitation are not compatible with market conditions – at least, for the moment. The second case concerns resources yet to be discovered or organised, that is, those that do not exist as resources at present. This second type of resource may be thought of as "virtual" in that the market would have no reference base or point of comparison for resources that, as it were, do not currently exist.

Assets are factors that are "active", exploited on the market. They may be goods or services. Manpower available on the labour market constitutes a simple example of an asset, in the same way as the presence of facilities or infrastructure.

Resources or assets are said to be *generic* when their presence is independent of the production process or of entrepreneurial and social dynamics. The generic is therefore an exogenous given. A resource or asset is said to be *specific* if it results explicitly from actors' strategies and is allocated for a particular use. Consequently, a specific resource is (socially) constructed. Thus, among the potential site resources that a territory can use to differentiate itself from its neighbour, four cases may be identified, as shown in Table 2.1:

- Quadrant 1: The generic resource is a potential that is both non-exploited and given.
- Quadrant 2: The resource is activated on the market.
- Quadrant 3: The specific asset is constructed or created by the economic actors and given its value by the market.
- Quadrant 4: The specific resource is a revealed advantage resulting from the dynamic combination of actors' strategies. This resource, which until then was virtual, is the result of bringing actors confronted by a new situation or problem into a creative relationship that is not yet marketable.

The situations described in the four quadrants of Table 2.1 are the "polar" situations, meaning that it is rare to find a purely generic or purely specific asset or resource.

The convergence between the strategies of firms and territories is far from automatic. The firm can choose two strategies, depending on the type of assets it prefers:

1. The "low" strategy involves using generic assets. This means the firm determines its geographic location in terms of the classic conditions of

Table 2.1 A typology of site resources and assets

	Generic	Specific
Resources	1 Outside market Exogenous	4 Non-marketable Endogenous
Assets	2 Marketable Exogenous	3 Marketable Endogenous

Source: Colletis and Pecqueur (1993).

location: low production costs (cheap labour, presence of raw materials, available infrastructure etc.) or the abundance of production factors. In this case, the firm commits itself to the territory as little as possible, which enables it to relocate very rapidly, without too many expenses. The form and organisation of the space where it is located are of little importance.[5]

2. The "high" strategy involves the firm in the territory; the space is structured by building up specific assets, which may then provide a basis for developing specific resources. Going from quadrant 2 to quadrant 3, or even quadrant 4, means constructing a proximity network by setting up cooperative arrangements (whether marketable or not) with other actors (firms, financial establishments, research centres or training organisations) and seeking to benefit from relational quasi-rents in a space of geographic proximity.

Faced with these two possibilities, local public institutions responsible for promoting territorial dynamism always strive for asset specification for two reasons. First, the presence of specific assets (presence of specific engineering schools, research laboratories, skilled labour with specific know-how etc.) makes it possible to differentiate the territory and to give it an identity in a context of strong spatial competition. Secondly, the presence of such specific assets acts as a brake on firms' volatility (that is, their propensity to relocate depending on the lowest possible production costs). Thus, specific assets have a "reversibility cost" or a "reassignment cost". This means that the asset would lose part of its productive value

[5] It is this type of strategy that Hoover followed a few years ago by relocating a plant from Dijon to a new site in Cambuslang, Scotland. For the firm, salary costs were 37 per cent higher in Dijon for three reasons: a greater number of supervisory staff (+ 10 per cent), higher wage costs (+ 12 per cent) and the devaluation of the pound sterling (+ 15 per cent).

if it was redeployed for an alternative use. Thus, it is costly for a firm to relocate as it may not immediately find the same specific asset, at the same price, elsewhere. This brake on reversibility becomes accentuated over time if we consider that the firm chronologically improves the quality of its proximity relations (confidence reduces costs).

Finally, it should be observed that the specification of assets may be reinforced by the interplay with specific resources. In other words, the discovery of specific resources may produce a tangible result in the form of creating new specific assets. This is only true, however, in areas where a real industrial cultural identity exists.

Two issues therefore exist in relation to urban territories based on the changes that productive systems undergo. These two issues co-exist and constitute polar arguments. From the territorially least anchored site and one that is the least dedicated to a particular speciality to the localised productive system of the "Silicon Valley" type, there is a whole range of intermediate situations. In a context of strong economic growth, the urban area does not appear as a group of actors, but when growth, experienced as exogenous – a gift from the economic situation or the market – is no longer present, restructuring in the international division of labour reveals the advantage of resource specification strategies.

2.2.3 The Emergence of Specific Resources in Grenoble

The Grenoble urban area may provide an example of the strategies for specific resources and assets constructed by actors described above. Situated in an alpine valley at the confluence of the Isère and Drac rivers, Grenoble is the most important urban area in the Alps today, having experienced a remarkable history of development. From 1850 to the end of the 20th century, its population increased by a factor of 16: from 25 000 to 400 000! It may be considered that the criterion of population growth, in a zone hemmed in by mountains and limited to a form of agriculture that was not very competitive, constitutes a good indicator of economic growth.

Let us try to read Table 2.1 in the light of the history of Grenoble's economic development. The fact that the area is hemmed in by mountains led to the choice of economic activities that could create a strong added value in light materials and would therefore be easier to transport in fairly difficult local conditions. During the 19th century, glove-making met these requirements and thus became an activity adapted to the mountain context of the Grenoble region. In this case, the generic resource (quadrant 1), represented by labour that was both available – outside the periods of intense agricultural activity – and cheap, was able to become a generic asset (quadrant 2).

However, the glove-making industry developed to meet only its own needs without producing know-how that was reusable in other activities. Another event proved to be crucial for the future development of the Grenoble urban area. This was the discovery and exploitation of so-called *white coal* (*houille blanche*) or hydroelectric power. Aristide Bergès, an engineer, saw the great potential for electrical energy locked up in the power of waterfalls, and in 1869 installed the first turbine powered by a high waterfall near Grenoble. The exploitation of hydroelectric power became competitive with other forms of energy in the region and throughout the world in 1883. In the table, we now shift our focus from quadrant 1 to quadrant 2. Water flowing from the mountains is a resource that exists but has not been activated. Its commercial exploitation gives it the status of an asset that remains generic in that it is possible to reproduce this resource identically wherever there is a waterfall. The specification process, which may result in the passage from quadrant 2 to quadrant 3, intervenes as soon as electric power in the Grenoble urban area becomes a reference in France, and its control an objective on which local institutions focus their attention. A number of dates mark significant stages in this development. In 1895, the municipality of Grenoble and the *Université scientifique* offered a municipal course on electricity, thereby sealing a close and quasi-permanent relationship between the university milieu and political institutions.[6] In 1925, an international exhibition on electricity reinforced this heritage of knowledge and know-how about the mastery of electricity. In the 1950s, engineering schools were set up and a state research unit created, following the efforts of Louis Néel, winner of the Nobel Prize in Physics. A form of specificity was established. In the fields of specialised mechanics (Neyrpic turbines) and the control of electricity (high and low voltage with Merlin Gérin), the Grenoble urban area acquired a specificity in the associated technologies that enabled it to accumulate skills. At the beginning of the 1970s, successful negotiations between local actors and state public funding authorities led to the creation of a *Zone of Innovation and Scientific and Technical Research* (ZIRST), which functions to develop hi-tech firms dedicated to prototypes rather than mass production.

This group of achievements has created a form of irreversibility (albeit fragile in the global economic context) where activities are expressed in a local culture in which the principal actors know and recognise each other. We are close to the "industrial atmosphere" that Marshall spoke about with regard to his industrial districts. This culture constitutes an accrued advantage for the area, a non-marketable resource that is active and has

---

[6] This relationship sometimes extended to the army. Some research centres worked for the navy and the air force during the Second World War.

been forged specifically in the Grenoble economic space. It corresponds to quadrant 4, which activates and feeds quadrant 3.

This illustration of the asset specification process (passage from quadrant 2 to quadrant 3) may appear far too positive and therefore epiphenomenal. In reality, the interesting virtuous circle in the case of Grenoble only operates for part of the activity. This part pulls the other activities, as will be seen later, but this does not prevent other branches from participating in this process. The territory is rather like a sieve: some actors belong to the specification path, while others do not. Champ and Rousier (1997) clearly showed that the global dynamics of the Grenoble technological pole concealed strong internal disparities. The growth of a city is not accompanied by a homothetic evolution of each of its constituent parts. Some activities are leaders and pull others along with them when they are in a process of asset specification.

Up to this point, we have dealt with static situations. In the following section, we will explore the question of the genesis of resource transformation. How does territorial identity develop from the identification of the resource? Our analysis adopts the "proximity economics" approach (Torre and Rallet, 2005), which identifies the role of situations of proximity between actors as a way to explain innovation and the performance of territories. In particular, in this *proximity* approach, knowledge of specific resources depends on "coordination mechanisms, which provide support for the agents and which define the conditions of their interdependencies" (Pecqueur and Zimmermann, 2004, p. 29). The next section therefore attempts to explain the process of territory creation as a coordination mechanism giving rise to a special governance that, in the case of the city, cuts across several sectors and several categories of actors.

2.3 TERRITORIAL CONSTRUCTION AND DECONSTRUCTION OF CITIES' ECONOMIES THROUGH URBAN GOVERNANCE

The matrix proposed in Table 2.1 can be used to situate the position of one site in relation to another and to show the state and quality of the resources mobilised at any given moment. At this stage in the discussion, it is important to understand how specific resources emerge. They do not appear spontaneously but result from the work of actors when finding a solution to production problems. The basic assumption rests on the empirical observation of the functional separation on a given site between the interest of the firms and the interest of the various actors on the site.

Territories, when they exist, are therefore in competition with each other, independently of the competition between firms.

Analysis of the constitution of coordination among actors, with a view to realising a territorial competitive advantage, is part of a meso-economic approach aimed at forming groups, which are the territories, following a process of discrimination (section 2.3.1). This process has given rise to models of governance (section 2.3.2), which can be illustrated in the Grenoble context (section 2.3.3).

2.3.1 Meso-economics and the Discrimination of Actors by Groups

In everyday terms, the meso-economic level would fall somewhere between the micro and the macro levels, between the individual and totality (the national productive system). It was seen earlier that the reference space of the local could not be a small intermediate space between the global and the individual point. Similarly, the meso-economic level is not defined simply as the level of coordination of groups of actors, somewhere between inter-individual coordination (micro-economy) and the aggregation of choices in a regulated ensemble (macro-economy). In fact, the group clearly constitutes the type of collective organisation constructed by actors (organisations or networks of organisations) that constitutes the territorial space, but the coordination of groups (internally, among each other, with regard to the global productive system) is not sufficient to determine the meso-economic level. Thus, the groups of actors have already been treated as individuals in a micro-economic perspective respecting the principle of methodological individualism. It is in this way that the theory of clubs developed by the Public Choice School (Sandler and Tschirart, 1980) and the approach of Olson (2009) can be situated. The latter is based on the principle that groups can be treated as persons even if the behaviour of the group may differ from the behaviour (and the interest) of the individuals comprising the group. These approaches are reinforced as the groups are assumed to be homogeneous (trade unions, political parties, firms). In this case, we have to distinguish large groups from small groups. Thus, for Olson, small groups are more efficient than large groups, particularly for benefiting from the externalities produced by collective goods. In our spatial perspective, a territory, when it exists, is composed of a group that is neither large nor small but composite, and whose members may themselves belong to different sub-groups. More recently, the French school of "l'économie des conventions" has also abided by methodological individualism: "the only actors are persons, regardless of whether they are considered members of a collective group or institution or exercise a representative function for a group" (Dupuy, 1989).

The irreducible nature of the micro/macro opposition between methodological individualism and holism excludes the possibility of any intermediate approach assuming some sort of compromise between micro and macro. The meso-economic approach, the objective of which is to coordinate the actors making up groups, is therefore not intermediate between the individual and the totality: it is of a different nature and autonomous with regard to the micro/macro dilemma.

To specify this nature, we propose the following hypothesis: the meso-economic approach deals not with groups as such but with the emergence and (always animated) formation of groups of actors engaged in an economic strategy of production or consumption. Such an approach would differ from pure micro-economics, which deals with the coordination of individuals and accepts the existence of groups as actors having their own strategies instead of one that is unique and distinct for each group. It is also distinct from the macro-economic approach as the latter deals with the flows and the circuit generated by the aggregation of all the actors. The groups may have very different motivations and adopt different processes for grouping together to obtain an advantage that each member would benefit from (pressure group, trade union, firm). Institutional sociology has developed from the idea that individuals' identity strategies help to produce groups. What is striking in empirical observations of the organisation methods of economic institutions is the coalition strategies between different groups around a question relating to production.

So, does the meso-economic approach to economic space involve the analysis of the processes of construction of an "inside" in relation to an "outside"? The territory will result from this process of discrimination. A territory, which may be provisional and incomplete, is the conjunction of abstract common space constructed by groups and a physical space when the latter contributes to the development of the resource that is the foundation of the "inside" in relation to the "outside". The territory thus constituted has a special function of repelling actors who do not come from within these limits. The discrimination process acts as a cognitive filter limiting, as far as possible, the radical uncertainty affecting each individual.[7]

The link between the meso-economic approach and groups has already been identified in an institutionalist perspective (Granovetter, 1994). Granovetter bases his reasoning on the question raised by Coase in his seminal article on the nature of the firm in 1937: why do firms exist? Coase replied to this question by identifying the transaction costs and justifying

[7] On the question of the territory as a cognitive filter and the relations of trust between actors, the literature on "proximity economics" has advanced a number of hypotheses. See, in particular, Pecqueur (1997).

the internal organisation of the firm. The latter is no longer a black box, which raises the question of the role of economic institutions from the market to the hierarchy. In this same perspective, Granovetter asks a second question:

> This question is similar to Coase's, but takes firms rather than individuals as the object of inquiry, asking why it is that in every known capitalist economy, *firms do not conduct business as isolated units* [our emphasis], but rather form cooperative relations with other firms, with legal and social boundaries of variable clarity around such relations (Granovetter, 1994).

This second question relating to the reason for inter-firm cooperative relations shows that there is a need for strategic alliances and, more generally, for cooperation, in so far as there are potential rents to be extracted from the economy. Coalitions in a competitive context do have the virtue of creating relative advantages that make it possible to obtain rents of different types (collective goods produced by public authorities, environmental or landscape amenities, position of oligopoly or even a solution to strategic games that the competitive market does not know how to tackle).

Granovetter then defines the groups of firms referred to in his second question as "business groups". A business group is a long-term association that links very different firms, as well as their owners and managers. According to Stackam, cited by Granovetter, this type of association differs from other forms of groups in three respects:

1. considerable diversity of the firms (not necessarily in the same field or of similar size);
2. pluralism (diversity of actors with different levels of wealth and a different heritage);
3. an atmosphere of loyalty and trust generally associated with relations among members of the same family.

These characteristic groups are clearly reminiscent of Marshall's industrial districts within which social and community links are forged. Such groups are, however, more frequent: they exist in the form of *chaebol* in Korea, *keiretsu* in Japan, *grupos económicos* in Latin America, or *clusters* in Africa and India. We could also add *local production systems*, which in the industrialised economies can be considered extensions of the district model (Courlet and Pecqueur, 2013). The business groups essentially concern groups of firms but maintain relations with other economic actors. The actors of these groups maintain forms of solidarity that are based more on reciprocity than commercial exchanges and integrate relations with other organisations. In particular, Granovetter identifies the relations between the business groups and the banks and the state. The role of the state is important as it provides a structure of authority with respect to the forms of ownership for the firms in the business group and the financial institutions. It appears that the state plays an important coordinating role when the business groups are in strong competition with one another.

2.3.2 From the Discriminating Group to Governance

Analysis of the business groups is clearly linked to the notion of governance, in the sense used by Williamson, and of arbitration by institutional configurations of the groups' sometimes contradictory strategies.

However, this approach remains related to the firms and to interfirm cooperative agreements. The debate that started more than twenty years ago on the spatial implications of economic development (the theory of location revisited by economic geography with its forerunners: Stöhr, Aydalot, Weaver, Becattini etc.) invites us to widen the path opened by Coase's question on the "why" of the firm. The subsequent question from Granovetter concerned the "why" of the evidence of the interfirm and group cooperative agreements that resulted. We propose extending these investigations by asking a third question: on the understanding that these cooperative agreements exist and have already been observed on numerous occasions, what is the purpose of the cooperative agreements between firms and the local institutions at plant sites?

By enlarging the question of cooperation between groups in this way, we go beyond those coalitions that are simply struck with other firms to include combinations of diverse groups in a complex society. The links between institutions of a different type, such as firms and banks or regional authorities, may be treated as group-to-group relations or as the constitution of a much more extensive "ensemble" that discriminates between members and non-members and organises itself according to specific modes of organisation.

In the first perspective, groups identified by their function (firms produce goods and services, local authorities produce collective goods and services, and banks provide monetary and financial services) coordinate their activities using different methods. Institutional economics has clearly shown that coordination through the market under the realistic hypothesis of contractual non-fulfilment, does not always make it possible to save on transaction costs and has therefore identified other methods of coordination, namely hierarchy or quasi-integration. The metaphor of the network is often used to illustrate the method of coordination that is neither on the market, where the agents face each other in a one-to-one relationship, nor a hierarchy where coordination is internalised by the groups. Network analysis nevertheless remains a convenient framework for observation rather than a method, given its essentially descriptive character. The real methodological tool proposed by Williamson (1994) is that of governance.

For Williamson, governance links individual behaviour with the institutional environment. Confrontation with rules and uncertainty implies different methods of coordination. At the root of the demonstration, there are a number of specific assets. The neoclassical analysis is generally based on a type of standardised goods and services between anonymous agents (the personality of the contracting parties is not important). There is, however, "a specificity of assets when a long-term investment (tangible or intangible) has to be undertaken to sustain a particular transaction and when this investment cannot be redeployed on another transaction" (Coriat and Weinstein, 1995). Assets may therefore be dedicated to a particular use. In this respect, the transaction is "situated"; it is neither anonymous nor instantaneous but part of the location in which it takes place. The place becomes an element of the context of the transaction (something that Williamson never specifies).

It seems to us that, in this case, the specific asset is an imposed constraint that distances the firm (taken as an individual) from its economic optimum. We are left with the issue of minimising costs under the constraint of the specificity of assets. The perspective remains the treatment of coordination between groups.

For us, territory may be defined as the social construction of a composite, or even a temporary group, structured around shared resources, and where, in most cases, some of these resources are linked to (or come from) a defined physical space. Since this approach is different, it is necessary to return to the notion of governance as a mechanism of coordination by breaking away from the sole perspective of cost minimisation but keeping the perspective of the creation of a collective advantage for a group, including the beneficiaries of this advantage. In a context of competition between territories (territory taken here as the result of the constitution of a group), the relative advantage for the group may be obtained by proposing an *offer of specificity*. This offer is based on non-reproducible knowledge, which is knowledge that is not likely to exist elsewhere or to be duplicated. Crevoisier (1998) insists on this "particularising" approach that calls into question the assumption of the unicity of the economic process. It is then the capacity of certain territories to distinguish themselves from others that produces a dynamic advantage. Thus, this perspective takes us back to a special approach to governance.

Indeed, the specification of assets places both private and public actors in synergy. Groups with different statuses coordinate with one another, producing varying degrees of clarity and results. Abdelmalki et al. (1996)

remind us of Friedberg's definition of the organisation and affirm that it is suitable for defining territory "as the result of organised action and as an institutional creation". According to them, Friedberg views the organisation as a "mixture of formal devices and emerging structures of a spontaneous or natural character, in the sense of being non-intentional, and of a built character, that is intentional or wanted. The 'organization' phenomenon always incorporates and superimposes nature and culture, constructed or emergent properties, constraint and contract, intention and chance" (p. 185).

As it happens, territorial governance[8] is characterised as the essentially dynamic process aimed at formulating and/or resolving production problems that, in most cases, are original in nature. This process implies the existence of a composite institutional compromise in which the partners are, on the one hand, economic (and socio-scientific) actors and, on the other hand, public actors, whether local or not.

The compromise lies in two concomitant dimensions: the local and the global. This means that the process of territorial governance makes it possible to link actors located not only on the same geographic site but also in the same time; it links the local actors and the global macro-economic levels of the national and even supranational. This point can easily be observed in the case where, for example, regional authorities negotiate subsidies from the European Union (e.g. the LEADER programme) to then help local actors to benefit from them through a feedback effect. Therefore, territorial governance is based simultaneously on a set of local and global compromises linking global productive and institutional forms.

2.3.3 The Case of Grenoble: A Specific Form of Territorial Governance

The Grenoble urban area has been the subject of numerous analyses, given that it represents a success story in the field of high technology and involves original combinations of strategies from different actors (large firms, start-ups, university institutions, research organisations). This success does not concern all the activities of the Grenoble urban area. Other industries that are more traditional but still part of the town's historical culture, such as agri-foodstuffs, have practically disappeared. This clearly illustrates the role of territorial governance that we are seeking to show here. The constructed territories do not necessarily concern all the populations present on the territory's physical base. It is instead necessary to think in terms of the groups of actors linked together around

---

[8] Territorial governance is a subject of reflection in itself that interests economists, geographers and political scientists alike. For a recent summary, see Le Galès (2000).

a shared culture (here, the know-how related to semi-conductors and nanotechnologies, resulting from a long and particular history) and of the common problems to be resolved.

De Robertis (2003) published a comparative analysis of the local systems of Tricase and Prato in Italy and Grenoble in France, based on an exhaustive survey. He identifies the major stages in the structural evolution of these towns since the 1950s. Table 2.2 presents his results for the Grenoble urban area.

Table 2.2 Evolution of the local economic system in Grenoble

	Market	Organisation	Strategy
1950–60s	Development of hydroelectric power, electrochemistry and electrometallurgy.	Large Fordist-type firms.	Adaptation of traditional industry to new technologies available.
1970s	Investment in research and innovation gradually transforms production. Traditional products become less important.	Arrival of multinational firms and public investment in research. Appearance of specialised SMEs.	Further adaptation of structures.
1980s	Traditional products in decline. Two areas of specialisation identified among new and emerging products: information technology and electronics.	Externalisation and increasing specialisation of SMEs. Labour becomes more skilled. Average salaries increase.	Investment in research and innovation gradually transforms production. Traditional products become less important.
1990s	Reduction in production of material goods. Grenoble recognised as technological pole. Large firms and networks of SMEs turn towards exports.	Installation of a spatial system of the “core and ring” type: Multinationals act as a focus for dynamic, efficient SMEs anchored in research activities.	Reduction in public investment (national policy) imposes a search for new solutions to maintain the site’s leadership (MINATEC).

Source: De Robertis (2003).

Let us complete Table 2.2 based on the De Robertis survey, ending at the beginning of the 21st century, with the evolutions that have taken place over the past 20 years. The emergence of nanotechnologies during the 2000s can be considered the most recent bifurcation in the industrial development path of Grenoble. Here again, we can easily observe the specific organisation of productive activities, following the model of the "triple helix" (Leyesdorff and Eztkowitz, 1996), which highlights the relationship between the university, industry and public authorities. From a strategic point of view, the investment in MINATEC, a major firm in the sector of micro- and nanotechnologies, is doubled by the wider ambition of the *Grenoble Innovation for Advanced New Technologies* – GIANT project. This urban project aims not only at fostering technological sciences in the north-eastern part of the city but also at developing the city (and its image) around this site. Its long-term objective is to create 1000 industrial jobs and produce 1000 researchers and 1000 housing units, thus mixing innovative industrial activities and the population (http://www.giant-grenoble.org).

This panorama of the major developments calls for a few comments on the governance process: the described economic activities have a certain unity in that they concern industries that originally developed from hydroelectricity. The territory of new technologies has evolved over time, and it may be observed that a bifurcation has occurred in the types of production, the methods of production and the collective strategies as the territory has adapted to the globalisation movement. The constitution of an "inside" (the Grenoble scientific, industrial and university community) and an "outside" (the international market of semiconductors and nanotechnologies) is clearly, in the Grenoble case, the expression of an asset specification process that strongly distinguishes this community from the rest of the population and, for example, from the traditional branches of activity mentioned above.

For Grenoble, it is possible to speak of a mixed model of governance focused on a mastery of high-technology activities. Here a combination of public and private financing, public research, large private firms and small local firms may be found. The conditions of equilibrium between the public and the private change with time, as seen in Table 2.2, but are based on the construction of local cognitive networks that have developed over the long term.[9] In the preface to the book by Bernardy de Sigoyer and Boisgontier (1988), Professor Louis Néel, who was one of the key

---

[9] A complete analysis of this development will be found in the text by Bernardy de Sigoyer and Boisgontier (1988), which, although not recent, has lost none of its relevance. In fact, recent changes in the urban area only confirm the results of its analyses.

figures in the development of institutions in the Grenoble area, recalls the endogenous character of Grenoble's development. He states that local initiatives have been the basis for numerous innovations, whether at university research centres or in industry, and that the Paris region never set up large industries in the Grenoble area nor opened branches of its research laboratories there, "in the desert".

In short, parallels may be drawn between the dynamic Grenoble urban area and a technological district in the Marshall model through the phenomena of activity discrimination (the shift from hydropower to nanotechnologies via successive bifurcations) and asset specification. There is obviously some divergence in that the former is an urban area and therefore much more complex and varied than an industrial district. "Territorial governance" only applies to the part of the urban activity placed in synergy. It may be comparable to the cluster proposed by Porter (1998), who states: "a cluster is a geographically proximate group of interconnected companies and associated institutions in a particular field, linked by commonalities and complementarities. The geographic scope of a cluster can range from a single city or state to a country or even a group of neighboring countries" (p. 78). The definition may apply to the activity that has developed around the electronics, semiconductor and micro- and nanotechnology industries in the Grenoble urban area.

However, recent difficulties in striking the right balance between technological and urban (social) innovation might indicate the end of the triple helix model as the sole strategy of territorial resource specification. Grenoble maintains its position as the major city for technological research and innovations in Europe, but it also shows some signs of weakness (Besson et al., 2015). The increase in employment in research and development is lower than in a number of comparable French cities, such as Toulouse, Nantes, Rennes, Montpellier, Bordeaux, Lyon, Nice, Lille and Toulon. These towns appear to be catching up to Grenoble, while the latter seems to suffer, with some delay, from the 2008 economic crisis, as is proved by the closing down and demolition of numerous industrial sites inside the city centre. Some cities, such as Nantes, are rather following the path of old industrial towns in England, like Newcastle (Bailey et al., 2004). In fact, the ongoing process of specification of cities in competition brings out new developments based on creativity, rendering the sole articulation between research and industry insufficient. Since the work of Scott (2000) on the Hollywood media industry and Florida's theory of the creative class (2002), the *creative city* has turned out to be a central model of urban innovation, and Grenoble might have missed processes of resource revelation and specification in the cultural domain.

2.4 CONCLUSION

Based on the case study of the city of Grenoble, we have tried to present and discuss the specification process of territorial resources in this chapter. The use of the French conception of territory makes it possible to consider territory as the result of a particular form of coordination between various (territorial) actors. This coordination should be seen as a particular method of creating specific resources and assets out of latent (as yet unrevealed) resources. In the case of Grenoble, the assemblage of industrial, public and university actors aiming at fostering innovation has a long history. This history is marked by the continuous creation of specific territorial resources and assets, which has enabled Grenoble to stay competitive in the national and global urban production processes. Out of the acquired know-how in mastering electricity, which arose from the exploitation of hydroelectric power at the beginning of the 20th century, this coordination process has constantly been able to create a Grenoble-specific "milieu" of knowledge, which turned out to be a specific resource that is not replicable by other cities. The recent (relative) slowdown in the growth of the micro- and nanotechnology sector shows that specific resources will constantly be renewed.

Territorial coordination thus goes beyond analysis in terms of networks in that the discrimination process orients the network thus formed and is based on a long history of the site, which also orients the network. Territorial coordination is not content simply to present examples of governance for which a typology can be drawn up but is a key to analysing ongoing changes in the global regulation of the world economy. Thus, the analysis of the forms of governance linked to the purpose of the groups that make up territories appears as an investigative method that should make it possible to reconstruct the paths of the groups of actors that produce a territory.

REFERENCES

Abdelmalki, L., Dufourt, D., Kirat, T. and Requier-Desjardins, D. (1996), "Technologie, institutions et territoires: le territoire comme création collective et ressource institutionnelle", in Pecqueur, B. (ed.), *Dynamiques territoriales et mutations économiques*, Paris: L'Harmattan, pp. 177–94.

Aydalot, P. and Keeble, D. (2018), "High-technology industry and innovative environments in Europe: an overview", in Aydalot, P. and Keeble, D. (eds), *High technology industry and innovative environments. The European experience*, London: Routledge, pp. 1–21

Bailey, C., Miles, S. and Stark, P. (2004), "Culture led urban regeneration and the revitalisation of identities in Newcastle, Gateshead and the North East of England", *International Journal of Cultural Policy*, **10**, 47–65.

Becattini, G. (2004), *Industrial districts: a new approach to industrial change*, Cheltenham, UK and Northampton, MA, USA: Edward Elgar Publishing.

Bernardy de Sigoyer, M. and Boisgontier, P. (1988), *Grains de technopole: micro-entreprises grenobloises et nouveaux espaces productifs*, Grenoble: Presses Universitaires de Grenoble.

Bernardy de Sigoyer, M. and Debarbieux, B. (2003), *Le territoire en sciences sociales. Approches disciplinaires et pratiques de laboratoire*, Grenoble: Maison des Sciences de l'Homme.

Besson, R., Linossier, R. and Talandier, M. (2015), "De la technopole à l'équilibre métropolitain", in Novarina, G. and Seigneuret, N. (eds), *De la technopole à la métropole? L'exemple de Grenoble*, Paris: Le Moniteur, pp. 27–75.

Camagni, R. and Capello, R. (2013), "Regional innovation patterns and the EU regional policy reform: toward smart innovation policies", *Growth and Change*, **44** (2), 355–89.

Champ, J. and Rousier, N. (1997), "L'économie de la région grenobloise: une dynamique globale de pôle technologique, de fortes disparités spatiales internes [The economy of the Grenoble region: a dynamic technological pole with marked internal spatial disparities]", *Revue de Géographie Alpine*, **85** (4), 37–56.

Charbonneau, F., Lewis, P. and Manzagol, C. (2003), *Villes moyennes et mondialisation: renouvellement de l'analyse et des stratégies*, Montreal: TRAMES, Université de Montréal.

Colletis, G. and Pecqueur, B. (1993), "Intégration des espaces et quasi intégration des firmes: vers de nouvelles rencontres productives?", *Revue d'Économie Régionale et Urbaine*, **3**, 489–508.

Colletis, G., Courlet, C. and Pecqueur, B. (1990), *Les systèmes industriels localisés en Europe*, Grenoble: Institut de Recherche Economique sur la Production et le Développement, Université des Sciences Sociales.

Coriat, B. and Weinstein, O. (1995), *Les nouvelles théories de l'entreprise*, Paris: LGF – Le Livre de Poche.

Courlet, C. and Pecqueur, B. (2013), *L'économie territoriale*, Grenoble: Presses Universitaires de Grenoble.

Crevoisier, O. (1998), "Structures spatiales différenciées de financement des grandes entreprises et des PME regionales", *Revue d'Economie Régionale et Urbaine*, **4**, 625–40.

Crevoisier, O. and Camani, R. (2000), *Les milieux urbains: innovation, systèmes de production et ancrage*, Neuchâtel: EDES and GREMI.

Del Biaggio, C.D. (2015), "Territory beyond the anglophone tradition", in Agnew, J., Mamadouh, V., Secor, A.J. and Sharp, J. (eds), *The Wiley Blackwell companion to political geography*, Chichester: Wiley, pp. 35–47.

De Robertis, S. (2003), *Spazio produzione regolazione: strategie post(?)fordiste nei sistemi locale di Tricase, Prato e Grenoble*, Milan: F. Angeli.

Dissart, J.-C. and Vollet, D. (2011), "Landscapes and territory-specific economic bases", *Land Use Policy*, **28** (3), 563–73.

Dupuy, J.-P. (1989), "Convention et common knowledge", *Revue Economique*, **40** (2), 361–400.

Elden, S. (2010), "Land, terrain, territory", *Progress in Human Geography*, **34** (6), 799–817.

Florida, R. (2002), *The rise of the creative class*, New York: Basic Books.

Granovetter, M. (1994), "Business groups", in Smelser, N.S. and Swedberg, R. (eds), *The handbook of economic sociology*, New York: Princeton University Press and Russell Sage Foundation, pp. 453–75.
Gumuchian, H. and Pecqueur, B. (2007), *La ressource territoriale*, Paris: Ed. Economica.
Judet, P. (1980), *Les nouveaux pays industrialisés*, Paris: Éditions Ouvrières.
Kitchin, R. (2014), "The real-time city? Big data and smarturbanism", *GeoJournal*, **79** (1), 1–14.
Koop, K. (2014), "Conventional or alternative development? Varying meanings and purposes of territorial rural development as a strategy for the Global South", *Geographica Helvetica*, **69**, 271–80.
Lacour, C. (1998), "Un renouveau de l'analyse urbaine", Foreword in Philippe, J., Léo, P.-Y. and Boulianne, L.-M. (eds), *Services et métropoles: formes urbaines et changement économique*, Paris: L'Harmattan.
Le Galès, P. (2000), "Régulation, gouvernance et territoire", in Commailles, J. and Jobert, B. (eds), *Les métamorphoses de la régulation politique*, Paris: LGDJ, pp. 203–40.
Leydesdorff, L. and Etzkowitz, H. (1996), "Emergence of a triple helix of university, industry, government relations", *Science and Public Policy*, **23** (5), 279–86.
North, D.C. (1991), "Institutions", *Journal of Economic Perspectives*, **5** (1), 97–112.
Olson, M. (2009), *The logic of collective action*, Cambridge, MA: Harvard University Press.
Pecqueur, B. (1997), "Processus cognitifs et construction des territoires économiques", in Guilhon, B., Huard, P., Orillard, M. and Zimmermann, J.-B. (eds), *Economie de la connaissance et organisations: entreprises, territoires, réseaux*, Paris: L'Harmattan, pp. 154–76.
Pecqueur, B. (1999), "Les processus de bifurcation de l'activité économique en milieu urbain: le cas de l'agglomération grenobloise", in Fontan, J.-M., Klein, J.-L. and Tremblay, D.-G. (eds), *Entre la métropolisation et le village global*, Quebec: Presse de l'Université du Québec, pp. 125–38.
Pecqueur, B. and Zimmermann, J.-B. (2004), *Économie de proximités*, Paris: Hermès-Lavoisier.
Porter, M.E. (1998), "Clusters and the new economics of competition", *Harvard Business Review*, **76** (6), 77–90.
Remy, J. (1966), *La ville: phénomène économique*, Paris: Les Éditions Ouvrières.
Sandler, T. and Tschirart, J.T. (1980), "The economic theory of clubs, an evaluative survey", *Journal of Economic Literature*, **XVIII**, 1481–521.
Scott, A.J. (2000), *The cultural economy of cities: essays on the geography of image producing industry*, Thousand Oaks, CA: Sage.
Torre, A. and Rallet, A. (2005), "Proximity and localization", *Regional Studies*, **39** (1), 47–59.
Vanier, M. (2008), *Le pouvoir des territoires*, Paris: Economica-Anthropos.
Williamson, O.E. (1994), "Transaction costs economics and organization theory", in Smelser, N.S. and Swedberg, R. (eds), *The handbook of economic sociology*, New York: Princeton University Press and Russell Sage Foundation, pp. 77–107.

3. Reconsidering the ground: new opportunities for shrinking cities. Lessons from the cases of Dessau and Halle

Charline Sowa

3.1 DOES URBAN SHRINKAGE OPEN UP NEW LAND RESOURCES?

Since the second half of the 20th century, many cities have entered a phase of urban shrinkage, which "refers to a concomitant process of demographic and economic decline with a structural impact on two constitutive elements of the city, the density of the population and its economic functions, thus generating considerable social effects" (Cunningham-Sabot et al., 2014). Examples include Liverpool, Manchester, Essen, Leipzig, Pittsburgh, Detroit, Saint-Étienne and Roubaix. Broadly speaking, the events that shaped contemporary society during this period – economic crisis, demographic shift, political transition and conflict, deindustrialisation, suburbanisation, migration and natural or industrial disasters[1] – all had a hand in these changes to the urban dynamics. The subprime mortgage crisis served as another searing reminder, as life dried up overnight in several North American cities. Today, because of the number and range of cities affected, urban shrinkage is regarded as a global phenomenon (Oswalt, 2005).

The rise of these shrinking cities around the globe also led to a great many people taking notice of the frantic urbanisation that has been taking place in our territories for decades. The large-scale consumption of land resources is highlighted by a general state of abandonment, as is the large number and diversity of neglected urban spaces (Figure 3.1),

[1] Many research projects focused on urban shrinkage – which have proliferated around the world since the 2000s and favour a multidisciplinary (geography, urban planning, sociology, political sciences, economics etc.) and collaborative (networks, research programmes, study day, collective works etc.) approach – have shown as much.

Source: Photographs taken by Charline Sowa in the United States and Germany, 2014–15.

Figure 3.1 Series of photographs showing a variety of neglected urban spaces

such as buildings, plots, open spaces, public spaces and infrastructure. They account for between 20 per cent and more than 80 per cent of the urban area in some parts of shrinking cities and represent real social and spatial fractures – conflict and danger zones – in the heart of the city. Photographer Alex MacLean's pictures of Detroit, which show entire neighbourhoods hollowed out because they no longer display any signs of activity, illustrate this situation perfectly. In this particular case, more than a third of the city is currently abandoned, which corresponds, by way of comparison, to the surface area of inner Paris. Moreover, this state of abandonment reveals a kind of sclerosis in the urban space. It is the product, on the one hand, of the landowners' withdrawal and, on the other hand, of the absence of a forecast regarding their future and of their disconnect from the dynamics of urban change (deconstruction/

reconstruction). The only transformational activity that these spaces have undergone is demolitions for "security" purposes, or natural deterioration because they have been abandoned or as a result of natural hazards. This new urban condition has an adverse impact on the image of the city, while neglected urban spaces are often the receptacle for spontaneous renaturation and a diversification of the fauna and flora in urban environments.

Thus, neglected urban spaces raise many questions with regard to their future. While metropolitan areas are facing extremely heavy land pressure because of the lack of available space, what should be done about all these artificial spaces that are underutilised, or even completely abandoned, yet so distinctive in shrinking cities?

If we look at this another way and consider the potential of these neglected spaces, they constitute, because of their footprint and their current state, a significant new land resource in the heart of urban space. Nevertheless, in the face of shrinkage and contemporary socio-economic and ecological issues, this resource invites us to ask ourselves many questions about these possibilities, which we will attempt to answer: what are the opportunities that it offers with respect to contemplating the territory's future? How can these neglected urban spaces be transformed? Is it necessary to retain all these built-up spaces when drafting the urban strategies? Can the ground return to its original state? Is it possible to work towards a de-urbanisation[2] of the territories? These questions also demonstrate the importance of refocusing debates taking place around urban fabric on the issue of the ground, its management, the development of its quality, its status and its uses. This has implications for how these neglected spaces are considered within the transformation of urban space and how the latter adapts to the population's real and future needs. In addition, their spontaneous renaturation invites us to rethink open spaces and the role that plants and other living organisms play in this process of urban change.

It becomes very important for communities to seize neglected spaces for themselves to reconsider how to transform them and, more generally, the territory as a whole. We hypothesise that the land, namely the neglected urban spaces, offers fresh perspectives to restructure the city, a reassessment of open spaces in the urban setting and a definition of new ecosystems to improve the urban environment for the remaining population.

To respond to these questions and test our working hypothesis, we will analyse two urban projects that rely on neglected urban spaces to

---

[2] By "de-urbanisation" we mean the process by which an urban space vanishes as a result of the built-up space and infrastructure being dismantled, concrete removed and ground cleaned up, which leaves room for spaces that are renatured or even completely free from being occupied by man.

reinvent the urban environment. The two cases that were chosen are in Germany and were examined within the context of my doctoral research.[3] Furthermore, they are part of an approach taken by the local community to accept and work with urban shrinkage. The goal of this study will be to understand how neglected urban spaces are integrated into the project process and to identify the type of transformation that they are facing. Then, a comparison between them will make it possible to identify their similarities and differences in order to develop some ideas regarding the consideration and management of the ground and open spaces in redefining cities that are facing the prospect of shrinkage.

For each of these cases, the analytical work uses a combination of different types of data: articles and works that present the creators' and researchers' written projects; available urban planning documents and development plans; aerial views of the city and of some areas before and after they were transformed; photographs taken in the field; observations collected through interviews conducted with actors involved in coming up with the strategy. The first phase of analysis consists of understanding the project's framework and guidelines and the way in which the neglected urban areas have been treated, as well as the tools used to do so. The second phase identifies the specificities of these projects in relation to the type of space produced by the transformations of neglected urban spaces; thus, lessons can be drawn regarding the reassessment of the ground and open spaces in the process of transforming and adapting the urban space. Different tools, including mapping and redrawing, support the analysis to understand the processes of transformation or the analytic photo collage to reveal the state of the urban space after redevelopment.

3.2 A LOOK AT GERMANY

Communities' and different public actors' acceptance of urban shrinkage is a key point in managing the ground differently and in reconsidering neglected urban areas in the development of urban space – as much in how the city is organised as in how its morphology and landscapes are transformed. New territorial strategies have emerged over the past 15 years, as both researchers and communities gained a better understanding of urban shrinkage. Some municipalities have decided, for example, to

[3] My research focuses on the urban fabric at the beginning of the 21st century in shrinking cities by examining the practices of urban reshaping in particular. By studying these practices, I have had to examine the lessons that could be learnt from these experiences in order to imagine the city of tomorrow. This chapter allows for some of the results to be revisited.

rely on identified spaces composed primarily of vacant buildings, parcels of land and abandoned street blocks to reduce the city's density, trim the built-up area and imagine a more compact and "green" city (Baron et al., 2010: 295).

In Europe, Germany is one of the forerunners not only in the development of these new strategies but also in the implementation of architectural, urban and landscape projects in shrinking cities. These kinds of pilot projects were able to see the light of day thanks to a constructive intellectual and political framework that was being assembled. Indeed, in parallel with the advances made in terms of research, different systems were put in place on the local, national and international scales. First of all, the different editions of the *Internationale Bauausstellung* (IBA) provided a favourable framework for architectural, urban and landscape experimentation in several shrinking regions in Germany. In this regard, we should note the *IBA Emscher Park* (1989–99), the *IBA Fürst-Pückler-Land* (2000–10) and the *IBA Urban Redevelopment 2010* (2002–10). Next, the *Stadtumbau Ost* urban restructuring programme, launched in 2002 has helped numerous shrinking East German cities to implement housing policy and urban strategy favouring the restructuring of the city. Finally, the widely publicised *Shrinking cities* international research programme has contributed to identifying the process of urban shrinkage and considering these cities as new areas in which to test innovative ways of living and of thinking about architecture. Indeed, the aim of this programme was to carry out a study on shrinking cities, to catalogue the innovative projects and to propose development strategies for regions from the former East Germany that have been severely affected by shrinkage since the 1990s.

In order to tackle our research topic, we focused our attention more specifically on two initiatives by the municipalities of Dessau and Halle (Saale), both of which are situated in the German state of Saxony-Anhalt. A so-called shrinking region, the state lost close to 1.5 million inhabitants between 1989 and 2000 (Oswalt, 2005: 627). Various factors played a role in this, including the demographic and political transition, deindustrialisation and an exodus to the suburbs and the western part of the country (Zepf et al., 2008: 14).

Beyond being geographically close to each other (40 km), these two cases make it possible to observe two ways of thinking about and working with urban shrinkage by restructuring and resizing the city at different spatial scales and reassessing neglected urban areas. The main goal was to transform neglected built-up areas into open spaces by changing the status of the ground, demolishing buildings, redefining uses and so on. These approaches – both opposing and complementary in the new imagined urban model – were developed during the same period, resulted in strong urban strategies, were defined through urban planning documents and development plans and were put into action on the ground by demolishing buildings and rehabilitating and redeveloping open spaces.

The first strategy that was examined, called the "urban cores-landscape zone", is in Dessau and explores the concept of an *archipelago city*. It has led to the creation of a plan to redevelop the landscape corridor conceived as part of this strategy (*Entwicklungskonzept Landschaftszug*), which will also be of interest. The second strategy analysed forms part of the Halle-Neustadt urban renewal plan (*Stadtumbaukonzept Neustadt*) in Halle-sur-Saale (Figure 3.2) and is based on the concept of a *compact city* to restructure the city and the Neustadt neighbourhood.

3.3 DESSAU, A NEW KIND OF TOWN CENTRE

Thanks to industrial activity (mechanical, gas), the town of Dessau underwent rapid development in the 19th century and became a hot spot for German industry at the time of the GDR. Together with Halle (Saale) and Leipzig, it covers a vast industrial area dubbed the "Middle German Chemical Triangle". The establishment of the Bauhaus School in the 1920s and 1930s also earned it international recognition. Although the school has since been closed, the building has preserved this reputation by serving as the headquarters of the Bauhaus Foundation since the 1990s.

Despite the economic dynamism that has been a feature of the city for decades, Dessau saw two phases of population decrease during the 20th century. Between 1940 and 1945, it lost close to 40 per cent of its population, and more than 80 per cent of its city centre was destroyed (Oswalt and Mittmann, 2010). Since the end of the 1980s, it has faced further demographic decline, with figures dropping from 101 262 inhabitants in 1989 to 78 360 in 2005 – a loss of more than 20 per cent of its population. Even though Dessau's annexation of Roßlau in 2007 contributed to a demographic increase in the city, which totalled 90 707 inhabitants as a result, this act did not stabilise the situation; on the contrary, by 2014 Dessau-Roßlau had only 83 616 inhabitants left (Steglich, 2010).

In the early 2000s, Dessau decided to take action in response to the decline in its population. Its relationship with the Bauhaus Foundation and its participation in the *IBA Urban Redevelopment Saxony-Anhalt 2010*, which was organised by the state of Saxony-Anhalt, enabled the city to make its approach part of a useful reflective framework at the local and regional levels. The IBA, which spans eight years and is organised by the particular state, offered support and guidance to participating communities to explore other ways of considering urban shrinkage in the

Source: Drawing by Charline Sowa.

Figure 3.2 A location map of Dessau-Roßlau and Halle (Saale)

transformation of cities. Thus, in 2001, the municipality, together with the Bauhaus Foundation and the IBA's organising team, defined the guidelines of its new strategy, which it called the "urban cores-landscape zone", within the framework of preparatory workshops at the IBA. The aim of this strategy was to stabilise and strengthen certain urban centres and, in addition, to make the rest of the city less dense in order to offer a new natural and landscaped environment. To a large extent, it was also fuelled by Mathias Ungers and his students' reflections on Berlin as an *archipelago city* in the late 1970s (Oswalt and Mittmann, 2010), which is one of the first project manifestos dealing with shrinking cities.

The reduction of density led to a new kind of city centre, namely the *landscape corridor* (Figure 3.3). The corridor's footprint and path are based on a distribution of the neglected urban areas: often former residential or industrial zones, located in the heart of the city and in flood-prone areas, that could be demolished (Oswalt and Mittmann, 2010).

Sketched out in broad strokes in 2001 within the context of the urban strategy, the landscape corridor was approved in 2003 when its scope was incorporated into the masterplan (*Flächennutzungsplan*). It can be seen in the creation of urban restructuring zones. In 2005, the urban and landscape project defining the corridor was launched as part of a plan conceived by the Station C23 agency. Covering an area of around 90 hectares, this plan coordinates the different demolition and development efforts (open spaces, public spaces. . .) undertaken within the corridor, including those that fall under the IBA: a pedestrian pathway crossing the entire corridor (the *Red Thread* project), as well as cooperative public spaces (the *400m² Dessau* project). The plan simultaneously deals with the reduction of density, the evolution of visual cues and the appropriation of new open spaces by the inhabitants.

The neglected urban spaces were identified as potential resources to make the city less dense and to offer new spatial and landscape qualities by renaturing the ground. In the masterplan, this consideration resulted in a zoning change for the sectors whose density should be reduced: the dense built-up zones were defined as those that had to be turned into spaces with low built-up density and strong green spaces. This signalled significant progress for the community's delivery of the shrinkage project.

In the plan and on the ground, the definition of a corridor spurred a sector change for the ground, the demolition of buildings and partial land consolidation to create a large number of open spaces to replace the neglected urban areas. The latter were converted to parks, recreation and relaxation areas. But for many, the strategic choice was to leave them unchanged after demolition and let them gradually transform into urban prairies covered in herbaceous plants (Figure 3.4). They cover the biggest

Source: Sketch based on documents from the Station C23 agency: Charline Sowa.

Figure 3.3 Urban strategy and scope of the landscape corridor

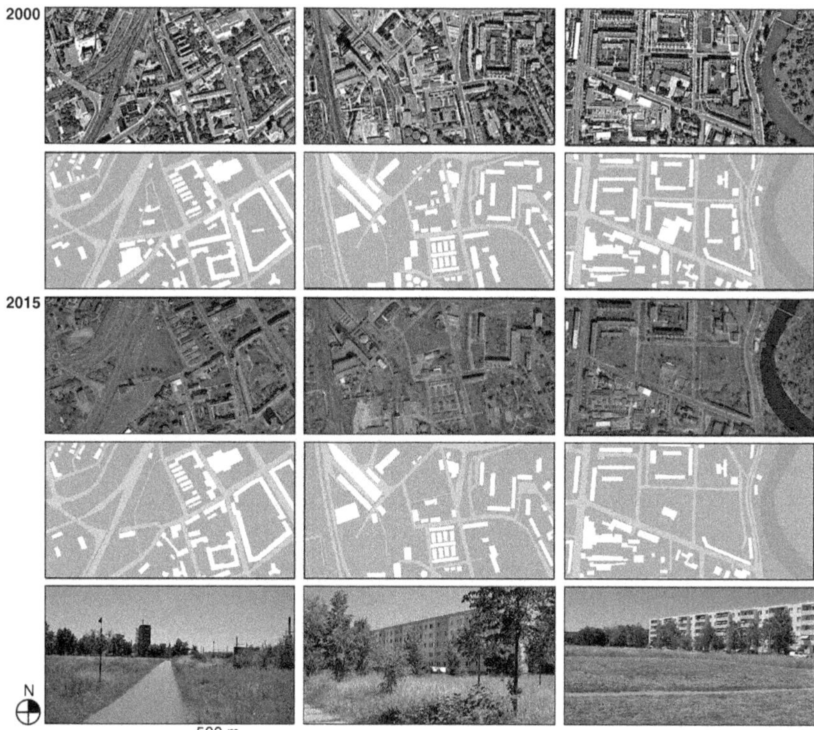

Source: Graphic analysis and photographs: Charline Sowa.

Figure 3.4 Process of reducing density in different sectors of the corridor

plots of land. Thanks to this series of developments, in the centre of the city and close to their homes, the inhabitants now have access to new spaces where they can carry out various outdoor activities which hadn't been possible in these areas before (gardening, walking area, skate park etc.).

Besides being an architectural, urbanistic and landscape response, the corridor, with regard to the way in which it was conceived and projected in the case of Dessau, is also a solution that is "of a technical and scientific nature [in order to] facilitate the circulation of water (to avoid the risk of floods), facilitate the circulation of living species and thus promote biodiversity" (Banzo, 2015). Thus, its implementation contributes to the ecological revival of the ground. It is also a financial solution that reduces the costs of managing and maintaining the urban space. Indeed, most of the developments require little in the way of investment (Wiechmann et al., 2013).

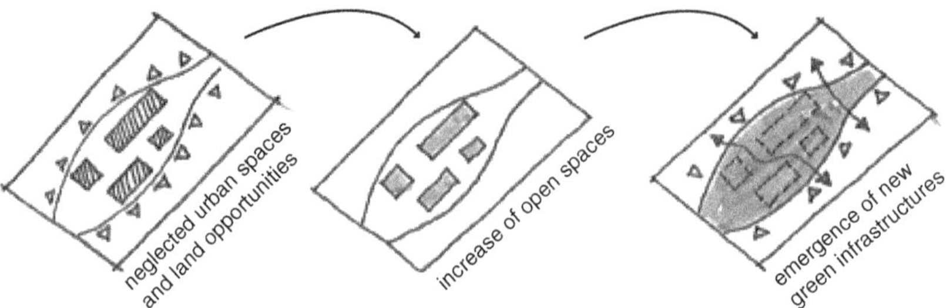

Source: Mapping: Charline Sowa.

Figure 3.5 Creation process of green infrastructure

The analysis reveals that the corridor is not only a system of parks. Rather, it corresponds to a complex "green" infrastructure composed of open spaces with various roles, statuses and uses. It plays a part in the process of reconstructing the urban framework and the existing urban fabric (Figure 3.5). By reconnecting the centre with the river, the corridor is the link between different polarities and between the territories outside the city. It serves as an interface and connection space between two parts of the city – meeting and recreation spots for the residents – and as the belly of the city by offering spaces to grow food to bring the locals together (Sowa, 2017). As a result, the corridor helps to redefine interactions between the social, economic and ecological systems. It is conceived as a new way to catalyse urban life, and thus, the inhabitants' cues regarding the urban environment are also redefined.

3.4 HALLE (SAALE), THE BUILT FOOTPRINT'S LOOSE OUTSKIRTS

Halle (Saale), a former university city that is more than 1200 years old and today has a population close to 233 000 (Oswalt and Mittmann, 2010: 608), forms a conurbation of around 2 million inhabitants with Leipzig. As in Dessau, the territory's urbanisation picked up speed in the second half of the 19th century with the development of the chemical and the steel industry and salt and gas mining operations. After the Second World War, the city grew, with vast collective housing projects (*plattenbau*) on its outskirts, such as the Neustadt neighbourhood, located west of the historical city centre, which had to accommodate more than 100 000 inhabitants.

Along with the city's urban expansion, the population in Halle (Saale) started to shrink in the 1950s, a process that only accelerated in the 1980s, as the population decreased from 290 000 to 230 000 in 1990. Despite the annexation of outlying areas at the beginning of the 1990s, the city continued to shrink, losing close to 25 per cent of its population – or around 80 000 inhabitants – in the space of 15 years (De Gasperin, 2011). In 2003, it was left with more than 30 000 empty homes, or 20 per cent of the housing stock (Fachbereich Stadtentwicklung und -planung und Netzwerk Stadtumbau, 2007).

Even though it was one of the testing areas of the *IBA Urban Redevelopment Saxony-Anhalt 2010*, which raised awareness of the shrinkage, Halle (Saale) only tackled the situation much later. It was thanks to the *Stadtumbau Ost* programme that the city started to change its outlook on the process, the management of vacant buildings and the restructuring of the most neglected and run-down neighbourhoods.[4] Thus, in 2007, the municipality drew up its *Integrated Urban Development Concept 2007–2015* (*Integriertes Stadtentwicklungskonzept*), in which it developed a strategy for urban contraction based on the *compact city* model. This strategy's objective was to facilitate urban management and reduce the housing stock's and the vacant buildings' state of disrepair (and the management problems it causes), as well as the social and spatial isolation of the most vulnerable sections of the population. To do this, demolitions and renaturing actions go some way towards making the outlying neighbourhoods less dense, until some areas are completely empty. At the same time, a choice was made to strengthen the hubs (through rehabilitation, even densification, of the buildings and improvement of the public space). The specificity of this strategy lies in its implementation. The process of urban contraction is conceived on two spatial scales: that of the city and that of the outlying neighbourhoods (Figure 3.6).

Our focus turns more specifically to how the strategy was implemented in Neustadt, which has lost close to 45 per cent of its population since the 1980s (De Gasperin, 2011).

The strategy of urban contraction resulted in an *urban restructuring plan* for the neighbourhood (*Stadtumbaukonzept Neustadt*). As is the case across the city, the plan intends to reduce the neighbourhood's density, starting with its outskirts, by favouring the dismantling of buildings. These sectors mainly comprise vacant buildings, as well as abandoned plots and blocks. In the middle of the neighbourhood, the activities relate to the renovation and modernisation of the buildings and housing (work on the façades: materials, colours, insulation, adding balconies), as well

4 From an interview with Detlef Friedewald and Antti Panian, urban planners for the Halle (Saale) municipality, which was conducted on 6 July 2015.

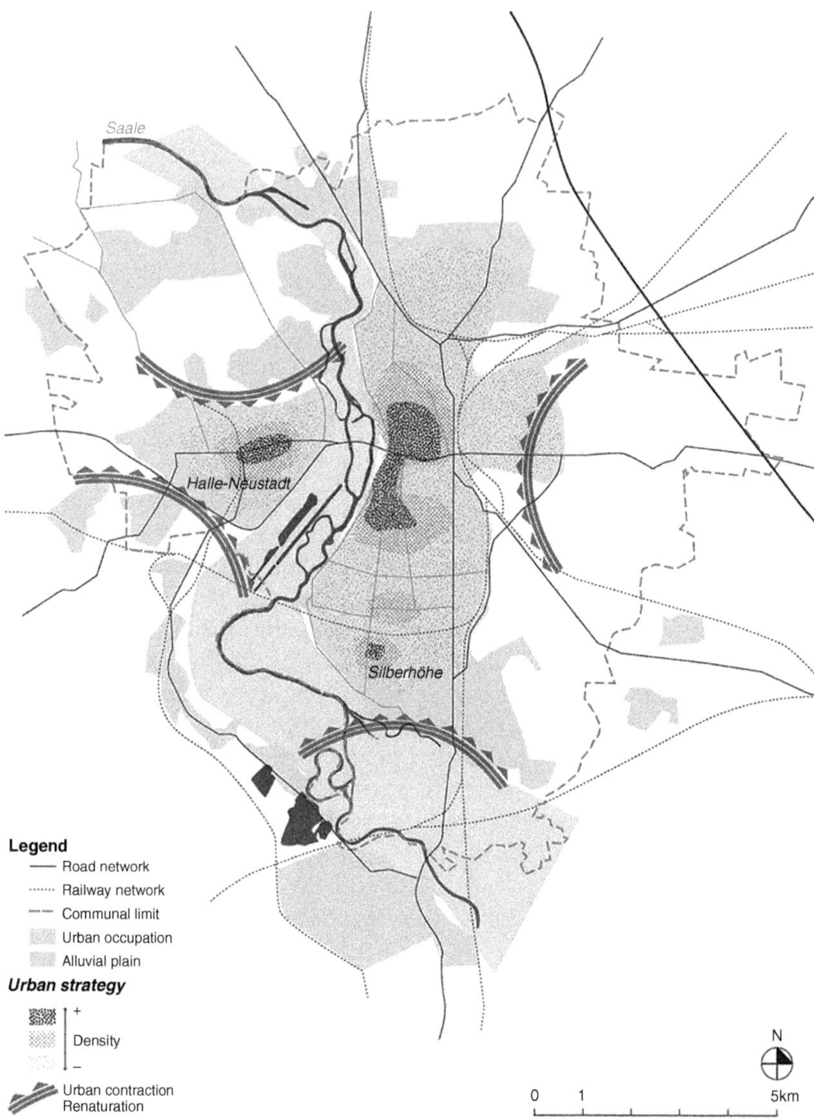

Source: Sketch based on strategic documents obtained from the Municipality: Charline Sowa.

Figure 3.6 Urban strategy followed in Halle

as the renewal of dilapidated buildings through demolition and/or new construction.[5]

Beyond proposing broad strategic guidelines, the zone change of the neighbourhood's different sectors was of paramount importance to the renovation plan. The built-up spaces on the outskirts became areas of strong restructuring and greening (*Umstrukturierungsbereich* / *Ausweitung von Freiflächen*). By creating open spaces where there are no plans to construct new buildings, and which the owners have to manage (landlords, condominiums), the ground is, as it were, liberated: buildings are dismantled, concrete and pollution are removed from the ground, all activities disappear (habitat, trade, leisure etc.).

Nevertheless, the quality to be given to these new open spaces is not clearly defined in the restructuring plan. The plan's implementation suffered from owners' lack of interest in these spaces and the public authorities' inability to invest, in the absence of financing and authority over the land – except for roadworks and some scattered parcels in the area. This situation produced a lack of reflection on and investment in the open spaces – in the plan's guidelines, in the definition of urban and landscape recommendations and in the development of these spaces after demolition.

Thus, a form of *loosening* in the urban space can be observed where these new open spaces appear. Urban discontinuities are formed. The owners are not looking to keep these spaces in the urban fabric by redeveloping them: rather, they seem to be moving towards the natural spaces on the periphery. Indeed, most of the plots were left unchanged and naturally looked like unspoilt prairies and forests (Figure 3.7). In addition, these *loose spaces* are no longer spaces that people pass through. They are generally difficult to access: the emergent vegetation forms a physical barrier and a landscaping closure that defines new boundaries between the spaces. The individual is not invited to conceive of some reappropriation. For example, no adjustments have been made to encourage people to stay and hang out. The city's physical boundaries tend to move towards the city centre thanks to the creation of these forest spaces and prairies.

In the case of Halle, the community's political will to renature certain parts of the city, along with different actors' (voluntary or involuntary) withdrawal from the territory, highlights the possibility of envisaging a gradual and controlled "de-occupation" of the ground and of the urbanised space, in order, on the one hand, to occupy necessary space for the population's real needs and, on the other hand, to recycle the neglected artificial spaces by removing concrete and renaturing them.

[5] From an interview with Detlef Friedewald and Antti Panian, urban planners for the Halle (Saale) municipality, which was conducted on 6 July 2015.

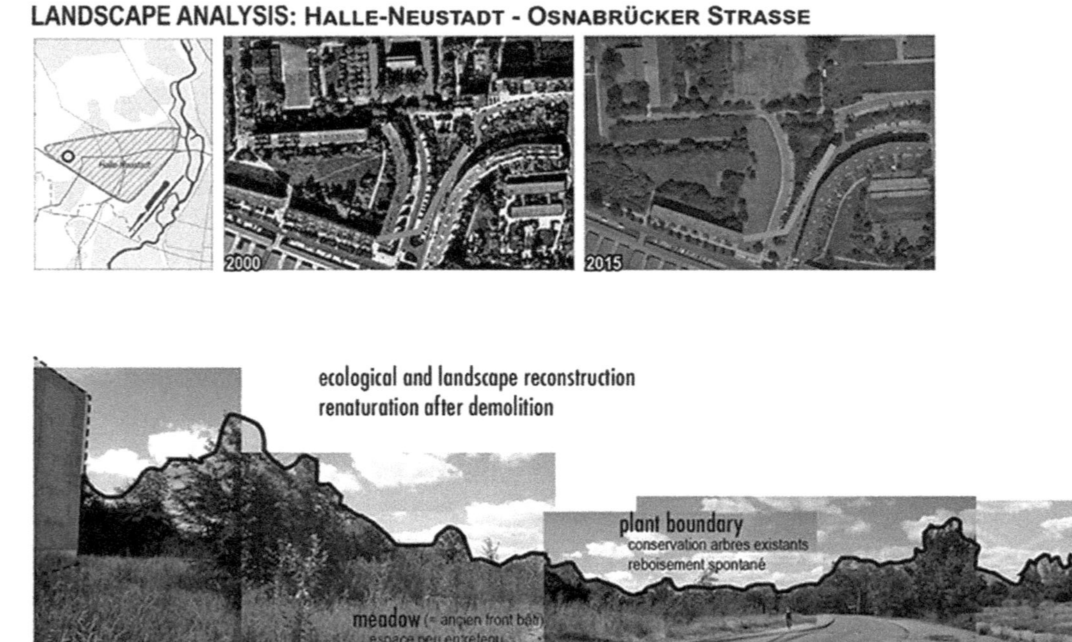

Source: Photo collages: Charline Sowa.

Figure 3.7 Evolution of the uses and of the landscape in different sectors of the Neustadt neighbourhood

But this de-occupation calls into question the identity of these new open spaces: should they still be considered as spaces that "belong" to the city, or are they really incorporating the adjacent natural environment? Can we consider this process a form of de-urbanisation?

3.5 FROM NEGLECTED BUILT-UP SPACE TO OPEN SPACE: RECONSIDERING THE GROUND AS A LEVER FOR ACTION

For both of the cases studied here, it was essential to reassess the neglected areas because of their change in status and use, which transforms them from built-up areas to open spaces in projects examined here. This took place as much on the regulatory level as in the urban planning stages, making real examples out of them in terms of urban shrinkage planning.

Moreover, this change in status and use seems to contribute to the neglected ground no longer being an object of speculation: unlike buildable land reserves, it is not given priority in either the short or the long term. On the contrary, there is a visible kind of disinterest in its market value. Its social and ecological values are primarily the ones that are emphasised. We observe this as much in the management choices as in the development choices, both at the architectural and urban design level and at the regulatory level in the urban planning documents. The cases even offer a glimpse of the possibility of constituting what we have dubbed, within the framework of our research, *ecological reserves* in the urban space. In other words, certain spaces are no longer meant to be rebuilt in order to preserve the ground and meet the current ecological challenges. Indeed, the transformation of empty plots into open spaces and their proliferation are part of the ground's re-permeabilisation and decontamination, better flood control, the construction of ecological corridors, the redefinition of urban ecosystems and the enrichment of biodiversity in an urban setting by promoting a reoccupation of the space by living organisms. In this regard, the case of Dessau is particularly pertinent.

The major difference between these two cases can be found in the manner in which open space is incorporated into urban space. This has had repercussions for the way in which ground is managed in urban reconstruction but also for the type of urban strategies conceived.

In the first case (Dessau), the open space that was created is assimilated into the urban fabric as a new component, structuring how the city is organised (infrastructure). A reduction in density means an increase in the number of open spaces within the existing urban fabric with the goal of bringing new architectural, urban and landscape qualities: new relationships between built-up areas and open spaces; fewer buildings that face other buildings; ventilation and brightness; new visual breakthroughs and urban connections; a weaker built-up footprint on the landscape; access to green, leisure and recreational spaces close to homes, and so on.

The second case (Halle) is comparable to an approach called "amputation": the open spaces are detached from the urban fabric (loosening process) and gradually return to being natural spaces. In this second approach, the de-occupation of the urban space means a tangible decrease in the size of the urban footprint. This is a real paradigm shift in the face of the urban development patterns that can currently be observed around the world.

By contrast, the discussion around de-urbanisation has to be nuanced because, first of all, these spaces are not really considered to be natural spaces in the development plans, even if they tend to look that way on the landscape level. Next, even if they are unoccupied and unmanaged, it is still possible that these open spaces can be redeveloped as leisure or productive spaces for the long term, all while continuing to respond to the urban strategy. For example, one plot has already been tested in Halle: it was transformed into a logging area to produce firewood. Thus, this restoration of neglected spaces to their "initial" state is fragile.

By projecting and changing their status and use, the neglected spaces are reintegrated into a new life cycle and new spatial and temporal dynamics – in other words, into a "*process*, simultaneously open to both the past and the future" (Chesnaux, 2001: 110).

Urban design researcher Brent Ryan,[6] utilising the notion of *patchwork urbanism*, examines this idea of an open process and of how both neglected urban spaces and open spaces can contribute to the spatial configuration. He sees it as a vision of urban change that is necessary today, from the moment that the shrinkage and the deconstruction of certain parts of the city are accepted. Indeed, it offers architects and urban planners the opportunity "to reconsider ideas about housing, neighbourhoods, and urban patterns, and for policy makers to consider new opportunities for placing public development interventions strategically and comprehensively" (Ryan, 2012: 217–18) and to meet the needs of a greater number of people. He defines *patchwork urbanism* as a dynamic process that is "shifting and changing over time as abandonment, demolition, and new development each make their mark" (Ryan, 2012: 214) and in which a diverse array of spaces – built-up and open, inhabited and abandoned – all alternate, intersect and co-exist with each other (Ryan, 2012).

---

[6] His work mainly focuses on the transformation of shrinking cities in North America.

In fact, as the case studies demonstrate, the integration of all the city's states of occupation and vacancy is in its infancy. The project's flexibility is still rare: solutions remain focused on actions with short- and medium-term goals in response to the surplus of buildings and ground and the socio-economic issues. Strategies are not adapted over time on the basis of new data about the territory.

In both cases, the community's lack of land management is one of the main obstacles to this type of approach: from defining the project (programme, use, development) to implementing it, from adapting it over time according to the evolution of needs and demand to managing spaces after changes have been made. This is clear in Halle in the effects of the disengagement of different actors from the implementation of the strategy but also the inability to propose a development and programming project for the created open spaces. In the case of Dessau, the community tried to make up for this lack of land control by proposing an alternative kind of reappropriation of the ground. The IBA team, in collaboration with the municipality and the landowners, defined a parcel system to be superimposed onto the existing one. This new system's plots are 400 m^2 (20 × 20m) and located at the edge of the landscape corridor, close to residential areas (Station C23, 2009). They have no legal status and are delimited by a right of use that is assigned by the owners (private, lessors) to occupy part of their land. They are offered free of charge to any inhabitants who wish to have them (citizen, family, business, youth group etc.) in exchange for developing and maintaining these spaces in order to make the inhabitants responsible for their environment (Wiechmann et al., 2013). In the long term, however, most of the proposed plots were neglected by the users again, and the owners also have the right to prohibit their plot from being occupied.

3.6 CONCLUSION: APPROACHES THAT ARE STILL MARGINAL BUT ISSUE NEW CHALLENGES TO THE URBAN FABRIC IN THE 21ST CENTURY

The two case studies illustrate innovative approaches to conceive of shrinkage and rethink the city. To achieve such evolutions in thinking about urban space and defining new urban strategies, it will be necessary to consider neglected spaces in urban space not as marginal spaces but as real spatial assets. They offer new areas in which to invest, but as the case study showed, unlike in cities that are booming, they are not land resources that need to be built on and made more dense. They are a cornerstone for redefining a less dense urban environment oriented towards qualitative open spaces. Indeed, with their footprint, the neglected areas offer an opportunity to imagine new open spaces in initially dense urban contexts. By becoming open spaces, they are also vectors of a new idea of urban life, of new amenities and new landscapes. Finally, by giving the ground a new status, new uses and new qualities, the neglected spaces have held "the role that, in the past, fell to the garden, in other words, to be a testing ground and focal point for new ideas" (Secchi, 2000 [2011]: 128).

At the scale of the city, this type of approach remains marginal. The tests that can be observed in many shrinking cities in Europe and the United States are mostly carried out on a small scale – a plot or a city block – and are largely focused on an economic revival of the ground in order to meet the needs of basic necessities and resocialisation. We note the development of community gardens and the increasing number of agricultural activities (e.g., vegetable garden, orchard) and (solar, wind) energy projects in previously neglected urban spaces. At present, France has no comparable urban strategies. Activities involving the dismantling of neglected spaces form part of the silent approaches of urban restructuring (Miot and Rousseau, 2017). In the United States, the big strategies that drive the restructuring and resizing of a city (*smart shrinkage*), like those of Youngstown, Detroit and Buffalo, are struggling to be implemented (Beal et al., 2016). The quality that has to be given to open spaces continues to be a secondary concern. This means it is necessary to turn the urban strategy into an urban and landscape project in order to start the real work of urban planning and collaborating with the territory's different actors. It is this aspect, in particular, that makes the difference between the urban development strategies and actions taken in Dessau and Halle (Saale). It is partly for this reason that both researchers and designers involved in shrinking territories in Germany and the United States consider the initiative in Dessau the most successful urban shrinkage project ever undertaken, even though it was carried out more than 10 years ago. A combination of factors contributed to the implementation of such a large-scale strategy. Without these conditions, the feasibility of such a project will be mixed.

It is still difficult to find projects as successful as the one in Dessau, except in theoretical projects led by multidisciplinary teams of architects, urban designers and landscapers. Examples include *The city in the city. Berlin: a green archipelago* (1977), *Decamping Detroit* (Detroit, 1995–96) and *Fiber City 2050* (Tokyo, 2005) projects. These references lay a firm foundation for how to think about urban shrinkage and to use it as an opportunity to reinvent the contemporary city. In particular, they influenced the work of the Stoss agency when it drew up the *Strategic Framework Plan* for Detroit (2012), in both the planning guidelines and the scales of work: from the city to the plot.

In all these cases, this new consideration of the ground highlighted by the two cases reveals, in our opinion, two important elements that have to be incorporated into the management of urban space and the production of the city at the beginning of the 21st century as it faces the current socio-economic and environmental issues.

The first element is the need to consider abandoned areas no longer merely as land reserves but as a territorial resource with a high social and ecological value. The cases that were studied perfectly illustrate this change of positioning with regard to the ground and its management. This is as much an issue of the waning speculative value of the ground and the acts of demolition as it is of the creation of leisure and meeting spaces and ecological reserves. This suggests new opportunities in the way that future urban development is to be conceived.

The second is the need to apprehend and think about urban space in its entirety (built, open, public, collective, private, vacant, occupied spaces etc.) and to return to a ground project as Bernardo Secchi means it: a project involving both land and open spaces, triggering the reinsertion of the city in its own process of manufacturing and formal and functional transformation at different spatial and temporal scales (Secchi, 1986; Secchi, 2000 [2011]). The studied urban strategies thus point to the urgency of tackling a city that is increasingly "dispersed, fragmented and heterogeneous" (Secchi, 2000 [2011]: 128), inscribing it in multiple urban cycles, valuing a custom-made city and facilitating its adaptation to the dynamics of both shrinkage and growth, each of which has advantages, potentials, constraints and threats.

BIBLIOGRAPHY

Banzo, M. (2015), "L'espace ouvert pour recomposer avec la matérialité de l'espace urbain", *Articolo-Journal of Urban Research*, **6**, accessed 7 November 2016 at https://articulo.revues.org/2708.

Baron, M., Cunningham-Sabot, E., Grasland, C., Rivière, D. and Van Hamme, G. (2010), *Villes et régions européennes en décroissance. Maintenir une cohésion territoriale?*, Paris: Hermès Science Publications.

Beal, V., Fol, S. and Rousseau, M. (2016), "De quoi le 'smart shrinkage' est-il le nom? Les ambiguïtés des politiques de décroissance planifiée dans les villes américaines", *Géographie, Economie et Société*, **18**, 211–34, accessed 20 November 2017 at https://www.cairn.info/revue-geographie-economie-societe-2016-2-page-211.htm.

Bernt, M. (2009), "Partnerships for demolition: the governance of urban renewal in East Germany's shrinking cities", *International Journal of Urban and Regional Research*, **33**(3), 754–69.

Brückner, H. and Stein, M. (2007), *Pixelation: Urban Redevelopment as a Continuing Process*, Dessau: Bauhaus Dessau Foundation.

Burkholder, S. (2012), "The new ecology of vacancy: rethinking land use in shrinking cities", *Sustainability*, **4**(6), 1154–72.
Chatel, C. (2011), "Une mesure du déclin démographique des villes allemandes de 1820 à 2010", *Géocarrefour*, **2**, 81–90.
Chesneaux, J. (2001), "Mémoire urbaine et projet urbain", in Paquot, T. (ed.), *Le Quotidien Urbain. Essais sur les Temps des Villes*, Paris: La Découverte.
Cunningham-Sabot, E., Roth, H. and Fol, S. (2014), "Décroissance urbaine", *Encyclopédie de Géographie Hypergéo*, accessed 10 May 2019 at http://www.hypergeo.eu/spip.php?article59.
De Gasperin, A. (2009), "Les villes des nouveaux Länder: la requalification dans le difficile contexte du déclin", *Vertigo*, **9**(2), accessed 19 January 2016 at https://vertigo.revues.org/8716#tocto1n2.
De Gasperin, A. (2009), "Rénovation et réhabilitation des grands ensembles dans les nouveaux Länder: quel avenir pour la ville socialiste?", *Revue Géographique de l'Est*, **46**(3–4), accessed 1 May 2014 at http://rge.revues.org/1469.
De Gasperin, A. (2011), "La restructuration des grands ensembles dans les villes des nouveaux Länder: une double lecture de la transformation de quartiers fortement touchés par le déclin démographique", *Géocarrefour*, **86**(2), 103–12.
Desimini, J. (2014), "From planned shrinkage to formerly urban: staking landscape architecture's claim in the shrinking city debate", *Landscape Journal: Design, Planning, and Management of the Land*, **33**(1), 17–35.
Fachbereich Stadtentwicklung und -Planung und Netzwerk Stadtumbau, Stadt Halle, Saale, (2007), *Integriertes Stadtentwicklungskonzept. Gesamtstädtische Entwicklungstendenzen und Entwicklungsziele*, Halle: Stadt Halle.
Großmann, K., Bontje, M., Haase, A. and Mykhnenko, V. (2013), "Shrinking cities: notes for the further research agenda", *Cities: The International Journal of Urban Policy and Planning*, **35**, 221–5.
Hesse, M. (2006), "The compact city: a model for Eastern German cities?", in Oswalt P. (ed.), *Shrinking Cities 2, Interventions*, Ostfildern-Ruit: Hatje Cantz.
Masboungi, A. (2013), *Métamorphose de l'ordinaire: Paola Viganò, Grand Prix de l'urbanisme 2013*, Marseille: Parenthèses.
Miot, Y. and Rousseau, M. (2017), "Décroître pour survivre? Démolitions et transition énergétique à Vitry-le-François", *Métropolitiques*, accessed 20 November 2017 at http://www.metropolitiques.eu/Decroitre-pour-survivre.html.
Oswalt, P. (2005), *Shrinking Cities 1, International Research*, Ostfildern-Ruit: Hatje Cantz.
Oswalt, P. (2006), *Shrinking Cities 2, Interventions*, Ostfildern-Ruit: Hatje Cantz.
Oswalt, P. and Mittmann, E. (2010), *International Building Exhibition 2010: Less is Future. 19 Cities, 19 Themes*, Berlin: Ministry of Regional Development and Transport of Saxony-Anhalt.
Richardson, H.W. and Nam, C.W. (2014), *Shrinking Cities: A Global Perspective*, Oxford: Routledge.
Rink, D. (2009), "Wilderness: the nature of urban shrinkage? The debate on urban restructuring and restoration in Eastern Germany", *Nature and Culture*, **4**(3), 275–92.
Ryan, B.D. (2012), *Design after Decline: How America Rebuilds Shrinking Cities*, Philadelphia, PA: University of Pennsylvania Press.
Sassen, S. (2014), "Land as infrastructure for living", *Topos*, **88**, 68–73.
Secchi, B. (1986), "Il progetto di suolo", *Casabella*, **521**, 19–23.

Secchi, B. (2000), *Prima Lezione di Urbanistica*, Rome: Laterza & Figli, trans. in Secchi, B. (2011), *Première Leçon d'urbanisme*, Marseille: Parenthèses.

Sowa, C. (2017), *Penser la ville en décroissance: pour une autre fabrique urbaine au XXIe siècle. Regard croisé à partir de six démarches de projet en France, en Allemagne et aux États-Unis*, thesis, Université Grenoble Alpes.

Station C23 (2009), *Stadtumbau Dessau-Roßlau – Entwicklungskonzept Landschaftszug*, Leipzig: Stadt Dessau-Roßlau.

Steglich, U. (2010), *International Building Exhibition Urban Redevelopment Saxony-Anhalt 2010. Dessau-Rosslau*, Dessau: Ministry for Region Redevelopment and Transport Saxony-Anhalt.

Vigano, P. (2012), *Les Territoires de l'urbanisme: le Projet Comme Producteur de Connaissance*, Geneva: MetisPresses.

Wiechmann, T., Vollkmann, A. and Schmitz, S. (2013), "Making places in increasingly empty spaces. Dealing with shrinkage in post-socialist cities – The example of East Germany", in Pallagst, K., Martinez-Fernandez, C. and Wiechmann, T. (eds), *Shrinking Cities: International Perspectives and Policy Implications*, Oxford: Routledge, pp. 125–46.

Zepf, M., Scherrer, F., Verdeil, E., Roth, H. and Gamberini, J. (2008), *Les Services Urbains en Réseau à l'épreuve des Villes Rétrécissantes: l'évolution des Réseaux d'eau et d'assainissement à Berlin–Brandebourg*, Paris: PUCA.

4. Mining the past? Alternative forms of heritagisation and local resources in mountain territories (France, 18th–21st centuries)

Karine Basset, Caroline Darroux and Pierre Judet

4.1 INTRODUCTION

History and anthropology have long been interested in the social uses of the past, primarily for political or identity purposes (Hobsbawm and Ranger, 1983), but also, more recently, in how the past is transformed into an object of consumption and how it is introduced as such into the capitalist economic system (Lowenthal, 1985). Moreover, since the 1980s, the continuous and accelerated expansion of the heritage field, which is typological, chronological and spatial, has led to the proliferation of social science work examining the mechanisms, actors, meanings and effects of multiple processes of heritagisation. The major development that can be discerned by reading these works is the shift away from an emphasis on the purely idea-related (even ideological) dimensions of manipulating the past to a growing interest in the material and economic effects that it produces in the territories concerned. This evolution corresponds to the historical trajectory of the concept of heritage, whose chronology appears to be well-established: "Having first been considered a conservation tool, then an essential element of the constitution of the nation [. . .], heritage has become a resource to construct and develop territories" (Landel and Senil, 2009: 2).

According to some analysts, this situation is characteristic of a more global evolution marked by the transformation of industrial capitalism into what Luc Boltanski and Arnaud Esquerre call an "enrichment economy" (Boltanski and Esquerre, 2016 and 2017). These sociologists refer to a type of economy characterised by an appearance of the production of value of previously excluded domains such as arts, culture and heritage in the capitalist process. What these fields have in common is that they generate profit by exploiting the past – that is, "enriching things that are already there" rather than producing new things. France is a fertile ground in which to observe this phenomenon, which is noticeable especially in West European countries affected by deindustrialisation, and concerns both urban spaces and rural areas.

In France, however, there is a difference between using the agricultural past as a resource and doing the same with the industrial past; the former benefits from the support of a national narrative – relayed by institutions and certain local elites – that, since the 19th century, has valued France's peasant origins (Lebovics, 1992). Rural upland areas stricken by the decline of agro-pastoral economies have been particularly affected by this politico-symbolic approach of conferring the status of "reserves of the past" or "reserves of nature" (that is, from an original past) on these spaces that are not adapted to productionist modernisation. Thus, the mountain is established as a territory of nostalgia, or even as a geographical ideal for a "communitarian critique of progress" (Lasch, 1991: 78), which, since the second half of the 20th century, has been fertile ground for exploiting the "mine of the past". The latter is transformed into a heritage resource in various forms: rediscovery and enhancement of objects from "artisanal" and "traditional" manufacturing, preservation of housing or renovation-construction according to the standards of an architecture that is supposed to reveal the "marks" of yesteryear, creation of "new traditional festivals", enhancement of landscapes by hiking, creation of regional natural parks and so on. By contrast, it is much more difficult for the industrial history of the mountain regions' valleys to join the representation of "the national authenticity". The movement of including the industrial past in the process of heritagisation is not recent but remains, as far as mountain territories are concerned, relatively little documented. The industrial heritage of mountain territories, as an active element of social memory, is subject to a double invisibility, because of the devaluation of this phase of modernity in the historical narrative of France (Andrieux, 1998) and its non-adequacy to a certain (both naturalistic and sacralising) imaginary of the mountain enlisted in the service of identity constructions in Europe (Walter, 2004).

Another aspect of the question of exploiting the past as a resource for mountain territories relates to the very strongly institutionalised nature of heritage, an area in France that is primarily the prerogative of the state. It derives from what Laurajane Smith describes as the construction of an "authoritative speech of inheritance", which influences the way in which we all think and write about what heritage is (Smith, 2006). The question of the ways in which social actors build their legitimacy to define what constitutes heritage – in other words, the way in which one arrives at the *valuation* (Dewey, 2011) of things' heritage and, consequently, their ability to be a "specific resource" for a territory – is also central.

In the 21st century, this state institutionalisation of heritage relates to a more global (and accelerated) process of seeking territorial distinction at all levels, in which the classical forms of heritagisation are associated with a "race for labels", namely the granting of a tag that is both distinctive and supposed to attest to "territorial excellence". It has value in the global competitive market for territories, but its potentially perverse effects cannot be ignored (Brochot, 2008). This raises the question of the existence of differentiated, even alternative, ways of constituting the heritage resource, with increasingly hegemonic patrimonial (heritage) forms "operating through the institutional production chain of heritage controlled by the nation-state (Heinich, 2009), by the decentralised public authorities or by the major economic actors".[1] According to some analysts, these "alternative heritagisations" would be favoured in present-day metropolitan territories facing the tensions of the neoliberal paradigm of urban entrepreneurialism (Cousin et al., 2015). However, many rural mountain territory actors were already at the forefront in the 1950s and 1960s, on the one hand to try to reconcile the preservation of natural and built heritage with economic development – a conciliation regarded precisely in opposition to the "any development" promoted during the Glorious Thirties or the nostalgic museification – and, on the other hand, to claim to take into consideration the endogenous terms of designation of what constitutes heritage. The study of the historical trajectories of some pioneering movements in terms of heritage and local development (Basset, 2009 and 2010) highlights the prefiguration, in particular during the 1960s, of the current exacerbated debate regarding the two types of opposing uses of heritage: "Keeping-for-selling and keeping-against-selling" (Franquesa, 2013).

The aim of the two case studies presented in this chapter is to understand these aspects of turning the past into a resource by starting with urban and rural mountain territories, which have been little examined from this angle. Here we think of a dual nature of the notion of "territorial resource" (Gumuchian and Pecqueur, 2004), which covers the dual nature of "heritage": an "objectifiable" entity that is both material and immaterial and likely to generate economic value, and a symbolic entity.

In both cases, it is a question of retrospectively reconstructing the historical trajectory of heritagisation – of the industrial activity of an

---

[1] According to the terms used in arguments of Open session 99 – Association of Critical Heritage Studies 2016 Conference, "Patrimonialisation alternative / métropolisation alternative?", Call for papers, *Calenda*, published 24 August 2015, http://calenda.org/337171.

urbanised alpine valley in one case and of the archaeological and landscape history of a Burgundian massif on the other – and starting by pulling together corpora from various sources (historical monographs, archival documents, press articles relating to the watchmaking activity of the valley in the first case; and scholarly discourse, reports and institutional communication documents, as well as oral and photographic archives, in the second). These corpora help to bring out the discursive elements and those involved in turning the past into a narrative but also to understand the events and the contexts that change the meaning of this process of creating a narrative.

In view of the questions raised above, the industrial trajectory of the Arve Valley seems to us to be of particular interest. Indeed, building up the past as a resource has been achieved early and evades the modalities of heritage-making as they have traditionally been described. It has to be noted that, while the heritage of the industrial past often seems to follow the decline or even the death of industrial activity itself, with cultural exploitation taking over from economic exploitation (Peroni, 2001: 255), the Arve industrial valley offers an original case of "permanent heritagisation" that accompanies the very development of productive activity since the 18th century.

The heritage trajectory of the Bibracte/Mont Beuvray site, located in the heart of a depopulated rural region, confirms the ongoing tension and issues surrounding the definition and exploitation of the site's heritage value. The opportunity for participatory action research, carried out as part of a labelling process under the umbrella of the Grands Sites de France, also makes it possible to observe "in real time" the repercussions of turning the past into a resource and to analyse the issues in terms of handing over and mobilising territorial actors. This work has been scientifically supported by a multidisciplinary research team, formed within the framework of the ITEM LabEx under the direction of K. Basset and V. Peyrache-Gadeau, to understand the social process by which collectives produce a territorial distinction by mobilising places and landscapes. Here, two types of data are collected and analysed using anthropological methods. On the one hand, participant observation is used, particularly in the context of participatory days (Darroux, 2017): interactions between the institutional actors managing the heritage areas and the inhabitants of the communes affected by the Grand Site management. On the other hand, discourses collected in the framework of semi-structured surveys are analysed using methods inspired by *grounded theory* (Strauss and Corbin, 2003). We observe that, in this very contemporary territory, albeit still far removed from the effects of metropolisation, an alternative path, eager to escape both an exogenous definition of the local resource and an unambiguous conception of "enrichment", attempts to invent itself.

4.2 HERITAGE IN SERVICE OF THE INDUSTRY: THE ARVE VALLEY (HAUTE-SAVOIE, FRANCE)

The coherence among the heritage processes is generally part of a long-term process that is rarely taken into account in analyses of the topic. This is the case observed in the Arve Valley (Haute-Savoie), where, since the 18th century, the heritagisation of industrial activity has been a weapon to be used both internally and externally by local elites wishing to preserve the valley's industrial character.

4.2.1 A Troubled Valley in the Grip of Change

As the world's leading centre of bar turning, the industry of the Arve Valley is so vibrant that it merges with the "local social group" (Judet, 2004: 126). Flowing from a subcontracted watchmaking activity for Geneva introduced in the 18th century, it has undergone a series of crises throughout its long history, and the changes it is experiencing today raise concerns for its future. Built over two centuries, the imaginary world of a rugged, beautiful and preserved alpine mountain leaves little room for industry and the enhancement of its history, whose material traces and intangible heritage are nevertheless important. But in this alpine world dominated by tourism, the central Arve Valley defends its industry at all costs (Judet, 2015).

The Arve Valley is a subcontracting industrial valley that manufactures rather sophisticated parts and sets of pieces for various contractors, including primarily French and German car manufacturers. It contains around 600 companies of all sizes that employ no less than 14 000 people. While the bar turning industry in Savoy withstood the difficulties of the 1970s and 1980s, economic globalisation, particularly since the 2000s, has caused the simplest and least profitable activities, which long made the world of small business and local crafts a prosperous one, to be relocated. Foreign capital often seeps into the major institutions, which weakens them and may cause the valley to lose control over its activities. Whatever their size, companies are restructuring from the bottom up. Between the two main development pathways that are possible (on the one hand, technological development and "mechatronics"[2] and, on the other hand, one that would aim primarily at lowering the cost of labour), the industrial players in the Arve Valley have chosen the former. But this orientation

[2] Mechatronics integrates computer technology into the production of machine-made metal parts, while bar turning is the machining of metal parts through chip removal (turning, drilling, tapping and milling of metal parts).

has to tackle some major problems: a lack of skilled labour, which the valley can no longer provide, the greatest difficulty for skilled workers to establish themselves, and the unemployment in unskilled labour. In this context, there is an ever greater appeal to the valley's past. This move, which expresses nostalgia for an idealised past, can serve to assert the cohesion of the local productive system and to show the advantages of industrial territory when it comes to seeking the help of political authorities. While this trend is particularly evident today, it has been around almost since activity started two centuries ago.

4.2.2 The Emergence of the Discourse over the Industry's Origins

As Boltanski and Esquerre (2016) point out within the framework of an enrichment economy, the value of a "thing" is tied to the creation of a narrative that highlights the greatness of this thing from the perspective of its past. However, in the case of the Arve Valley, this storytelling has been observed since the earliest days of the development of industrial activity.

The manufacturing of timepieces was brought to the mountains of the Arve Valley at the beginning of the 18th century by migrant merchants who were originally from there, when Geneva manufacturers eager to reduce their costs were relocating part of their production operations. The activity subsequently spread throughout the Cluses basin. According to local tradition, someone named Ballaloud was behind this adjustment, and this character very early on embodied the values of an industrial and sedentary society based on work and the family, contrary to the practice of temporary emigration that was not looked upon kindly by ecclesiastical and political authorities. Although the enlightened 18th-century elite of Geneva (e.g. de Saussure and Sismondi) were not interested in the history of watchmaking, the story of Ballaloud has become part of the local memory. Following the annexation of Savoy by revolutionary France, it was used in a memorandum addressed to the Convention by a Jacobean watchmaker from Savoy named Dufresne to show the age of the industry in Cluses and demand the establishment of a watchmaking trading post (Judet, 2016).

4.2.3 The Cluses School of Watchmaking Dedicated to Developing the Heritage Story

The restoration of royal Sardinian power in Savoy after the defeat of Napoleon, which was accompanied by a customs barrier being set up between Geneva and Savoy, and the Cluses fire of 1844, which destroyed the city, almost eliminated industrial activity. After a hard struggle, the municipality of Cluses, which at the time benefited from the help of the Sardinian state in rebuilding the city, managed to secure the opening of a royal watchmaking school to revive its activity. The trustee of the city, Firmin Guy, relied on the industrial past by evoking "Clusiens' innate taste for mechanics" (letter from Firmin Guy to the steward of Faucigny, 24 October 1844, quoted by Deville, 1948: 20). Once the school was established, the fire in the city was at the forefront, and the event is illustrated by the work of a Clusien painter based in Paris, Claude Hugard, whose painting – one of the centrepieces of Clusien heritage – was offered to the city by its author and today hangs in the wedding hall of the Town Hall. After being the subject of dispute for many years because of the expenses it entails, especially for municipal finances, the School of Watchmaking finally won out. To plead its own cause, it has had to develop the history of watchmaking, which it makes its own by centring on two significant events: its birth with Ballaloud and its rebirth with the fire of 1844 and the founding of the school. After France's annexation of Savoy in 1860, it became the most important and most characteristic building in Cluses. The narrative scheme established by the School of Watchmaking was taken up by local monographs, whether written by the clergy or the lay camp.

The First World War and the massive orders for turned metal parts (shell fuses and precision mechanisms) for national defence offered the Savoyard industry, experiencing great difficulty since the end of the 19th century, the possibility to shift from watchmaking to bar turning. These transformations, which do not call into question the structures of the social fabric, do not mark a break in the local historical narrative, which continues to develop and materialise. In 1929, acting on the proposal of Charles Poncet, who was the general counsel and director of the School of Watchmaking and one of the major players in the industrial reconversion, the City Council unanimously decided to name one of the streets in Cluses after Ballaloud. The Cluses National School of Watchmaking brought together a collection of objects by professors and pupils that were presented at the big national and international exhibitions, as well as exemplary works created elsewhere. This pedagogical approach, which includes a heritage dimension, favours the "beautiful objects" that come from watchmaking.

4.2.4 From the School of Watchmaking to the Museum of Watchmaking and Bar Turning, the Paradoxes of Heritagisation

The increasing mass consumption of durable and semi-durable goods, especially automobiles, which are becoming the leading customer of the

Savoyard turning industry, makes the Arve Valley one of the French "industrial district" models (Courlet, 2002). These successes are accompanied by a deepening of the story of the industry's past and the latter's heritagisation. In 1960, when the National School of Watchmaking was transformed into a multi-purpose high school, it sparked a protest by the Alumni Association, firmly established in Cluses, which led to the idea of creating a Museum of Watchmaking. In 1978, after many twists and turns, the industrialist César Dépéry and many bar turners from the Arve Valley who had attended the school formed an interim commission for the museum. They collected tools and machines used in watchmaking and bar turning to ensure "the protection of the art and science of watchmaking, switchgear and bar turning" ("Musée d'horlogerie et du décolletage: une association se crée", *Le Messager*, 20 May 1988).

While the economic climate changed and "globalisation" was raising serious concerns, the municipality of Cluses acquired a large part of the Carpano plant as part of an urban renewal operation. This prestigious plant in the valley has subsequently been home to the Museum of Watchmaking and Bar Turning. But the subcontracting nature of the Cluses basin is a handicap for its heritage policy. Indeed, while there are local products and bar turning machines used in the valley inside the museum, the essence of the exhibited "beautiful objects" includes watchmaking products that do not always have a direct relationship with local activity. The process of "enriching" the value of objects produced locally can only be done here in a roundabout way: even as the museum celebrates the antiquity and authenticity of the local watchmaking activity, it has to resort to "beautiful pieces" manufactured elsewhere in order to attract tourists.

Lacking a prestigious material heritage, the story of the valley's industrial history takes the lead. Today, this story relies on disparate elements that it makes coherent: characters (Ballaloud, Firmin Guy), some art objects (the painting of the Cluses fire), prestigious objects (watches and clocks often manufactured outside the valley), objects relating to industrial activity, the building of the former School of Watchmaking and a museum. This narrative construction is used to defend the valley's industrial activity. But it also has an internal memorial function: by recalling the value of the local social group that supports this activity. This story is shared by the hard core of the local workforce consisting of the main bosses and skilled workers who attended the Cluses School of Watchmaking many years ago. The closing of the School of Watchmaking opened a new era – that of the Museum of Watchmaking and Bar Turning. But even though Cluses is located on the road to Mont Blanc, it is hard to imagine that the founding of the museum would lead to the territory being transformed to draw more tourists.

This evolution raises the question of the social function of this museum, which is now controlled by the municipality (it was initially managed by an association dominated by the industrialists who had attended the school) and whose aim seems to continue to be to serve as a museum for a living industry. With a scientific council (in the process of being set up), this might be the site of a new way of exploiting the heritage resource, understood as the possibility of developing and transmitting, by taking a step back, a shared critical knowledge of the industrial past and the crises faced by local society in order to draw lessons for the future. Some of these crises include threats of deindustrialisation after the fire of 1844, the eve of the First World War and competition exacerbated by the current economy of globalisation.

4.3 AWARDING A LABEL TO A TERRITORY, BETWEEN A DESIRE FOR NATIONAL DISTINCTION AND THE DESIGNATION OF A LOCAL RESOURCE: THE CASE OF THE BIBRACTE/MONT BEUVRAY SITE

The long-term heritagisation process observed around Mont Beuvray appears at the antipodes of this exploitation (essentially for "internal" use) of the Arve Valley's industrial past to such an extent that the scientific investments and policies outside local society dominate there.

The valley of Mont Beuvray is located south of the perimeter of the territory of the Morvan Regional Natural Park, created in 1970 on a contract basis for a renewable period of 12 years. In 2017, during the third renewal of the charter, there were 117 member municipalities (in 1970, there had been 64). "Regional Natural Park" is a national label created specifically from the notion of heritage resource, since it is both a matter of preserving and enhancing the distinctive natural, cultural and landscape qualities that are fragile but likely to contribute to local development. Since the discovery of the Bibracte archaeological site, buried under the forest of its summit cap, at the end of the 19th century, "Beuvray" (its local name) has undergone its own heritage trajectory within the park. In that trajectory, the inhabitants' socio-cultural habits and practices, pioneering speeches legitimising certain scientific and political figures, successive rankings and financial resources of the state are all interwoven. Today, however, this distinction of Mont Beuvray as an iconic site is occurring in a demoralised territorial atmosphere, and the demands of neo-rural installation do not succeed in counterbalancing a sense of inevitable desertification. The progression of the coniferous forest, with its perceptible effects of landscape closure and the commercialisation of landscapes, seems to be the landscape metaphor for this decline. Here the heritage, whether it be natural or cultural, struggles to constitute itself truly as a resource capable of founding a policy of territorial development, even though the symbolic value of these places is affirmed by the expression of the population's many attachments to this territory, as described below.

4.3.1 The "Singularity" of Mont Beuvray: Between Heritage Memories, Cultural Memories and Ordinary Attachments

There are modes of designating "heritage" at Mont Beuvray that are both socially differentiated and subject to contradictory processes of localisation and deterritorialisation.

Starting in 1864, the unearthing of the remains of an ancient city, quickly identified as Bibracte, the capital of the Aedui, immediately launched a politico-scientific process of heritagisation that was interrupted by the Great War before being resumed in the 1980s. The construction of the historical value of the site, in the context of searching for the nation's origins and the birth of a so-called "national" archaeology,[3] was initially done by taking local memory into account, since the testimonies of the population had provided archaeologist J.G. Bulliot with riddles on the ground and traces of an ancient settlement (Figure 4.1). Throughout the 20th century, local culture still conveyed the memory of a sacred place, through the healing or divinatory properties of certain fountains and pilgrimages, but also from a place of congeniality, through the recollection of agro-pastoral practices, the development of coal mining techniques or flotation of firewood (to supply Paris). Finally, the holding of great fairs from the 6th until the beginning of the 20th century affirmed, through oral transmission, the importance of Mont Beuvray in the public space.

At the end of the 1980s, Mont Beuvray really gained renown as a prime heritage site, when President François Mitterrand proclaimed it a site of "national interest". It also benefited from successive rankings and protections – as historical monuments (1988) and natural sites (1990) – while the state retained ownership over the heart of the classified site (968 ha). This space is permanently open to the public and has been managed, since 2008, by an institution dedicated to this task: the Public Institution for Cultural Cooperation (EPCC) of Bibracte. In France, an

---

[3] On this question, see the articles by K. Pomian, "Francs et Gaulois", and O. Buchsenchutz and A. Schnapp, "Alésia", in the volume of the collection *Les lieux de mémoire*, edited by Pierre Nora (Nora 1997).

Source: Private archive, © Collection Bibracte, Mémoires du pays de Glux association.

Figure 4.1 Postcard, festival on Mont Beuvray, 20 September 1903

EPCC is a public institution tasked with facilitating cooperation between local authorities to manage cultural public services; the EPCC's activities must be of interest to each of the legal entities involved and contribute to implementing the national cultural policy. The site is also subject to relatively intense scientific exploitation and cultural enhancement, starting with the development of two major facilities. The first, the Centre for European Archaeological Research (in addition to accommodation and restaurants, technical workshops and reception areas for school children, among others) is located in the territory of Glux-en-Glenne, a small rural community of about 100 inhabitants during the winter and visited by several hundred researchers from all over the world during the summer. The second facility is a museum, built at the entrance to the archaeological site, which houses objects from the excavations of Bibracte and on which it offers up-to-date knowledge, including what is known about "the Europe of oppida" (Figure 4.2). Today, the site of Mont Beuvray, placed within vast scientific networks and attracting about 80000 visitors a year because of its renowned excavations, seems to shine much more brightly at the European level than at the national level, where it remains largely ignored by the general public.

Source: Private archive, © Collection Bibracte, Antoine Maillier, 2004.

Figure 4.2 Bibracte Museum, 1995

Scholarly "heritage memories" (Morisset, 2009) and forms of cultural memories that still show up in different practices have been superimposed onto this long trajectory of a century and a half. Thus, employees of the EPCC, in the service of unearthing the historical memory of the ancient city, frequently exhibit contemporary curative practices, while recent surveys show residents' strong attachment to and almost daily use of trails across the mountain (Delhommeau, 2017). However, the heritagisation of the archaeological site has led to a specific form of management across an entire heritage operating chain (conservation, scientific study, restitution to the public and economic enhancement), which seems gradually to have moved away from the usual modes of attachment to the place. Some farmers lament the fact that the space, which used to be an agro-pastoral area, is used for tourism. In addition, there is often tension relating to the technical management of the regional natural park, which calls into question certain agricultural and forestry uses because of the necessity for sustainable management.

In this context, the managers clearly perceived national labelling as a way to promote the heritage resource: unlike the other French candidate sites for the "Grand Site de France" (GSF) label, the Bibracte managers use the relative under-visitation of the site and the museum with regard to their expected regional socio-economic impact and claim that there is potential for development that can be exploited (*"Grand Site de France" labelling application file*, Glux-en-Glenne, 2007). The GSF label, awarded for a renewable period of six years, is:

> the recognition of management that applies the principles of sustainable development . . . [combining] the conservation of the landscape, the "spirit" of the site, the quality of the visitors' experience . . . and the participation of the inhabitants and partners in the life of the Grand Site. [The label] may be revoked if the site manager does not respect its terms. (www.grandsitedefrance.com/en/the-label)

One stage in the heritagisation of the site, officially named Bibracte/Mont Beuvray, was reached in 2008 when the ministry in charge of ecology awarded the site the label that falls under the Environment Code. This meant that cultural aspects (the buried city) and natural aspects (forest, geomorphological qualities of the mountain, plant biodiversity and fauna) were brought together into a single system of value creation with the goal of preserving the landscape. From then on, multiple actors have emerged with economic and scientific, as well as social and political, interests. These particular aspects came together in 2013 during the process of applying for the renewal of the Grand Site de France label. The two managing institutions, namely the archaeological site and Morvan Park, engaged in management that they wanted to be "integrated" in "concerted" governance, in accordance with the recommendations of the label. This new stage prompted a period of uncertainty and repositioning for the various actors, in which new ways of jointly defining the singularity of the places can be experienced.

4.3.2 From Exemplary Place to Common Landscape: Collaborative Action Research to Define a Hybrid Resource

Territorial labels, such as "Grand Site de France", implement processes that make it possible to distinguish part of the territory, here by virtue of its outstanding landscape, and to highlight the heritage dimension in the interest of setting an example. The attribution of a landscape value is governed by national and international legal instruments that calibrate the value of both rarity – a certain vision of the unique "work" that human and natural history have produced by interacting with each other (World Heritage Convention in 1992) – and of the ordinary resource that this landscape comprises on a symbolic level as a marker of territorial identity (landscape law of 1993 in France), and on the economic level, by favouring the introduction of activities such as tourism, in particular (Florence Convention of 2000).

The initial application for labelling (2007) considered the landscapes of Beuvray merely as a setting for the "landscape in itself", that is, the archaeological site (a landscape management plan adopted in 2005 sought "to make the site of the Gallic city of Bibracte more readable and more attractive"). But in 2013, the managers particularly emphasised the idea of considering the production of landscapes in a project dynamic, on the scale of a zone encompassing the site and its inhabited periphery (eight municipalities, in total). It would involve local actors, inhabitants and users in "a shared approach to agricultural and forestry issues" and in participatory action research that would make it possible to "guide and structure all the action that will be deployed to involve the inhabitants in the management and valorisation of the labelled area" (Dossier de demande de renouvellement du label GSF, 2013, pp. 44 and 54). This approach contrasts with the population's previous lack of involvement in managing the site and defining what constitutes its value. Heritage is now being asked to "make territory", in accordance with a clearly identified overall process of territorialisation of the heritage (Di Méo, 1994; Micoud, 2004).

The action research approach that is used to redefine the objectives of the Grand Site is based on the idea of working to create a hybrid space for the definition of the territorial resource within a heritage area set up according to a top-down approach.

The initial results of a comprehensive analysis of interviews conducted with people involved in various ways in the management of the Bibracte/ Mont Beuvray site (technicians-managers, farmers, inhabitants and other stakeholders) make it possible to identify variable and gradual representations of what constitutes the territory's heritage value. At one end of the scale, the quest for the *singularity of the inhabited space* is evoked: the place, with its landscape qualities, is recognised for its ability to favour particular types of "human existence", to produce singular sensibilities and relationships with others in both time and space. At the other end of the scale, the existence of standard procedures for conservation and management will be defended in the name of the legitimacy of the state and public authorities to guarantee the "spirit of the site" over a particular space – above all, for its monumental qualities and symbolic influence.

But, on the ground, one realises that these definitions and positions are not specific to particular categories of actors. Most of these actors or people concerned are likely to adopt one or another posture according to the various social roles they play, sometimes all at once: territorial/scientific actor, manager/inhabitant/scientist, inhabitant/scientist, researcher/decisionmaker. They all handle the strings of their hybrid posture with experience and combine in their own way the needs of local singularity with the external requirements generated by the norms of the public recognition of an "exemplary place" (Micoud, 1991).

Starting with this observation, the goal of collaborative action research is to care for the strings of this hybridisation and to utilise it to have a driving force for action by opening spaces to share points of view on what is of interest to everyone in this landscape. Through individual and collective meetings, farmers, forest owners and inhabitants, as well as territorial managers, scientists and technicians, define the elements that make sense for them, which they care about and on which, through some environmental, symbolic and practical aspects, they depend. The organisation of guided tours at sites selected for their collective interest and fragility lets people see the methodical development of the local resource thanks to everyone's contribution and sharing of specific knowledge. A process begins that reveals what the notion of "common landscape" can encompass: the close and careful observation tied to historical documentation, tourists visiting the places and the collective dimension of the memory effort can all lead to a commitment and actions among the population to make the places "readable" for everyone. Thus, in Glux-en-Glenne, the participants decided to re-open a pathway around the place from which the driftwood used to be sent out, in memory of an activity that occupied a significant place in the social and economic local space and whose importance in terms of representing the place's identity was collectively highlighted.

In such an approach, the construction of a heritage resource is no longer only relative to a hotspot created as such and valued through scholarly memory. It is, thus, no longer just constructed from the (literal) viewpoint of this "iconic site", that is to say, from the mountain's summit towards its inhabited periphery, but in the opposite direction, from the "bottom" towards the "top"; it gives new visibility to other landscape components of the locality and somehow "reterritorialises" the feeling of heritage associated with the places and landscapes of Beuvray.

4.4 CONCLUSION

Using the methods of history and anthropology, we have sought to understand the empirical modalities of mobilising the past and how it is exploited as a resource in the Arve Valley and Morvan, as well as their importance with regard to current territorial issues. In both cases, this has led us to reconstruct historical heritagisation trajectories with very specific characteristics, both of which question the usual readings of the past's use as a resource.

If no territory today, let alone that of the mountain, escapes the multiple tensions of heritagisation, neither the powerful dynamics of the enrichment economy nor the movements of deterritorialisation-reterritorialisation at the metropolitan levels are enough to report on them. The long-term observation of past modes of investment in territories that are poorly represented in the stories and images of the "true mountain" (the industrial alpine valleys, the depopulated border of the Massif Central) complicates our understanding of the many ways and multiple objects with which a heritage resource can be built to benefit a territory that aspires to overcome its fragilities.

In the industrial valley of the Arve, it is the productive activity itself, put into a narrative form, that anchors and configures the locality in the fashion of a foundational and permanently refoundational myth. The heritagisation process that has accompanied the industry's development for two centuries reminds us of the primary function of heritage activity, namely the symbolic function of anchoring a group of individuals in time and space for the purposes of identity and social cohesion. At the same time, this exploitation of an industrial past (still present here) for internal use does not escape the conditions created by contemporary capitalism: it is also about calling for the manna of wealthy tourists by having timepieces of choice attract them, even if it means sacrificing the "authenticity" of local production.

In the case of the Bibracte/Mont Beuvray site, the tensions associated with the heritagisation of an "iconic site" allow a public dimension to reappear in the designation of the heritage value: actors with diverse interests undertake to discuss and to act on what matters to them in their immediate environment. Taken in the global logic of exploiting the mine of the past (the buried city and its forest setting), the actors in the "Grand Site de France" project are seeking a compromise to answer the problem of maintaining a landscape constituted by cultural heritage but also to the inhabitants' more or less formulated desire to take charge of what is, in their eyes, the singularity of the place.

It is important, however, to continue the observation of the changes underway in the two fields investigated here and in particular to deepen the analysis, which we have only sketched here, of the role of social science research in these dynamics. We can advance the idea that these two cases may indicate to us, *in fine*, a change of a patrimonial "regime of authenticity", understood by Lucie Morisset as "the given balance between the relationship that a society maintains with Time, its relationship with Space (or its way of objectifying space) and the relationship it has with the Other (or its way of identifying it or being situated in relation to it)" (Morisset, 2009: 26). The heritagisation trajectory of the Arve's watchmaking activity currently appears to question the place of (historical) scientific knowledge alongside social memory in the constitution of a reflexive space capable of nourishing the thought of territorial becoming in the Beuvray Valley. At the same time, however, the committed heritage work is redefining the relationship with time, which is no longer limited by archaeological research. Here the collaboration of knowledge, the visits to the mountain expanded to its inhabited periphery and the taking into account of the ordinary perceptions of the inhabitant as the occasional visitor can create a big shift. Provided they continue and are generalised, these new forms of collaboration may in themselves constitute a new local resource.

ACKNOWLEDGEMENTS

This work was supported by the LABEX ITEM (ANR-10-LABX-50-01), within the program 'Investissements d'Avenir' operated by the French National Research Agency (ANR), research program 'Singulariser les Territoires de Montagne' led by Karine Basset and Véronique Peyrache-Gadeau.

REFERENCES

Andrieux, J.-Y. (1998), "Les nouveaux champs de la mémoire: le patrimoine du travail et de l'industrie à la fin du XXe siècle en France", in Andrieux, J.-Y. (ed.), *Patrimoine et société, Rennes*, Rennes: Presses Universitaires de Rennes, pp. 215–32.

Basset, K.-L. (2009), *Pierre Martel et l'association Alpes de Lumière: l'invention d'un territoire (1953–1983)*, La Tour d'Aigues: Editions de l'Aube.

Basset, K.-L. (2010), "Forms, stakeholders and challenges of participation in the creation of the Cevennes National Park (1950–1970)", *Revue de Géographie Alpine / Journal of Alpine Research*, **98** (1), accessed 3 October 2019 at http://journals.openedition.org/rga/1145. DOI: 10.4000/rga.1145.

Boltanski, L. and Esquerre, A. (2016), "L'économie de l'enrichissement et ses effets sociaux", *Teoria politica*, nuova serie, Annali VI, pp. 289–306.

Boltanski, L. and Esquerre, A. (2017), *L'économie de l'enrichissement. Une critique de la marchandise*, Paris: Gallimard.

Brochot, A. (2008), "Les territoires de l'excellence au risque du quotidien", *Strates*, **14**, accessed 2 October 2016 at http://strates.revues.org/6724.

Courlet, C. (2002), "Globalisation et territoire. Le cas du district industriel de la Vallée de l'Arve (Technic Vallée)", in Grange, D.J. (ed.), *L'Espace alpin et la modernité – bilans et perspectives au tournant du siècle*, Grenoble: Presses Universitaires, pp. 93–103.

Cousin, S., Djament-Tran, G., Gravari-Barbas, M. and Jacquot, S. (2015), "Faced with the creative metropolis. Heritage and tourism policies in Plaine Commune, in the northern suburbs of Paris", *Métropoles*, **17**.

Darroux, C. (2017), "Journée participative: paysage et patrimoine à Glux-en-Glenne, 11 juillet 2017", accessed 6 November 2017 at http://reflaction.hypotheses.org/category/recit-de-recherches-en-cours.

Deville, M. (1948), "Histoire de l'Ecole Nationale d'horlogerie", Cluses: Revue de l'Association Amicale des Anciens Elèves de l'Ecole Nationale d'Horlogerie.

Dewey, J. (2011), *La formation des valeurs*, translated by Bidet, A., Quéré, L. and Truc, G., Paris: Les Empêcheurs de Penser en Rond – La Découverte.

Di Méo, G. (1994), "Patrimoine et territoire, une parenté conceptuelle", *Espaces et sociétés*, **78** (4), 15–34.

Franquesa, J. (2013), "On keeping and selling. The political economy of heritage making in contemporary Spain", *Current Anthropology*, **54** (3), 346–59.

Gumuchian, H. and Pecqueur, B. (2004), *La ressource territoriale*, Paris: Economica.

Heinich, N. (2009), *La fabrique du patrimoine. De la cathédrale à la petite cuillère*, Paris: Éditions de la MSH.

Hobsbawm, E. and Ranger, T. (1983), *The invention of tradition*, Cambridge: Cambridge University Press.

Judet, P. (2004), *Horlogeries et horlogers du Faucigny. Les mutations d'une identité sociale et politique (1849–1934)*, Grenoble: Grenoble Presses Universitaires.

Judet, P. (2015), "Une industrie alpine? Alpes françaises, XVIIIe–XXIe siècle", *Histoire des Alpes, Storia delle Alpi, Geschichte der Alpen*, **20**, 59–81.

Judet, P. (2016), "Une patrimonialisation permanente. Le territoire et le récit de l'histoire industrielle (Vallée moyenne de l'Arve, Haute-Savoie, XVIIIe–XXIe siècles)", in Lorenzetti, L. and Valsangiacomo, N. (eds), *Alpi e patrimonio industriale*, Mendriosio Academy Press, pp. 193–210.

Landel, P.-A. and Senil, N. (2009), "Patrimoine et territoire, les nouvelles ressources du développement", *Développement durable et territoires*, **12**, accessed 9 December 2017 at http://journals.openedition.org/developpementdurable/7563.

Lasch, C. (1991), *The true and only heaven. Progress and its critics*, New York, USA and London, UK: W.W. Norton, translated (2002), Castelnau-le-Lez: Climats.

Lebovics, H. (1992), *True France: the wars over cultural identities, 1900–1945*, Ithaca, NY: Cornell University Press, translated (1995), Paris: Belin.

Lowenthal, D. (1985), *The past is a foreign country*, Cambridge: Cambridge University Press.

Micoud, A. (1991), *Des hauts-lieux. La construction sociale de l'exemplarité*, Paris: Editions du CNRS.

Micoud, A. (2004), "Des patrimoines aux territoires durables. Ethnologie et écologie dans les campagnes françaises", *Ethnologie française*, **34** (1), 13–22.

Morisset, L.K. (2009), *Des régimes d'authenticité: Essai sur la mémoire patrimoniale*, Rennes: Presses Universitaires de Rennes / Quebec: Presses de l'université de Québec.

Nora, P. (1997), *Les lieux de mémoire*, Vol. 2 *Les France*, Paris: Gallimard/Quarto.

Peroni, M. (2001), "Ce qui reste de la mine dans la région stéphanoise. La mine faite objet, la mine faite sujet", in Bensa, A. and Fabre, D. (eds), *Une histoire à soi: figurations du passé et localités*, Paris: Éditions de la MSH, pp. 251–77.

Smith, L. (2006), *Uses of heritage*, London, UK and New York, USA: Routledge.

Strauss, A. and Corbin, J. (2003), "L'analyse des données selon la grounded theory. Procédures de codages et critères d'évaluation", in Cerfaï, D. (ed.), *L'enquête de terrain*, Paris: La Découverte, collection Recherche, pp. 363–79.

Walter, F. (2004), *Les figures paysagères de la nation. Territoire et paysage en Europe (16e–20e siècle)*, Paris: Editions de l'EHESS.

ORAL SOURCES

Oral sources archived at the MPO de Bourgogne, Lai Pouèlée and Mémoires Vives foundations, particularly recordings no. 611, 1346 (hamlet of Rebout), 1305 (hamlet of Villechaise) and 1308 (hamlet of Anverse), as well as manuscript no. 1674 (Christiane Vilain).

Delhommeau, E. (2017), "Enquête sur le paysage culturel du Mont Beuvray", conducted from January to March 2017, Corpus REF0192, foundation: Grand Site de France Bibracte/Mont Beuvray (Labex Item, EPCC Bibracte, PNR Morvan), archived at the Maison du Patrimoine Oral de Bourgogne.

5. Are outstanding cultural heritage sites useful territorial resources for community development?

Jean-François Ruault and Magali Talandier

5.1 INTRODUCTION

Territories with heritage sites that have been identified and recognised at a national or international level for their outstanding qualities also have to participate in managing, promoting and transmitting heritage rich in potential as an asset for development but also loaded with day-to-day responsibilities. In France, outstanding locations listed as "Grands Sites de France" or UNESCO World Heritage sites attract many visitors but are intrinsically fragile. The public and private bodies tasked with managing them must cope with the many challenges they pose, as well as the opposition and tension they generate in a wide range of fields. The status of a large number of these heritage sites is equivalent to that of a public property or even a common good. By the same token, the recognition of their national importance and the role they play in various policies (particularly within the framework of the European Union) justifies financial support by the authorities. However, growing pressure on the use of public funds has cast doubt on costly local models or has, at the very least, compelled policymakers to reappraise the financial packages that had previously been put together at the local level.

So the overall picture seems very contradictory, with a mesh of conflicting motives and rationales in and around these remarkable places. Yet they undeniably (indeed, by definition) represent exceptional assets, an essential part of a territory's identity and attraction. The positive impact of natural and/or cultural amenities on the residential and tourist economy of such territories has already been highlighted (Talandier, 2014). Obviously, many resources are available to territories, which gives rise to many theoretical and empirical hypotheses.

More precisely, the notion of territorial resources belongs to the school of thought that defines local development as a process of player interaction liable to capitalise on the characteristics of a given place. In 2007, Bernard Pecqueur and Hervé Gumuchian proposed defining a territorial resource as "a constructed characteristic of a specific territory from the point of view of development" (Gumuchian and Pecqueur, 2007, p. 25). Each territory has resources specific to it, in a latent state, yet to be revealed and exploited. Through the concerted action of various players, the resource can be turned into a specific asset, a resource for the territory. The specificity of the resource once it is tapped – the fact that it exists only here in this form – protects the territory from competition and enables the players to derive territorial rent from it (François et al., 2006; Hirczak et al., 2008). More precisely, the fact that the resource exists here rather than somewhere else means there are favourable conditions in place to protect the territory from competition and to enable players to derive territorial rent from it (Mollard et al., 2007).

Thus, remarkable places have the potential to become a specific resource for territories, provided that the relevant players are aware of it, motivated and organised to maintain, conserve and capitalise on this part of heritage. The outstanding nature of the place may be sufficient to make the property or landscape specific and unique, but it will only become an asset if the players are sufficiently organised to capitalise on it and turn it into one of the territory's development factors. Thus, the capacity of such places to drive a local dynamic depends on both endogenous and exogenous factors, which in turn have an impact on both the resources and the places being studied.

The results presented here were obtained during a research programme carried out for the Plan Urbanisme Construction Architecture department of France's Ministry of Ecology and Sustainable Development (Talandier et al., 2019). The key issue addressed by this research is how heritage sites impact territorial development. It is underpinned by two assumptions that also determine our methodology:

- The first assumption concerns the tensions between players on the ground who have a stake in the economy, funding, society or the environment. Only a field study can provide a better understanding of the interplay between these agents.
- The second assumption relates to the stakes themselves, the areas of agreement and disagreement on these different issues, which may take particular forms depending on the type of site and the type of territory where they are located. So we have adopted an approach allowing for territorial and spatial differences in order to better analyse the impact of heritage sites on the surrounding territory.

In order to explore the question from various angles, we have adopted a mixed methodology, quantitative for all the sites and qualitative for targeted study sites. We explain this methodology in the first section of the chapter. In addition, this chapter questions the capacity of outstanding heritage sites to serve as a local resource and, in so doing, drive a territorial-development dynamic. The second section of the chapter discusses the results of quantitative analysis in more detail and measures the (lack of) impact of heritage sites according to their location. Drawing on surveys and field research, the third section explains which levers may be used to exploit a resource and outlines possible forms of action in this respect. The chapter concludes with a discussion of the hypothetical system by which a territorial asset – however remarkable – could have a noticeable or enduring effect on local development.

5.2 TOWARDS A HOLISTIC APPROACH TO THE RESEARCH QUESTION

5.2.1 A Mixed-methods Research Paradigm

Mixed-methods research argues that better findings could be expected by combining qualitative and quantitative methods rather than prioritising one research paradigm over another (Sieber, 1973; Johnson and Onwuegbuzie, 2004; Tashakkori and Creswell, 2007; Hay, 2016). This paradigm seems more reflective of the complex and systemic building process of social life in general and more relevant to issues related to the management of cultural heritage sites.

As a starting point, the issues in this chapter face two different paradigmatic research problems. The first (mainly quantitative) is about the impact of cultural heritage sites on local development; the second (quite qualitative) is concerned with efficient, if not innovative, means of managing such places sustainably. Obviously, some qualitative findings are also achievable for the first and quantitative findings for the second, but this is not expected to be the case. However, the two challenges are closely interlinked because of the suspicion that community development raises management capacity and, consequently, one can be treated separately from the other. Furthermore, both community development and management capacity are embedded in territorial specificities, which means at least multidimensional place-based (geomorphology, climate, land quality, geographical location, inherited natural capital etc.) and social-based attributes (historical trajectories, knowledge, institutions, infrastructures, adaptability etc.). As a result, the first mixed-methods research adaptation came from the research project coordinators – both economists – who decided to set up a multidisciplinary research team sensitive to economics, geography, sociology, political science, environmental planning and management. The second point was then to agree how to do interdisciplinary work collectively.

5.2.2 Interdisciplinary Agreements and Shared Use of the Territorial Resource Concept

For an interdisciplinary research team, working together is not always easy; some of the reasons include recurring, time-consuming dialogues, the costs of learning from each other, the need for the conciliation of paradigms and, inevitably, scientific arbitration (Johnson et al., 2007). The research team finally found its feet by ensuring four types of agreement: (1) adopting a common understanding of key concepts; (2) making room for all disciplinary sensitivities through the different stages of the research process; (3) allowing time to have scholarly conversations; and (4) exchanging and combining methods and findings before drawing any definitive conclusions.

The first steps in doing mixed-methods research are taken by coming to a collective agreement on what will be the representative sample of outstanding French cultural heritage sites and the adoption of the common concept of a *territorial resource*. The first decision was made easier, mainly by the shared belief that the UNESCO list of world heritage sites is an unrivalled international platform recognising outstanding heritage attributes, and secondly by the fact that the "Grand Site de France" (GSF) label was one of the most relevant for national recognition. The latter only concerns French cultural heritage sites that meet the necessary conditions of being among "the most prestigious and most visited", already a protected area, facing excessive tourist pressure and committed to large-scale governance issues. In the end, 76 French cultural heritage sites are listed in either one of the two statuses, and the research team unanimously labelled them as being "outstanding".

However, each disciplinary sensitivity is able to express its view differently about how to study and analyse the contribution of cultural heritage sites to community development or how to reveal sustainable ways of managing them. Should places be considered as recreation services characterised by their attraction or as cultural areas defined by identity? Can sale revenues account for community development, even if there is no change in the local living standards? Is site management capacity determined by skill transfers and knowledge spill-overs? Is it rather the result of experience acquired and endogenous empowerment? In the end, the concept of territorial resources provides a comprehensive, holistic and attractive concept to address the research question in an interdisciplinary way. If resources provide a means of subsistence to local communities, they do so as a by-product of human territoriality (Dyson-Hudson and Smith, 1978; Sack, 1983) because without land control, there is no possible extraction, transformation or economic valorisation of raw materials (Georgescu-Roegen, 1977; Hudson, 2005). As a consequence, the same raw materials don't provide equivalent resources to mankind but depend on locally used knowledge and technologies, which are the result of varying historical trajectories across territories in which a specific control and management of land have been established. Territory-specific resources are then major factors of regional development differentiation (Colletis-Wahl and Pecqueur, 2001; Dissart and Vollet, 2011). In the long run, the concept of territorial resources is an effective basis for multidisciplinary expression because its holistic nature does not lend itself well to fragmented views.

That is precisely why the second agreement is about integrating mixed views and methods at different stages of the research process. By maintaining a steady pace of almost two meetings a year throughout the research programme, the team collectively ensured the interdisciplinary nature of the different research stages, starting with the choice of a common methodological framework mixing methods from a macroscopic, quantitative overview to field surveys (see Figure 5.1) and using multi-thematic approaches (economy, governance, finance, environment, socio-cultural, heritage nature etc.).

The macroscopic overview includes analyses of secondary data regarding population, employment, income, local tax, local environmental protections and natural/technological risks, as well as data collection (national survey) from cultural heritage site managers in the representative sample. The multi-thematic secondary data were used to develop statistically both a typology of cultural heritage sites and a typology of an extended area, including cultural heritage sites and their adjacent inter-municipality institutions. The main idea was to compare the principal component analysis (PCA) of cultural heritage sites with the PCA extended to the surrounding area in order to examine the relationship between the two parts. It also provides the characteristics of and a means to interpret economic and financial impact analyses. The latter are another component of the macroscopic overview strictly interested in quantitative measures of community development. However, secondary data do not, in any way, help to give an overview of territorial resource capacity or, even more, sustainable site management issues. That is why the last part of the macroscopic stage of the research encompasses the conduct of a national site-manager survey from a selection of 76 French cultural heritage sites. With a participation

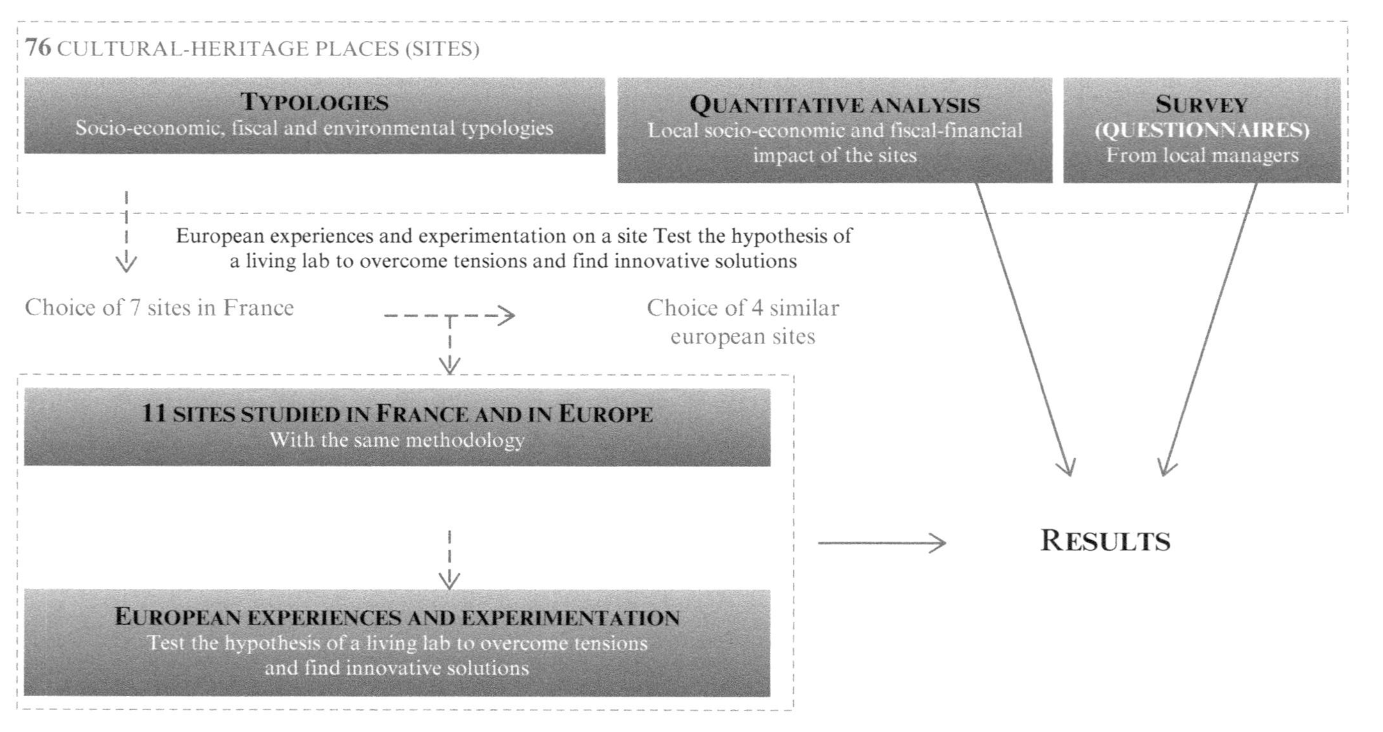

Source: Authors.

Figure 5.1 A mixed-method framework to study outstanding French cultural heritage sites

rate of 62 per cent and a low non-response bias to questions, a confident analysis is possible. All site managers were requested to present their view of the site's impact, as well as the tourist impact, on community development and environment, and of the benefits and disadvantages of managing such an "outstanding" cultural heritage site in the short and long term. In so doing, the macroscopic overview as a whole introduces various findings of which attributes bind similar outstanding cultural heritage sites, what differentiates them, how they are embedded in regional dynamics, how site managers currently perceive the impact of cultural heritage sites and what the main perceived issues are for sustainable management. Furthermore, each disciplinary sensitivity has been expressed through dedicated thematic views of territorial resources related to selected places in France.

Ultimately, the last two mixed-method agreements, which are scholarly conversations and a combined method analysis, were reached through a systematic collective presentation of findings and drawing up of definitive conclusions. Seven French case studies were selected from the representative sample of 76 outstanding French cultural heritage sites following a participatory decision process among the research team and after focusing on emblematic case studies for thematic key issues. In addition to the biannual meetings and cross-reading of science materials, field surveys were conducted with the basic rule of an interdisciplinary two- or three-person team. Most of all, each field team followed a common and interdisciplinary interview grid to provide homogeneous and cross-disciplinary science materials.

Obviously, mixed methods are not easy to implement by people who have never worked in such a way before. Lengthy discussions and tough decisions are inevitable. Furthermore, the representation of disciplinary sensitivities is still perfectible considering the absence of anthropologists, ecologists or even true historians. Ultimately, it is less easy to fully understand the cross-disciplinary conclusions but also more realistic to meet the research issue, which is what motivated the team in the first place.

5.3 SOCIO-ECONOMIC IMPACT OF HERITAGE SITES ON THEIR HOME TERRITORY

A distinction needs to be made between the problems, the stakes at play and the impact of sites on territorial development, but first we need to define the local conditions on which they depend. To this end, prior to the statistical study of territorial dynamics, we defined a typology of sites and territories. On the basis of this typology, we studied the impact of sites on local dynamics.

5.3.1 Diversity of Sites under Varying Territorial Conditions

Our typology of 76 remarkable sites in mainland France is based on a quantitative socio-economic analysis at various overlapping scales.

The smallest scale we considered corresponds to the *commune* (or municipality, France's smallest administrative unit) or *communes* where the site is located, then we looked at the site as a whole, then the one or more *établissement public de coopération intercommunale à fiscalité propre* (EPCI) (a framework for inter-municipal collaboration with the power to levy taxes) home to the site and neighbouring EPCIs. Thus, we can distinguish between the following five overlapping scales (see Figure 5.2):

1. each municipality that is home to a remarkable site (UNESCO, Grand Site de France);
2. all the municipalities that are home to the site;

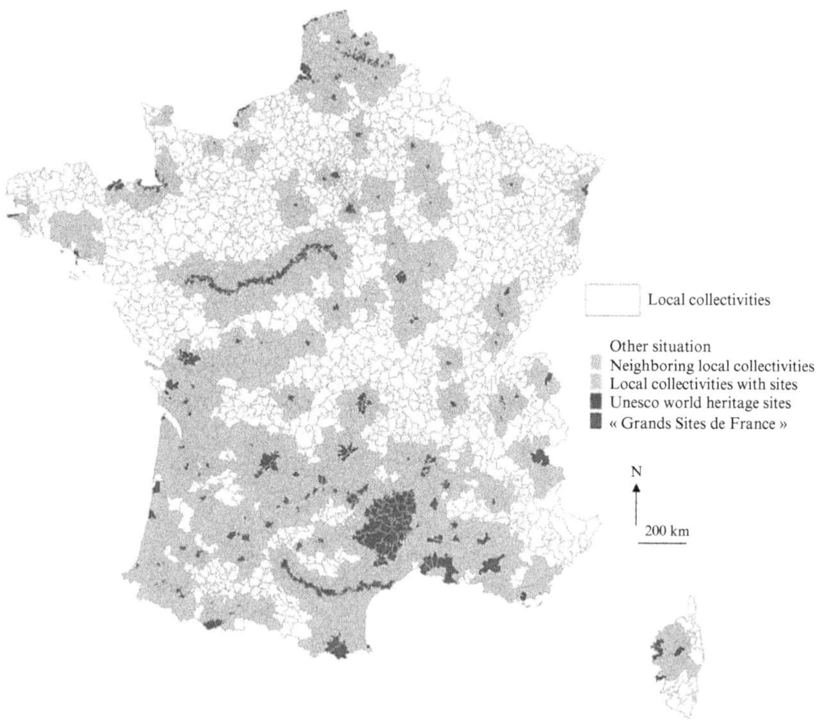

Source: Authors.

Figure 5.2 Remarkable sites in their territorial context, scales of analysis

3. the EPCI(s) hosting the site;
4. neighbouring EPCI(s);
5. the rest of mainland France.

When analysing the typology, we only took into account the first three scales; for the statistical analysis of territorial dynamics, we considered the last four. The aim of the typological approach was to identify the different configurations of sites in their immediate local environment. However, to examine how the sites impact on or interact with territorial development, a broader view is needed, which reveals possible territorial ratchet effects at much larger scales than that of the site itself or the host EPCI.

Using a funnel approach, the resulting typology is based on socio-economic variables. We start by trying to qualify the site's socio-economic environment at a local level, corresponding to the EPCI, then the profile of the site itself (one or more municipalities covered by the site) and lastly the degree of heterogeneity of the site itself (differences between component municipalities).

The local socio-economic environment is determined by PCA, followed by hierarchical ranking drawing on a database that indicates for each EPCI and then for each site:

- the weight of the various economic assets or driving forces;
- the tendency to convert such assets into income for people living in the territory;
- the intensity of the seasonal variations in visitor numbers;
- the territorial dynamics regarding population, jobs and income; and
- the profile of the local population.

On this basis, we produced a typology of local territorial environments at the scale of each EPCI home to a remarkable site. Then we carried out the second round of typological analysis by using the same variables to identify the specific features of the one or more municipalities making up the site. Next, we identified sites with a profile similar to – or, conversely, at odds with – their local environment and the EPCI in which they are located. Finally, we used a weighted variance analysis of each of the variables at the municipality level to highlight the heterogeneity of the sites. Details of the various calculations and results can be found in the final report on the study (Talandier et al., 2019).

Ultimately, our analysis revealed several types of site and territory (Figure 5.3).

Some sites attract large numbers of visitors and are located in territories that also receive many visitors. In attractive, dynamic territories, two types

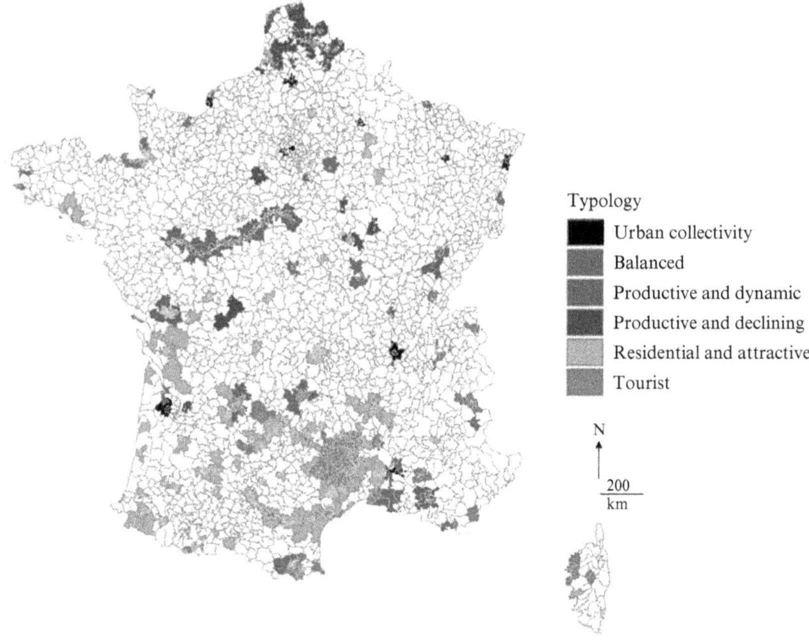

Source: Authors.

Figure 5.3 Socio-economic typology of sites in their territorial environment

of sites may be identified on the basis of their drawing power; here, the municipal make-up is fairly uneven. In formerly productive but currently declining territories, the sites themselves are either related to business and in decline or attractive to tourists despite the local environment. Dynamic productive territories are home to the greatest diversity of sites, with all the various types represented. Lastly, sites located in areas where the local economy is functionally balanced are either balanced or attractive to tourists.

So in northern France we see a concentration of EPCIs that are industrial, production-related and facing a relative decline in terms of their socio-economic and demographic dynamics. This type of territory is also found in rural areas of central France but at a lower concentration. What seems more interesting is when tourist attractions, such as the Somme Bay cultural heritage site, are located along the coast of the English Channel, in what at first blush might seem like a "difficult" environment. On its own, the presence of a particular site is obviously not sufficient to make a territory attractive and dynamic, but it seems worthwhile to examine the role and economic contribution of a tourist attraction in an unpopular area. There are places with thriving businesses all over France. Several EPCIs in this category are to be found in northern France. They include tourist or residential sites (Deux Caps and Dunes de Flandre, in the north of France) that may contribute to feeding a tourist attraction in a predominantly business environment. Our analysis shows the Marais Poitevin wetlands (located along the coast of the Atlantic Ocean, next to La Rochelle) to be primarily residential, but they are set in a fairly dynamic business environment. Here again, it would be interesting to see how combining the two trends produces (or not) a particular dynamic. There are several residential and tourist clusters south of the Loire River, and here it seems that the outstanding heritage sites do contribute further to this type of economy. This, in turn, raises the question of the degree of dependence on the tourist trade alone that these combined dynamics may sometimes create. Here again, it would be worthwhile to examine in greater detail the situation of these remarkable sites which, along with their host territories, are as attractive as both tourist destinations and residential locations. Lastly, some EPCIs seem more functionally balanced, in the sense that business and residential activities are relatively well represented. The remarkable sites located in this type of EPCI are balanced because they are in the core municipality (Roman theatre and triumphal arch in Orange; the Bourges cathedral), or highly attractive (Puy Mary, Pointe du Raz, Mont Saint Michel). So, does the contribution of tourism-based resources bolster the balanced character of a territory by supplementing other types of economic assets?

Whatever the answer, our initial results show that, for any consideration of the role and operation of remarkable sites, it is essential that allowance be made for the diversity of environments.

5.3.2 Sites and Territories, what are the Forms of Socio-economic Interaction?

We used the same scale as the one that was used for the analysis of typology to quantify territorial dynamics but shifted the smallest scale down to that of the municipality (or municipalities) hosting the site, followed by the host EPCI and any neighbouring EPCIs. The sites taken as a whole were compared with the average for all the remaining French municipalities.

We analysed the following variables: demographics (population, natural balance, migratory balance), jobs and per capita income; tourist reception capacity, measuring the number of visitors a given territory can accommodate in hotels, campsites and second homes compared with the resident population; salaried jobs in the private sector.

The period of observation ran from 2007 to 2013 or 2014 for salaried jobs in the private sector, a recent period of six to seven years marked by the financial crash and a rise in unemployment, its gravity depending on the part of France.

The analysis of the changes in the different variables, at different scales over the 2007–2014 period, yielded several results.

On the whole, the heritage sites are predominantly dynamic spaces located in similarly dynamic territories. It is apparent that these territorial entities, consisting of a site and its perimeter, evolve in a largely similar way, with the presence of tourist activities in particular – and, more broadly, an economic organisation – enabling them to weather the crisis in 2008. It is also worth noting that retail activities serving the demands of resident households or visitors account for 48 per cent of local jobs! But the fact that these sites are specialised in visitor or resident-oriented services has in no way discouraged growth in intermediate jobs, such as upper-grade (or highly qualified) business services.

A spatially situated analysis, which allows for the features of a given site and its environment, yielded interesting results, too, with three typical situations.

First, we identified sites contributing to the overall dynamic observed in France. Such sites are undoubtedly assets, but only assets among others. This is the case, for instance, with tourist attractions or residential centres in a tourist- or residential-oriented setting. The whole territory is attractive, with rising per capita income and the creation of new jobs, particularly in retailing, personal, hospitality and business services. By taking a closer look at these territorial-heritage configurations, we can see that sites largely serving the hospitality or residential market may be subject to a high demand for housing (large, positive migratory balance). This may conflict with the place's key function as a tourist attraction (and associated amenities), potentially leading to some young families with children or indeed less prosperous households being driven out by rising property prices. In the tourist–residential configuration, growth in the number of visitors is primarily due to the site itself, ultimately not spilling over into neighbouring territories to any great extent.

Secondly, by contrast, there are cases where neither the site nor its surrounding territory seems particularly prosperous. It is as if the predicament of the territory is increasingly penalising the site, failing to constitute an asset for the latter, regardless of how remarkable it may be. This is the case in particular with sites located in small or medium-sized towns currently jeopardised by their poor strategic position in economic terms but also by the lack of a clearly defined image and identity. They are competing with large metropolises on the one hand, and, on the other, with places that are more attractive to visitors and prospective residents. Under these circumstances, even a "remarkable" site cannot work miracles. Without the benefit of a minimum amount of commitment, drive and strategic thinking, the presence of a remarkable site is not enough to power territorial development. The site may be an asset for its host territory but only if the latter can secure a minimum amount of resources and drive.

Lastly, there are some positive, albeit not spectacular, signs worthy of note. The case of remarkable sites located in declining industrial territories is particularly interesting. These rustbelt territories are the victims of globalisation and the current emphasis on urban areas. The presence of a remarkable site does not reverse this overall trend, nor can it solve all manner of problems on its own, but positive signals are nevertheless apparent. For example, the tourist venues in these territories have confirmed their drawing power (potential for attracting tourists and jobs) despite the economic climate, and thus far the other municipalities belonging to the relevant EPCI have benefited from this trend. In the case of sites that are still mirror images of their host territory (productive and in decline), there has been very limited tourist development. The potential for attracting visitors has increased. Above all, the rise in the number of jobs in hospitality, retailing and personal services, as well as jobs in the arts, at the site itself and in the vicinity, is restoring the functional balance of the local economy. This slight lift, driven by tourism and the in-place economy and accompanied by a rise in intermediate activities in EPCIs, setting aside heritage sites, has dispelled some of the gloom in territories where unemployment and poverty remain the predominant features.

5.4 MOBILISING CULTURAL HERITAGE SITES AS TERRITORIAL RESOURCES

The survey of the managers of remarkable sites shows that heritage is both dynamic and socially constructed, which means it is shaped by time. However, such places may not be used carelessly to satisfy the needs of present generations, precisely because the heritage value is currently identified as valuable resources that require protection for the future. Time can affect, transform and enrich the heritage value, but putting it under a bell jar doesn't prevent anything from happening to it. That is why several authors have already suggested treating heritage as neither immutable (free from significant intervention by humans) nor perishable (for example, an exploited market good) (Soucy, 1996; Choay, 2001; Sgard, 2011). In other words, local communities should consider heritage as an evolving resource that is territorially managed and preserved for future generations.

However, in this way it becomes a complex economic asset involving costs and obligations, raising tensions between the community players (Varine, 2006) and possibly being called into question in the end (see section 5.4.1). The heritage value is not unrelated to short-term economic benefits, particularly with tourism (Zeppel and Hall, 1991; Prentice, 1993; Cuvelier et al., 1994; Benhamou, 2010), but the question of wealth (re) distribution then arises, considering the joint effort to manage it (section 5.4.2). Lastly, cultural heritage sites are attractive to recreational and various other social practices, but the public's sensitivity to ongoing degradation varies and is not directly committed to preserving the heritage value (section 5.4.3).

5.4.1 Economic Development and Protection Rules

The recognition of cultural heritage contributes to raising both landscape issues and protection needs. Consequently, the high number of regulatory instruments is one of the typical features of outstanding cultural heritage sites, as the national site manager survey highlights (Table 5.1).

Almost every cultural heritage site has protected national monuments and Natura 2000 rules. Nearly half of the sample is covered by national sensitive natural environments, and one-third by national architectural heritage managed areas. Therefore, each cultural heritage site is, on average, affected by at least four different regulatory instruments protecting heritage and the environment. Such instruments are not specific to outstanding cultural heritage sites, but such an accumulation of them is.

Table 5.1 Regulatory instruments to protect outstanding cultural heritage sites in 2016

Regulatory instruments	Survey sample
Protected national (natural or historical) monuments	93%
Natura 2000	78%
National sensitive natural environment	48%
UNESCO World Heritage Site	39%
National architectural heritage managed area	33%
Other instruments	26%
Regional natural park	26%
Biosphere reserve – UNESCO	13%
National natural park	7%
RAMSAR convention	7%

Source: National site manager survey.

Sixty-five per cent of the surveyed site managers feel that way and believe that regulatory instruments are less numerous outside their area of action.

During field interviews, local stakeholders were very knowledgeable about cultural heritage protection but simultaneously also very concerned about the resulting limited opportunities for economic development, considering the constraints on accumulation. The irritation of local elected representatives is frequently reported through an exhausting "accumulation of procedures" claim. Some of them accommodate this issue by "becoming complex project management experts" (Poitevin wetland). Others are much more critical: "We are constantly annoyed rather than helped. Public administration is a drag on community development" (Canal du Midi). They share concerns about the limited potential of local areas for urbanisation and the increasing time to process land use authorisation (Nord-Pas-de-Calais Basin, Canal du Midi, prehistoric sites and decorated caves of the Vézère Valley). Protection rules also produce many misunderstandings among landowners and economic players who are not fully allowed to use their property as they please (Canal du Midi, Ocres Mountains, Nord-Pas-de-Calais Mining Basin, Somme Bay).

Outstanding cultural heritage sites taken separately do not have such economic diversity; instead, each territorial context rather leads to a specific economic specialisation around one or a few economic services. These places are not particularly attractive to major business groups, and protection rules – sometimes in combination with a low population density – often discourage major investment.

Despite the fact that economic development and cultural heritage management are currently regarded as rivals by the people surveyed, some weak signals may be observed that indicate possible co-development. For example, the national site manager survey, as well as the macroscopic statistical overview, reveals that a wide range of economic services benefits from the existence of outstanding cultural-heritage places as a whole (Table 5.2): restaurants, hotels, leisure activities, building industry, retail, public services and so on. Moreover, at the local level, rules to protect cultural heritage provide something similar to "protectionist barriers" for traditional (extensive agriculture, local craft etc.) or emerging (organic market, ecotourism, high-quality or socially responsible products and services) economic activities that are otherwise endangered by mainstream business development. For example, landscape protection instruments prevented a huge warehouse development in the Nord-Pas-de-Calais Mining Basin and thus preserved agricultural land and valuable ecosystem services. All cultural heritage sites also create site management jobs and, frequently, provide training activities (Somme Bay, Poitevin wetland, prehistoric sites and decorated caves of the Vézère Valley etc.).

Table 5.2 In your view, which primary business sectors are positively affected by cultural heritage?

Primary business sectors positively affected	Survey sample
N/A	4%
Body-care services	4%
Personal assistance	9%
Public services	11%
Building industry	13%
Other*	15%
Food retail	15%
Hotels	20%
Recreation activities	59%
Restaurants	78%

Note: * Other: agriculture, site management, nature guides etc.

Source: National site manager survey.

Additionally, protection rules could potentially stimulate economic innovation and favour the strengthening of quality products and services through the branding of local know-how and heritage (Bessière, 1998; Cortright, 2002; Mollard et al., 2007; Sims, 2009). In the case of the Ocres Mountains, a social cooperative company is promoting ochre colours as a territorial resource, including traditional (paint, coating etc.) and creative goods and services (coloured concrete, graffiti, photography workshop etc.) and even know-how through specialised training. In short, to quote the site manager of the Poitevin wetland, his cultural heritage site is used as "a living lab and an experimentation field" for community initiatives and resource construction processes.

5.4.2 Unfair Distribution of Economic Benefits and Shared Commitment

When the magnitude of cultural heritage management costs is well known and a cause for concern, the magnitude of economic benefits provided by cultural heritage sites is often unclear, if not overestimated (Greffe, 2004). This is particularly true when it is primarily focused on the growth of inhabitants' disposable income benefits rather than on wealth creation, which can easily leak outside the local community (Talandier, 2013; Ruault, 2017). Both the national site manager survey and the field interviews provided some insights on the perception of economic benefits, including job creation, the valorisation of local know-how and the rise of property values. Nonetheless, such benefits are neither pervasive nor fairly distributed among local communities.

First of all, the impact on employment is globally judged as positive but moderate in cultural heritage sites as a whole, or possibly even low for 40 per cent of respondents. Job creation is rather stable or showing a slight increase for 35 per cent of site managers. More than 80 per cent of the jobs are full-time, and most of them are locally filled (80 per cent on average) but mainly seasonal. Therefore, no significant differences seem to be observable between total economic income benefits and inhabitants' disposable income, but it is not as much in most cases.

Secondly, half the respondents have developed famous local goods or services related to the cultural heritage site: cheese, pastry, local cuisine, traditional events and so on. An outstanding site, by attracting visitors, is indeed a medium of choice to make local know-how visible and build a new in-place market. Authentic goods and craft products can gain visibility from cultural heritage sites but also benefit from the extra market value for visitors. Frequently, there is a growth of local brands, which requires coordination between stakeholders and specification requirements and leads to brands such as "Les Saveurs du Marais" (Poitevin wetland), "Émerveillés par l'Ardèche" (Ardèche Gorges) or "LH" (Le Havre). However, the free appropriation of the cultural heritage image is also a growing issue for local managers, who commonly perceive such practices as potentially discrediting for local brands and damaging to consumer confidence. Consequently, some site managers and local elected representatives are currently trying to ensure more stringent specification requirements and create controlled label brands (Puy Mary, Poitevin wetland).

Thirdly, cultural heritage can also improve the perceived living conditions by providing amazing landscapes or natural amenities. At the same time, it reduces opportunities for new urbanisation. Hence, the existing property can increase in value and benefit local landowners. According to the national site manager survey, no fewer than 73 per cent of respondents consider the cultural heritage to have had a positive impact on property value and 30 per cent consider it to have had a very big impact (Jurisdiction of Saint-Émilion, Giens Peninsula, Pilat Dune etc.).

However, these different economic benefits are fairly distributed neither among cultural heritage sites nor inside them, which poses problems when seeking to ensure equal collective involvement. Outstanding cultural heritage sites are common goods involving significant costs that are difficult to bear efficiently without a financial sharing of responsibility. The trouble is that the latter is not easy to secure when only some benefit while others pay for it, or when economic benefits are simply low in the end. This is particularly true for economically dynamic cultural heritage sites that are often almost exclusively led by tourism and tourism affected by a spatial polarisation around a few favoured destinations. For example, only two or three coastal towns on the Somme Bay take full advantage of cultural heritage, while most of the inland ones are neglected. Thus, developing cultural heritage primarily as a territorial resource for tourism raises managerial and collective issues. That does not seem to be the most desirable community development perspective and certainly not the most favourable to sustainable place management. In the end, most interviewees argue that economic benefits are either of a low order or unfairly distributed among local stakeholders, which complicates cultural heritage management and financial commitment.

5.4.3 Attractive Destinations and Unengaged Public

Cultural heritage places are common goods and, consequently, accompanied by a duty of public access – perhaps even regulated. The amazing feeling of outstanding cultural heritage sites makes it attractive for various reasons (Table 5.3): contemplation of the landscape, nature sports, cultural events, spiritual quest, local cuisine and so on.

It comes as no surprise that most surveyed site managers have major tourist traffic – at least 500000 visitors a year, and even 1 million visitors a year or more for two-fifths of the sites. The national or international visibility of outstanding cultural heritage sites not only attracts visitors but also exposes protection rules and governance efficiency to the outside world. What these places have in common is that they are under the outside scrutiny of heritage advocates and have to be prepared to account for their successes and failures. Interviewed local representatives are well aware of their public exposure, their "global audience" (Ardèche Gorges, Canal du

Table 5.3 What are people's main motivations to visit?

Main motivations to visit	Survey sample
Other	4%
Spiritual value	11%
Gastronomy	15%
Identity	33%
Environment	46%
Leisure and recreational practices	52%
Cultural value	57%
Landscape	91%

Source: National site manager survey.

Midi), their "national or international aura" (Nord-Pas-de-Calais Mining Basin) and the "media coverage" of their actions (Le Havre). They perceive it as a moral obligation to do the best they can to protect their cultural heritage, which might make them more reluctant to join heritage management with economic development. In some cases, this global audience helps site managers gain support from local stakeholders and financial commitment. The Puy-de-Dôme cultural heritage is currently supported by a private foundation, with various donors including regional industrial leaders (e.g., Michelin, EDF, Volvic, Limagrain, Aubert & Duval, Echalier, Rockwool), which promotes Puy-de-Dôme to UNESCO. Above all, national and international heritage recognition builds global networks between sites and local communities. This makes the sharing of experiences between site managers possible, allows tourism and protection coordination projects, creates an awareness of new practices and sparks a useful collective momentum.

However, cultural heritage sites are first experienced by people – inhabitants and visitors – with individual motivations, which is certainly the most powerful driver for both cultural heritage management and resource construction processes. They can provide an additional workforce, ideas, political legitimacy and much more to secure future generation goals instead of immediate economic use. All outstanding French cultural heritage sites are (sometimes densely) populated. According to the national site manager survey, 63 per cent of the inhabitants living close to outstanding sites support management and heritage protection rules, and 15 per cent are greatly in favour of such rules (Table 5.4).

The local community's feeling of sharing a common history and belonging to an enviable living area goes a long way towards involving people at the local level (Poitevin wetland, Somme Bay, Ardèche Gorges etc.). In a case like Le Havre, there was an unexpected "pride building" process that started with the period of rebuilding following the bombing trauma during the Second World War and ended with a new pride in living in

Table 5.4 What is the local population's view of the cultural heritage site and its protection rules?

Local population's view	Survey sample
Not favourable	0%
Less favourable	13%
Quite favourable	63%
Very favourable	15%
Indifferent	9%

Source: National site manager survey.

a UNESCO World Heritage city. Inhabitants sometimes become local cultural heritage ambassadors (Le Havre, Poitevin wetland etc.), drivers of participatory funding (Somme Bay) or even micro-project directors (Nord-Pas-de-Calais Mining Basin).

However, these spin-off effects of national or international heritage recognition vary according to territorial context. Visitors are still slow learners and can be careless consumers. Indeed, site managers point to disrespectful visitor practices as the primary threat to cultural heritage value protection (Figure 5.4).

It is probably even truer for heritage places surrounding large cities or in established tourist areas where bad habits could already be in place and high-intensity tourist traffic hard to manage. For this reason, most site managers currently promote cultural heritage awareness, provide environ-

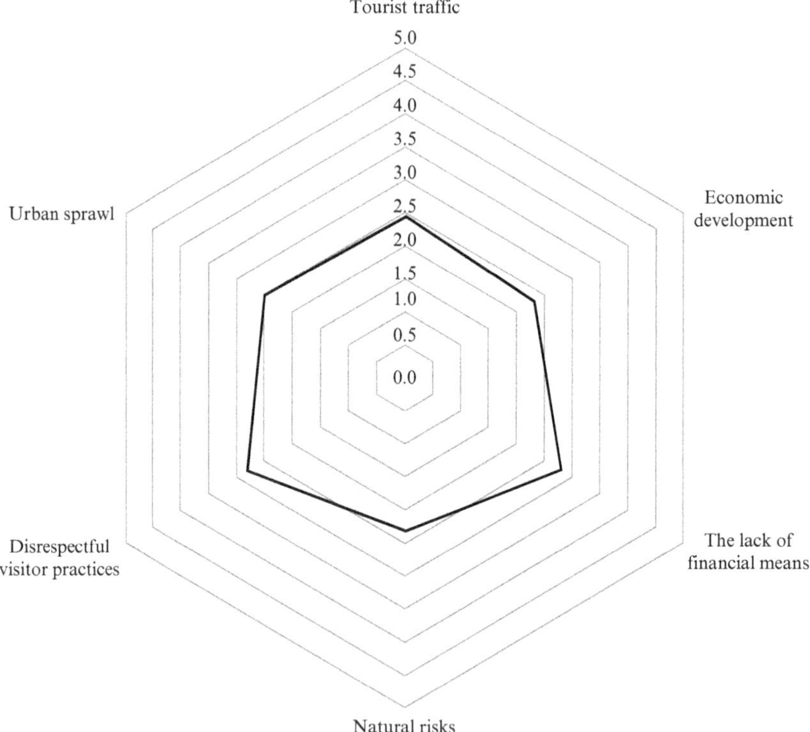

Source: National site manager survey.

Figure 5.4 What do you see as the main threat to cultural heritage value protection on a scale of 1 (no threat) to 5 (major threat)?

mental education, encourage alternatives to private transportation, build facilities such as public dustbins or erosion barriers, try to contain the flow of visitors and so on. However, eco- and heritage-friendly behaviour starts off slowly, and a lot remains to be done. Outstanding cultural heritage sites are territorial resources for current generation recreation practices, but current visitors are still mostly unengaged when it comes to protecting its value for those in the future.

5.5 CONCLUSION

Territories that have remarkable heritage sites are subject to substantial regulatory frameworks and must contribute to protecting their sites. As a result, they face a whole series of development constraints. So it is often far from easy to attract new business or for some activities to prosper. Furthermore, the survey of players on the ground underlines the failure to redistribute heritage rent socially, spatially and to other economic sectors. The economic spill-overs of these remarkable assets thus seem to be located in the hands of only a few key economic agents. However, as we have shown in sections 5.2 and 5.3, heritage sites can boost the local economy, although this is not always the case. Their positive impact on local jobs, attractiveness and income differs according to the local context. Our approach, with its mixed methodology, yields a better understanding of the factors driving or holding back such ratchet effects. So the remarkable – indeed, unique – nature of these sites is not enough to guarantee the development of the territories in which they are found. The cooperation of, support from and investment by public and private players in and around the site are essential to securing positive outcomes, but the manner in which the heritage sites are promoted is just as important. The functions of remarkable heritage sites must be diversified, for they have a huge potential for leveraging cooperation, with scope for greater profits that could be used to better manage and protect each site. Such diversification should seek to develop business that has a self-sustaining impact on the site itself – both its intrinsic qualities and those of heritage value.

Thus, our results question the concept of a territorial resource. The presence of a specific, exceptional resource activated by local actors is not enough to ensure local development. It is necessary to rethink the notion of a territorial resource as part of a more dynamic model and to extend it into the medium or long term in order to better accommodate successive interactions between the asset and development. In the case of remarkable sites, capitalising on their heritage value affords a way of keeping a record of past economic activity that has often produced little more than tourism. In

France, in particular, it seems a complex, conflict-ridden task to relaunch productive business in these key heritage venues. Yet it is probably essential for the host territory's development and the upkeep of heritage. Consider the Canal du Midi, in southern France: transport of goods ended in the 1980s, and for years now no barges have dredged its bottom. The canal has silted up and deteriorated as a navigable watercourse. Whatever the specific concerns may be, there is no discussion about redeveloping past activities "as they were", particularly if they are no longer viable.

The priority is to discover, or rediscover, economic, social and cultural activities that are often linked to the essence of a place. And there is no question of replacing tourist activities, which represent an essential source of revenue for territorial development. What is needed is to multiply the economic possibilities afforded by this exceptional resource. These new activities may give rise to a positive synergy between different sectors: agriculture and tourism; property and cultural services; manufacturing, construction and recreational activities; and logistics and hospitality, among others.

Ultimately, the aim is to turn the territory into a resource for heritage sites and vice versa by striking a balance that benefits both.

REFERENCES

Benhamou, F. (2010), "L'inscription au patrimoine mondial de l'humanité: la force d'un langage à l'appui d'une promesse de développement [The World Heritage List: the Power of the Language in Support of the Promise of Development]", *Tiers Monde*, No. 202, 113–30.

Bessière, J. (1998), "Local development and heritage: traditional food and cuisine as tourist attractions in rural areas", *Sociologia Ruralis*, **38** (1), 21–34.

Choay, F. (2001), *The Invention of the Historic Monument*, Ithaca, NY: Cambridge University Press.

Colletis-Wahl, K. and Pecqueur, B. (2001), "Territories, development and specific resources: what analytical framework?", *Regional Studies*, **35**, 449–59.

Cortright, J. (2002), "The economic importance of being different: regional variations in tastes, increasing returns, and the dynamics of development", *Economic Development Quarterly*, **16**, 3–16.

Cuvelier, P., Torres, E. and Gadrey, J. (1994), *Patrimoine, Modèles de Tourisme et Développement Local*, Paris: L'Harmattan.

Dissart, J.-C. and Vollet, D. (2011), "Landscapes and territory-specific economic bases", *Land Use Policy*, **28**, 563–73.

Dyson-Hudson, R. and Smith, E.A. (1978), "Human territoriality: an ecological reassessment", *American Anthropologist*, **80**, 21–41.

François, H., Hirczak, M. and Senil, N. (2006), "Patrimoine et territoire: vers une co-construction d'une dynamique et de ses ressources", *Revue d'Economie Régionale et Urbaine*, **5**, 683–700.

Georgescu-Roegen, N. (1977), "Inequality, limits and growth from a bioeconomic viewpoint", *Review of Social Economy*, **35**, 361–75.
Greffe, X. (2004), "Is heritage an asset or a liability?", *Journal of Cultural Heritage*, **5**, 301–309.
Gumuchian, H. and Pecqueur, B. (2007), *La Ressource Territoriale*, Paris: Economica.
Hay, M.C. (2016), "Applying methods that matter", in: *Methods That Matter: Integrating Mixed Methods for More Effective Social Science Research*, Chicago, IL: University of Chicago Press.
Hirczak, M., Moalla, M., Mollard, A., Pecqueur, B., Rambonilaza, M. and Vollet, D. (2008), "From the model of 'basket of goods' to a broader model of territorialized goods: concepts, methodology elements and issues", *Canadian Journal of Regional Science*, **2** (31), 241–59.
Hudson, R. (2005), *Economic Geographies: Circuits, Flows and Spaces*, London: Sage.
Johnson, R.B. and Onwuegbuzie, A.J. (2004), "Mixed methods research: a research paradigm whose time has come", *Educational Researcher*, **33**, 14–26.
Johnson, R.B., Onwuegbuzie, A.J. and Turner, L.A. (2007), "Toward a definition of mixed methods research", *Journal of Mixed Methods Research*, **1**, 112–33.
Mollard, A., Rambonilaza, T. and Vollet, D. (2007), "Environmental amenities and territorial anchorage in the recreational-housing rental market: A hedonic approach with French data", *Land Use Policy*, 24, 484–93.
Prentice, R. (1993), *Tourism and Heritage Attractions*, New York: Routledge.
Ruault, J.-F. (2017), "Beyond tourism-based economic development: a Paris-city region case study of transient custom", *Regional Studies*, **52** (8), 1122–33.
Sack, R.D. (1983), "Human territoriality: a theory", *Annals of the Association of American Geographers*, **73**, 55–74.
Sgard, A. (2011), *Le Partage du Paysage*, Dissertation, Grenoble: Université de Grenoble.
Sieber, S.D. (1973), "The integration of fieldwork and survey methods", *American Journal of Sociology*, **78**, 1335–59.
Sims, R. (2009), "Food, place and authenticity: local food and the sustainable tourism experience", *Journal of Sustainable Tourism*, **17**, 321–36.
Soucy, C. (1996), "Le patrimoine, ou l'avers de l'aménagement?", *Annales de la Recherche Urbaine*, **72**, 144–53.
Talandier, M. (2013), "Redefining the in-place economy and women's role in the local economy of highland areas", *Journal of Alpine Research/Revue de Géographie Alpine*, **101**(1).
Talandier, M. (2014), *Retombées socio-économiques des aménités paysagères et patrimoniales dans les territoires de France métropolitaine*, Paris: Research report PUCA.
Talandier, M., Navarre, F., Cormier, L., Landel, P.A., Ruault, J.F. and Senil, N. (2019), *Outstanding Heritage Sites – A Resource for Territories*, Paris: Edition du PUCA, coll. Recherche.
Tashakkori, A. and Creswell, J.W. (2007), *The New Era of Mixed Methods*, London: Sage.
Varine De, H. (2006), "Ecomuseology and sustainable development", *Museums & Social Issues*, **1**, 225–31.
Zeppel, H. and Hall, C.M. (1991), "Selling art and history: cultural heritage and tourism", *Journal of Tourism Studies*, **2** (1), 29–45.

6. Implementation of tourism diversification in ski resorts in the French Alps: a history of territorializing tourism

Emmanuelle George and Coralie Achin

6.1 INTRODUCTION

The French mountain areas experienced unprecedented tourism development in the 1960s and 1970s, often called the "Snow Plan" (Cumin, 1970), creating a significant and competitive European-level winter sports industry. During this 30-year boom period favorable to the development of a dynamic winter sports economy, what was termed "integrated resorts" were born (Knafou, 1978), created on virgin sites with an economic model founded on the concomitant development of ski lifts and tourist accommodation. From this time on, these functional resorts cohabitated with the village resorts opened in the first part of the twentieth century, developing progressively as financial and real estate opportunities arose. All of these winter resorts and the associated winter economy were a fresh impetus for these rural mountain areas and farmlands, which had been abandoned during the twentieth century and then, with the white gold, rediscovered, producing strong signs of economic and demographic dynamism. However, starting in the 1990s, the French mountain resorts ran into their first problems. With the snowless winters of 1989, 1990 and 1991 came the first stagnation in tourist numbers as well as economic and financial problems for certain sites and a setback in the dynamism of the winter sports economy. With the 2000s, the uncertainties intensified, going as far as questioning whether certain resorts should be kept open. In this context of strong local tourism stakes and new preoccupations in terms of sustainable employment (OMT, 1995), climate change arrived to accentuate tensions concerning the fate of the resorts and the areas making their living based on this mass tourism. These changes do not concern only French resorts; their foreign competition is also confronted with these trends, to a greater or lesser degree (Dawson and Scott, 2013; Scott and McBoyle, 2007).

Consequently, the resorts' capacity to adapt is put to the test and two main types of strategy have been adopted locally. Some prefer to secure the snow product, considered to be central to the winter tourist's visit, and reinforce artificial snow production tools. Others prefer to concentrate on the development of a diversified tourism. Often planned together, these two ways of thinking concern the vast majority of winter ski resorts situated in the world's various mountain areas. In France, the diversification of winter sports resort activities nonetheless took a particular direction in the 2000s, becoming mandatory for those Alpine resorts[1] qualified as mid-altitude resorts. Located at altitudes deemed too low to guarantee snow cover (GIEC, 2007), with a ski area and a mid-sized tourist accommodation, these resorts were singled out and consequently became the target of public policies centered on tourism diversification and the abandonment of exploitation of the snow product alone. This led public authorities to adopt measures for diversification. However, it is worth noting that these measures are context dependent (different political objectives to satisfy, different implementation modalities), illustrated in the first part of this chapter. Most particularly, through the notion of a local resource developed in the 2000s (François, 2008; Pecqueur, 2001), we will show how the diversification processes succeed in valorizing these resources. Initially, winter sports first exploited the local snow resource before they needed to respond to the new expectations of visitors by widening the range of local resources used. Both the environmental and landscape resources were thus valorized through new winter activities (snowshoeing, skijoring, etc.) beginning at the end of the 1990s. Beyond this, the development of infrastructure and additional services (swimming pools, museums, etc.) made it possible to diversify winter tourism. More recently in the 2000s, the notion of tourism diversification evolved toward an ambition, first backed by public policy decision-makers, of a deeper change in local economics, with an ambitious objective of promoting four-season tourism, quickly refocused on two seasons. The environmental and landscape heritage, as well as the cultural heritage, linked to the history of the area, whether agricultural or industrial (enhancement of mines, for example), became the local resources to develop. This notion of a local tourism resource has clearly changed over the past few decades, leading to further questions. At what scale should this diversification be developed? Who should be the actors? We will illustrate the responses to these questions

[1] Unless mentioned otherwise here, use of the term "Alpine" refers to the French slopes of the Alps.

in the second part of this chapter, with the situation of the French Alps and the array of public policies of the Valley Areas conventions (Espaces Valléens). We thus emphasize how the diversification processes unfolded, raising questions in terms of the type of activities promoted and the area or areas concerned in a renewed local context and finally the leaders of this new tourism.

6.2 TOURISM DIVERSIFICATION IN RESORTS: A POLICY ISSUE WITH VARIED IMPLEMENTATIONS

With today's global change, synonym of uncertainty and instability, resorts must define and implement effective adaptation strategies (Bosello et al., 2010; Elsasser and Bürki, 2002). The first adaptation strategy retained, chosen to sustain winter activity, essentially meant an unprecedented development of artificial snow infrastructures (Spandre et al., 2015) and ski slope re-profiling. At the same time, alternatives to the "all snow" product via diversification are today being sought. The French situation, however, stands out clearly. Already specific given the strong governmental intervention at the time winter resorts were created, the interventionist characteristic of the public actors is confirmed with this diversification, organized and partially funded by different localities. However, as a result of the funding thus allocated, the public authorities are attempting to disseminate a specific vision of diversification, first and foremost valorizing local amenities and resources, based on implementation within a broadened geographic area, going beyond the solitary resort.

6.2.1 From Winter Diversification to Diversification of the Economy: an Attempt at Clarification

Diversification today is at the heart of debate, yet since the early 1990s it has been considered most notably by government services in terms of developing a product that would be complementary or accessory to alpine skiing, aiming at expanding the resort's tourism activities. In this study, the SEATM (SEATM, 1993) defended the idea that the resorts could develop a more extensive and more sophisticated range of products, to extend the products and services in order to respond to several types of market. This diversification in no way challenges the single activity around which resorts have developed. Much more, diversification tends to consider itself a movement encouraging the complementarity of products or services in a virtuous circle of tourist visitation where the development of activities ancillary to alpine skiing generates an increase in the number of tourists visiting ski areas.

Today, although diversification can no longer be ignored (Achin and George-Marcelpoil, 2016), it struggles to find unanimity. In 2008, an article written by professionals of the sector, with a suggestive title "Skiing is everything is perhaps over but without skiing everything is over" ("*Le tout ski est peut-être fini mais sans le ski tout est fini*") (Reynaud, 2008), succeeded in advancing the idea that ski areas played a fundamental economic role. This has since been reaffirmed on many occasions, enhanced by a new local quantitative dimension. Studies by these same professionals confirmed that for every euro spent on purchasing a lift ticket, six additional euros were spent with the other actors in the resort: hotel owners, restaurateurs, ski equipment rental specialists, ski instructors, and so on. The arrival of ski lifts has irrefutably driven the local economies and the preservation of the quality of this production tool is a major preoccupation. Also, given the structuring role of the ski areas, valid questions have been raised concerning the economic model of diversification, and they persist. In 2015 the union of ski resort operators pointed out the economic limitations of diversification considering that, despite various attempts, new activities have not replaced skiing in its capacity to generate employment and economic repercussions. Therefore, mountain professionals have great reservations about the issue of diversification, but the different public authorities (national, regional and departmental) see it as *the* solution for winter resorts, considering that the future of tourism in the Alps is conditioned by the diversification of mountain resort activities and their complementarity between summer and winter (Comité de Massif des Alpes, 2006).

Yet, although the economic model of diversification remains uncertain, this is not for lack of searching for new avenues for development. Over the years, the notion of diversification has been enhanced (Achin, 2015). It is no longer only envisaged as a complementary product to alpine skiing, but it has opened up possibilities in other seasons as well as other activities and economic sectors. There are many initiatives to develop agritourism, local know-how, the local heritage, architecture and history of the areas. Consequently, diversification is based on an articulation between different activities, at the very heart of the local economic fabric. Local authorities have the choice between two extreme orientations (Table 6.1): exclusive winter diversification or non-exclusively tourism-based approaches for reconstructing their territorial economy (e.g. agritourism).

Despite a wide range of possibilities available to diversify tourism, diversification does not lend itself to a clear definition and/or a widely accepted vision. Far from obvious within the development of the ski

Table 6.1 Palette of local versions of diversification

	Winter diversification	Summer/winter diversification	Four-season diversification	Diversification of the economy
Objective advanced	Attraction of new winter clients	Profitability of facilities and extension of tourist season	Extension of tourist season toward year-round attractiveness	Balancing tourism with other local economic sectors
Examples of local initiatives	Snowshoe trails, skijoring	Mountain biking, hiking trails	Aquatic facilities, skating rink, swimming pool, rail toboggan	Snacks based on farm products, itinerary to explore local know-how, scenic ridge road, etc.

Source: Achin (2015).

industry, diversification is fumbling for solutions and often remains confined to the status of a simple complement to snow activities, with occasionally a vision of town planning that questions the place of tourism in the local economic fabric. Tourism has indeed been developed in close collaboration with the local areas and their actors. As such, the organization of mid-sized resorts has been considered close to the Local Productive System, and even described as Local Tourism Systems.

6.2.2 Local Tourism Systems in Movement

Coming out of the Second World War, France, like many other countries, entered a period of reconstruction. In this context, tourism asserted itself as a means to stabilize France's trade balance. Following Perroux's theory, which accompanied France's industrialization (Perroux, 1955), mountain hubs were progressively structured via the creation of ski resorts *ex nihilo*. During the 1960s and 1970s, these resorts went through a golden age, but, as we have seen, the first warning signs of global change rapidly led to enhancing more endogenous forms of development that could implement different resources that were under less threat than the snow resource. Equated with Local Tourism Systems (LTSs) (Becattini, 1992; Courlet, 2001), the resorts developed around existing villages tended to attract attention. For the most part situated in mid-altitude areas, these resorts were distinguished from the large resorts renowned in France based on two main organizational characteristics. First, there were no firms in a position of leadership controlling all the functions of the resort. On the contrary, the LTSs comprised a plurality of small companies structured around the ski lift operators, whose greater or lesser coordination guaranteed the operation of these tourist destinations. Then, while the resorts created from the ground up developed around a single tourist specialization and, most particularly, around winter sports activities, the village resorts preserved their pre-tourism economy. This therefore resulted in preserving a multifunctional area where tourism mixed with agriculture and craft industries to varying degrees.

With the haphazard snow cover and the evolving expectations of the resorts' clientele, this tourism development model has attracted a great deal of attention, because it is no longer (only) a time for seeking optimal functionality and rationality, but also for seeking authenticity and specificity (François et al., 2006). All resorts must therefore attempt to broaden and diversify their range of tourism activities by developing local resources, whether they stem from nature, local heritage, culture or a combination of these resources. It was hypothesized that these village resorts, developed and then managed at the heart of an economic and sectoral plurality, would have a greater capacity to integrate a dynamic of diversifying their activities (Gerbaux and Marcelpoil, 2006).

That being said, the renewal brought on by tourism diversification is by no means irrelevant. It seriously challenges the economic development of mountain areas, even questioning the structuring of village resorts (now considered mid-altitude mountain resorts) into LTSs. As will be detailed in the second part of this chapter, the actors, the leaders, the different levels of government intervention, as well as the drivers of local development will have to be renewed.

6.2.3 Public Actors and Diversification: a Close Relationship

Although diversification may be attempting to rethink the range of tourist activities on offer, this is not the prerogative of the local political and economic actors. Furthermore, since the 2000s most of the public actors have chosen to commit to accompanying diversification. This intervention is a lever for local areas with limited financial resources. Nonetheless, it strongly orients the choice and the projects of the resorts receiving assistance. Despite the more or less restrictive criteria, the public actors for the most part wager on a local approach with local options for diversification.

While the first assistance programs implemented for winter sports resorts were modeled on one-door policies, the 1990s were a turning point. At the same time as public action evolved toward generalization,

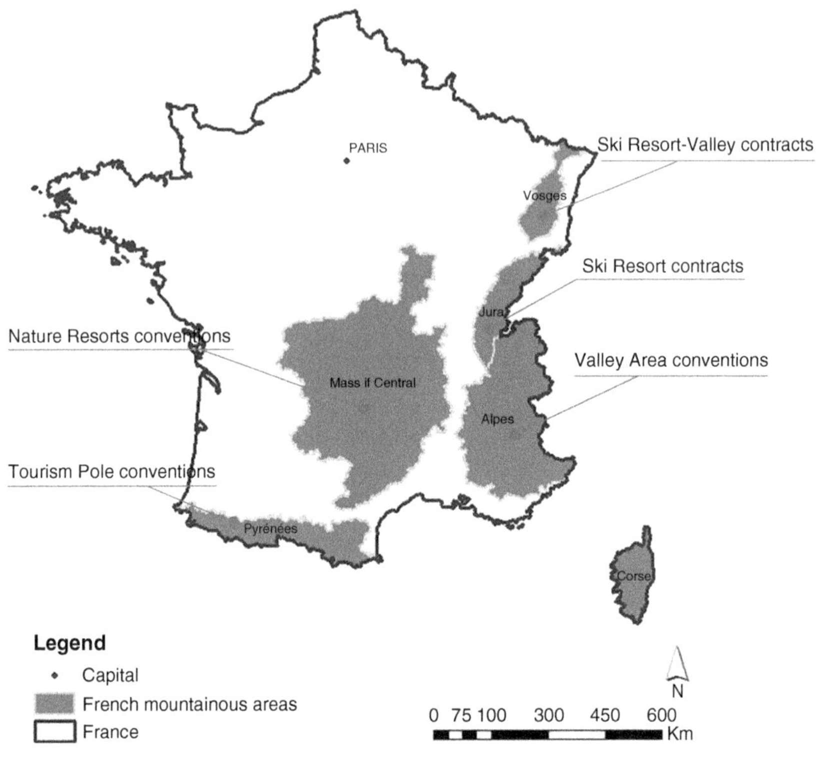

Source: Irstea-DTM (2017).

Figure 6.1 The different public assistance programs for mountain resorts

aid turned toward an organization of projects, the catch-phrase being one contract, one project, one locality. Locally, different versions were put in place, resulting in a variety of programs under different names in the various French mountain ranges, as illustrated in Figure 6.1. Specifically, these different assistance measures assumed that tourist development would be rethought at a local scale and therefore would go beyond the strict level of the resort, on condition that it remained coherent and pertinent. This resort level had nonetheless monopolized the attention of the public decision makers during the first few years during which such dedicated public assistance was implemented. Depending on the geography, the history of resort development, and the issues at stake, this "tourist area" was defined in a number of ways. In the Alps the term used was *espaces valléens* (Valley Area conventions), in the Vosges it was *station-vallée* (Ski Resort-Valley contracts), in the Massif Central *stations nature* (Nature Resort conventions), and in the Pyrenees *pôles touristiques* (Tourist Pole conventions). The point that all these programs had in common was the vision of an area aiming to unite under a common identity, resorts whose original vocation centered on winter sports as their anchorage point (Marcelpoil, 2007), within the aforementioned limits of coherence and pertinence.

Grouping the different financial partners (the different levels of local communities) and the local actors, these more or less formalized contracts with paradoxically no restrictive value in judicial terms, were progressively disseminated in France's mountain ranges. They sealed, so to speak, the grouping of actors around a tourist area and a multiannual tourism development project.

6.2.3.1 How should the tourism areas be delimited?

It is understood that the tourist area retained to implement diversification should be broader than an area that has thus far been based solely on winter sports, but the question of optimizing these borders is raised. Different strategies have been put into action, leading to the definition of "small" areas as well as others, including a maximum of 30 towns. In 2016 for example, the Auvergne Regional Council supported the creation of an area called a "Pôle de pleine nature" grouping 15 towns identified as "Grand Sancy", including two valleys on either side of the volcano of the same name, based on an association of municipalities created a few years before to manage tourism issues. However, it has been observed that unity within this vast area is difficult to achieve, given the local actors' tendency to stick to action plans on the scale of the three valleys. This choice of assistance is not specific since the Alps tend to adopt a similar pattern, whereas the Jura and Vosges mountains prefer intervention more centered on the resort, with the land development rationale aiming first and foremost to "connect" the ski area and the village of the primary municipality.

It can therefore be seen that the land use dimension of tourism diversification is accepted in all the massifs. On the other hand, the scale varies considerably and raises questions. An unavoidably delicate balance will have to be found between the definition of a broad perimeter that can include a vast diversity of resources potentially exploited by tourism, and the development of a sense of belonging to a new destination, as we have briefly described with the example of the Massif Central. This then leads to the consideration that the contours of the tourism area will not only be physical and that, on the contrary, bringing actors together around a tourism development process will guarantee a truly shared development strategy.

6.2.3.2 The local actors: pillars of the implementation of tourism diversification

For the most part structured around existing equipment and infrastructure, the tourist destination cannot be limited solely to this material dimension and must also encompass a human dimension. The requirement for diversification thus leads to inevitable changes in the system of actors involved, extending beyond the resort's actors. Like the hoteliers, admittedly the ski area operators have been mobilized, but new groups are entering the system of actors in this diversification, such as farmers and those working in culture and local heritage, notably in an environmental context.

Renewing the system of actors can be challenging for groups of actors who have never worked together. This requires getting to know one another better and developing new products and services. Over the longer term, for lack of a common culture, the goal is that a shared vision emerges of the fate of tourism within a defined area. In this context, the task of mobilizing the different actors turns out to be indispensable and vital, often orchestrated by the technician present on site, the person in charge of the assistance program. Nevertheless, more than fifteen years of experience with actions promoting diversification emphasizes just how difficult it is to federate these groups of actors around a common frame of reference as well as the precariousness of this type of dynamism.

The example given by the Pays de Luchon (Pyrenees) Tourism Pole illustrates this problem. Although the preparation of the first contract phase (2002–2007), and most particularly the drawing up of a local diagnosis undertaken by an outside consultancy, assembled a wide palette of actors, the time it took to launch the procedure and the complexity of the application processes are now said to have contributed to quelling this enthusiasm. Consequently, in the second contract phase (2008–2013) the pilot committees only included (once again) local elected officials, the ski resort operator, and the tourist information center director, thus returning to a more traditional form of tourism governance.

Despite the problems this involves, it cannot be denied that the effectiveness of the implementation of the local diversification project depends on gathering local actors. Without this, there is a risk that the diversification project will be driven by a small number of actors and *de facto* excluding certain stakeholders who are parties in the diversification. Indeed, it seems that with the diversification of activities increasing more than ever before, the complex relations between different local actors are a determining factor in the definition of a local project. These relations will be even more impacted by whether or not a single structure exists to manage the project.

6.2.3.3 Supporting structure and diversification project

The third, and essential, component of the assistance program for mountain tourism locations is the project itself. With two components, the tourism strategy itself and the action plan, the project reflects the dynamics around tourism that local areas wish to acquire for the coming years. Far from a simple formality, developing a tourism project requires collaboration of different stakeholders (elected officials, economic actors, local inhabitants) to ensure that the local population is involved to participate in the success of the project. These projects will be supported by an external research consultancy, providing useful information concerning the area's strengths and weaknesses. After a few years of operation, it seems that drawing up a tourism business strategy requires but also allows the actors to plan for the next 5 or 10 years to organize the future of the tourist activities in their location. On the other hand, hiring a specialized consultancy raises the question of preservation and development of the local area's specificities. Homogenization of tourist orientations and projects is frequently observed: is the proposal a true adaptation of the area's situation or a consequence of hiring outside professionals to respond to calls for supervised projects?

Ideally developed by and for all the local actors, the tourism project will then be managed by an intermunicipal structure. It will vary in its features according to the selected structure: an association of municipalities (*communauté de communes*), a regional nature park (*parc naturel régional*), a joint association (*syndicat mixte*) and a *pays*, an area defined by the Pasqua (1995) and Voynet (1999) laws. However, the choice of structure is not a neutral one and clearly defines the territorial organization to be retained. All of these structures do not have particular competencies in tourism, for example. They therefore can only set up tourism development actions if they do not encroach upon the competencies of another structure.

Finally, it seems that this issue of the project and the organization that manages it refers to how one should define a tourism area and its coherence with nearby tourist destinations. Here, no general rule can be applied, and although there may be a clear desire to succeed in defining tourism areas that are both pertinent and coherent, the absence of an easily transposed turnkey solution leads to challenging just how precisely they can be defined. Understanding the challenges related to the contours of the tourist area depends on the competencies of the bearing institution, and the stakeholders involved. Yet tension continues to exist between winter and summer tourist areas, the use of well-known brands (most often the names of ski resorts) and the development of a larger area similar to the Italian development strategies for the Dolomites or Val d'Aoste. It is no less true that no single response can be formulated for this question, particularly given that a balance between the functions, experiences and promotion of a given area should be found.

6.3 DIVERSIFICATION IN ACTION IN THE ALPS

To analyze the diversification processes at work, we based our investigation on a methodology combining several types of information source and several land scales.

Starting with scientific studies conducted on an international scale such as the work of the GIEC (Intergovernmental expert group on climate change, *Groupe d'experts intergouvernemental sur l'évolution du climat*), we undertook a double examination based on accounts collected from actors in the winter sports sector, notably ski resort operators, as well as public policy documents implemented in the different massifs, highlighting the level of importance accorded to winter sports and diversification. In practical terms, this combination of the scientific and technical literature emphasizes the clear gap between, on the one hand, the discourse around climate change, the potential impacts on winter resorts and their durability, and, on the other hand, the reality of current practices, their diversity, and finally the empirical bases of the processes.

Finally, by focusing on the Alps, and the long history of public assistance granted to ski resorts, the analysis was based on a two-phase methodology:

- A phase of systematic perusal of how diversification has been applied in the 35 valley areas validated for the 2015–2020 period (see Figure 6.2). This was based on the study of all the action plans defined by the local areas, to assess the place of diversification in the actions identified, an evaluation that will be presented below.
- An empirical phase through semi-directed interviews with the actors present in the Valley Areas' programs. These actors are the stakeholders in the Valley Areas, the towns involved, public or quasi-public actors as well as socio-professional actors in all their diversity. This also includes technicians of the regions and the CGET[2] involved because of their role in the Valley Area conventions.

[2] Commissariat Général à l'Egalité des Territoires, as representative of the national government, in particular responsible for the implementation of policy in the Alps.

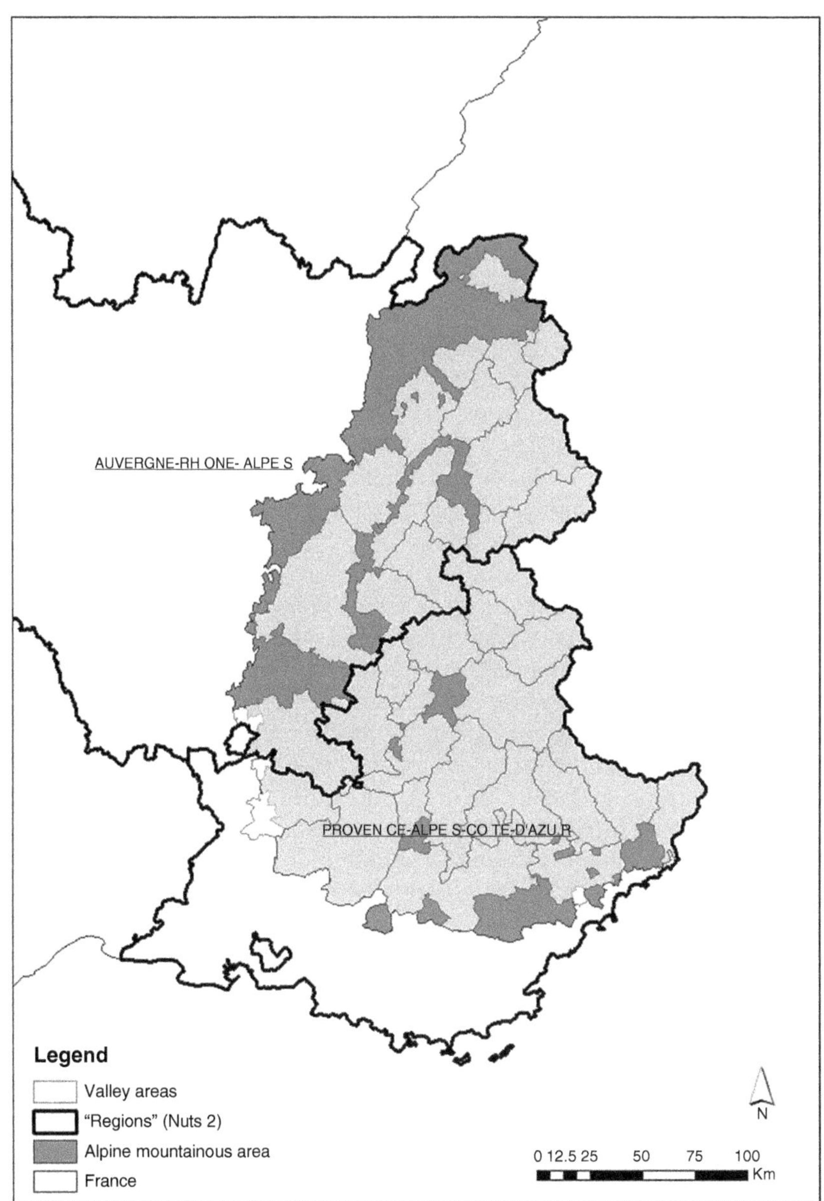

Source: Irstea-DTM (2017).

Figure 6.2 The Valley Areas in the Alps

6.3.1 Sequential Development of Diversification

As elsewhere, in the Alps the dilemma of the towns oscillates between supporting the pivotal local economic activity (skiing) and the obligation to diversify. The assistance programs adopted during the 1990s and rapidly reinforced the following decade confirmed this orientation toward multi-seasonal tourism. To understand these different programs and the stakes involved, three main periods can be identified, related to the different generations of public policy, generally implemented for a period of six years.

6.3.1.1 2000–2006: the early stages of diversification

Adopted in April 1995 for a period of five years, the Contrat Station-Entreprise (Regional Business-resort Charter) proposed by the Rhône-Alpes Regional Council[3] was the first public assistance program set up for winter sports resorts. As the exclusive beneficiaries, the mid-altitude resorts were presented as resorts with fundamental economic stakes for "fragile" economic zones. Only resorts with a scope other than purely local (on the order of 2000 tourist beds), or presenting a sufficient economic size to require land use planning at the scale of the living area, were targeted for this dedicated policy (Conseil Régional Rhône-Alpes, 1994). Among the eligible actions, projects strengthening and restructuring ski areas were favored in the assistance proposed, driven by new local organization modalities that could lead to the creation of reservation centers, or the definition of tourism organization providing better performance, or even, more marginally, the first offers of diversification. Above all, this program aimed to bring resorts into the market economy by considering them as a business. Renewed in 2000, via the Contrats de Stations Moyennes (Mid-altitude resort contracts), the new program confirmed the importance of adapting mid-altitude resorts to the vagaries of the weather, improving governance, and encouraging going beyond the resorts' immediate periphery. However, these objectives will be met only partially: summer diversification, for example, only amounts to 7 percent of the total public subsidies allocated.

Similarly, in the Provence-Alpes-Côte d'Azur (PACA) region, mountain contracts aimed to assist actions in resorts seeking to strengthen and modernize existing facilities, diversify and organize the tourist activities on offer, or improve facilities and the quality of accommodation with a view to increasing the number of visitors. Finally, analysis of the actions receiving assistance encourages one to relativize the reach of this mul-

[3] A consequence of the implementation of the territorial reform (NOTRe Law, 7.08.2015), most regions were obliged to merge. Rhône-Alpes merged with Auvergne to become the Auvergne-Rhône-Alpes region.

tisectoral approach. Only 46.6 percent of the financing allocated by the region between 2000 and 2004 targeted the development of ski resorts and among these, 65 percent provided finance to equip sites with snowmaking machines and hillside storage reservoirs.

6.3.1.2 2007–2013: stronger affirmation of diversification

With the renewal of procedures in the two regions over the 2007–2013 period, the place allotted to the diversification of tourist activities has grown. The analysis of new contracts, other than a few remainders of winter activity funding, highlights the nearly exponential growth of diversification operations. Mobilizing up to 50 percent of the funding allocated to local areas, diversification is delivered in the form of hiking trails, exhibits of the natural and cultural heritage, wilderness sports activities and games, or diverse actions to promote the area and its know-how. Diversification is therefore slowly moving into these areas motivated by a "carrot effect" that cannot be denied.

Another novelty: now the assistance no longer targets only resorts, but also other areas that have applied for targeted assistance based on two main objectives: the strengthening and diversification of activities whose purpose is to make the sites less dependent on the winter season and the reinforcement of local cooperative efforts as well as the expected development of support at the level of the valley or a relevant area. This means assisting the distribution of resources at the valley scale and limiting the concentration of tourists and the economic consequences in the winter sports resorts and, by extension, benefiting only a limited number of local actors. This requires that the programs put in place drive an increase in the power of inter-municipal action in local tourism organization.

6.3.1.3 2014–2020: Valley Areas for sustainable and high-quality tourism

Today, during the 2014–2020 contractualization period, in collaboration with the two regions, Auvergne-Rhône-Alpes and Provence-Alpes-Côte d'Azur, the Alps has renewed its assistance program for sustainable and high-quality tourism by labeling the 35 Valley Areas (Espaces Valléens), revealing the less important place accorded to winter sports resorts in this program: now areas without a resort are allowed to apply.

In this current public policy, once again diversification of tourism activities in the areas concerned is emphasized. To achieve this, heritage development actions, whether they be related to nature or culture, are strongly encouraged. The aim is indeed to make the range of tourism activities more specific at the scale of the Alps massif, and much more attractive when developing local resources than by promoting a standardized tourist experience, possibly with the creation of recreational parks in the mountain environment. Today, the incentive seems to have received a favorable response from the local areas, most of which have undertaken initiatives in this direction in their action plan. Nevertheless, prioritization of the projects requested stemming from a strict overall budget can only raise questions on the future of development actions in these areas. Indeed, since all of the applications for financing cannot be funded, will these actions be confirmed or abandoned and benefit instead those actions with confirmed economic profitability?

6.3.2 The Reality of Diversification via the Valley Area Program

To grasp the outlines of diversification as implemented in the Valley Areas, we collected all the action plans in order to identify, beyond the general orientations proposed in the tourism strategy, the type of tourism operations programmed. We then attempted to classify these actions into eight categories so as to distinguish the main components of the tourism activity: biodiversity, inter-Valley Area cooperation, diversification, governance, tourist accommodation and urbanism, tourism promotion, services for inhabitants, and, the last category, transportation and mobility.

Analysis shows that diversification concerns only slightly more than half of the actions planned in the Valley Areas (52 percent). This of course makes it possible to respond to the objective of the POIA[4] (2014–2020) seeking to accentuate development of the local areas' tourism resources,[5] but nonetheless raises the question of where diversification of the tourist activities on offer is situated compared with the other aspects of tourism development, much like the tourism promotion actions or the renovation and modernization of tourist accommodation.

Beyond this, we sought to identify the nature of these diversification actions by selecting nine subcategories, which aim to take into account how the operation is deployed locally, within the ski area (Resort Diversification) or, in a more diffuse way, over the entire area (Valley Area Diversification). In the same way, referring to the first scenario presented above, we distinguished the operations based on time. We thus differentiated the diversification operations that focused strictly on winter from those focusing on the four seasons. Finally, the last key to understanding the type of investments made, in the context of territorialized

---

4 Programme Opérationnel Interrégional du Massif des Alpes (Alps Interregional Operational Program).

5 Axis 1 and Strategic Objective 1 of the POIA notes that the tourism strategy should aim for sustainable development of mountain areas by valorizing aspects of the local heritage based on both nature and culture and by integrating objectives designed to protect alpine biodiversity and ecological continuity.

diversification, would be whether diversification is based on the acquisition of heavy infrastructure (water parks, museum exhibits, etc.), development of accessible sports tourism (mountain bike trails, running trails, etc.), or development of nature aspects as cultural elements of the local heritage. And last, we isolated the operations relevant to diversifying clientele (which does not affect the tourist activities) and the studies programmed (some of which will not generate concrete action).

This view highlights the diversity of the actions stemming from diversification. An important point concerns the dichotomy between the diversification illustrated by investment in physical infrastructures and the choice of diversification that is preferentially associated with a more diffuse tourism. More than 50 percent of the actions in the action plans stem from the orientation of diffuse tourism (actions valorizing the local heritage and developing tourism accessible to everyone), tending to illustrate a radical break from the winter sports tourism mode. However, this change cannot be idealized or overestimated, since the number of actions targeting heavy infrastructure make up only 10 percent of the total: the percentage of the budget allocated reaches 40 percent of the total funding planned, as shown in Figure 6.3. This undoubtedly illustrates the problems encountered by local actors, notably elected officials, when attempting to make the familiar model of the winter sports resort evolve. Symbols of heavy tourism

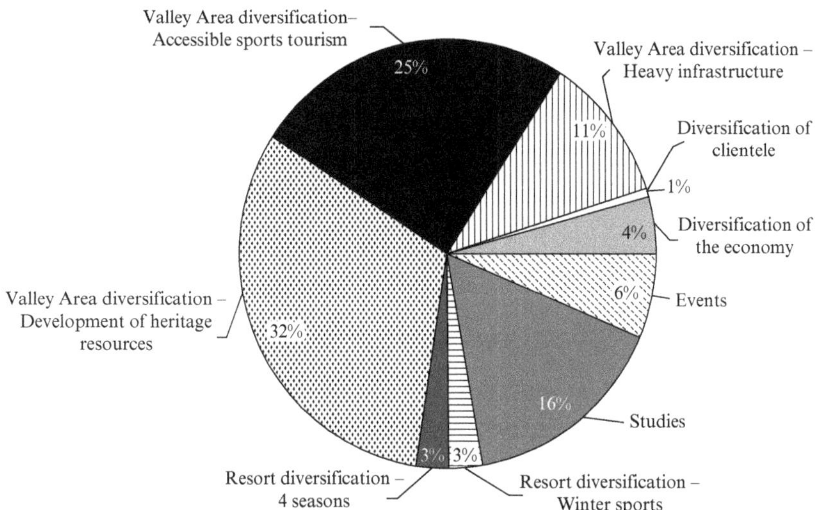

Source: Irstea-DTM (2017).

Figure 6.3 Subcategories of diversification actions in the Alps Valley Areas

infrastructure in mountainous areas, these actions have contributed to the acceptance of heavy infrastructure as indispensable tools for tourism development. With diversification, new orientations are being sought, in certain cases resulting in the creation of spas or water parks, museums on local heritage, or skating rinks and other mountain sports complexes. Yet although it has almost been accepted that this infrastructure is responding to the expectations of today's clientele, its future remains much more uncertain. The financial stability of the exploitation of this infrastructure, often in deficit, is raised, with particular intensity because of its possible abandonment by the tourists for whom it was intended. What will then become of this infrastructure once it has fallen by the wayside?

Beyond this, as mentioned above, current public policy tends to be encouraging tourism areas to be defined by increasingly widened borders, or even insisting on this. This territorialization of diversification, progressive since the 2000s and based on the NOTRe law, as well as the reform of intermunicipalities,[6] nevertheless raises questions. As illustrated by the maps in Figure 6.4, with the example of the Hautes-Alpes department, the Valley Areas have widened their boundaries with the 2014 call for applications. This has resulted in the combination of up to three Valley Areas, necessarily raising the question of how the different tourism strategies developed have been articulated to date. More precisely, with the combination of several large winter resorts within a single Valley Area, how well do these resorts and their actors work together in creating a single tourist destination?

More globally, widening the contours of the Valley Areas has sometimes led to creating project territories at scales that both tourism communication and planning could not handle. Also, rather than boosting the development of mountain areas, this mandatory extension sometimes acts as an additional constraint of public policies, which, despite having being implemented for several years, may not lead to adoption by the local community.

6.4 CONCLUSION

Analysis of the past fifteen years of the public assistance dedicated to resorts has highlighted the importance of diversification in the different mountain ranges in France, despite variable intensities and different histories.

---

[6] With the intermunicipal associations frequently acting as the management structures for the Valley Areas, the borders of the Valley Areas were frequently modeled on this widened institutional area.

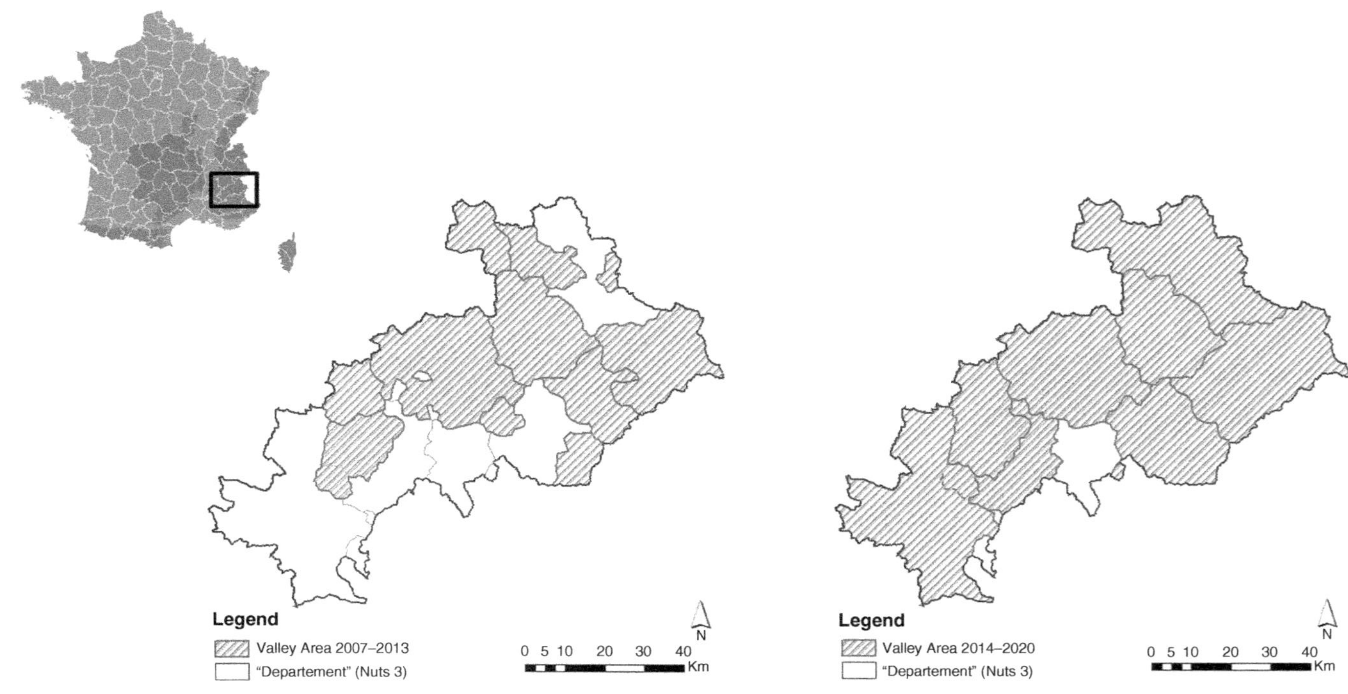

Source: Irstea-DTM (2017).

Figure 6.4 Valley Areas between 2007 and 2014: the example of the Hautes-Alpes Department

Tourism is diversified using a variety of actor systems and local resources. However, a few years after implementation in local areas presenting historic, geographic and/or economic diversity, a certain similarity appears in the choices of diversification. This similarity tends to be expressed at the department level or for all the mountain ranges, thus erasing the highlighted specificity and unicity of the local areas, despite a central preoccupation with abandoning the generic nature of this diversification in favor of more area-specific solutions. Consequently, are we not observing Act II of mountain sports facilities where products, within a relatively narrow range in fact, will be implanted from the ground up on sites where local specificities have been severely diluted for the benefit of white gold? On the other hand, to counterbalance this skeptical declaration on the nature of diversification, it is clear that we cannot blame these areas that have been structured around a capitalistic economy for two generations or more, which has created a fortune for the early pioneers and provided consequential improvement to these areas' standard of living.

The work carried out in the Alps raises the question of where diversification is situated in the resorts' adaptation policies. Depending on the local context, the history of tourism, or the vitality of the winter sports sector, the dynamics oscillate between making the exploitation of the ski area reliable and encouraging tourism diversification. It should therefore be noted that in France, the investments of the ski resort operators in infrastructure (ski lifts, artificial snow, slope grooming) have increased threefold since 1990, in 2016 reaching 302 million euros before tax. These figures show the resonance of the snow and skiing activity in the resorts' economic model and the ever-delicate balance between making the snow activity reliable and tourism diversification, as well as the difficulty in axing one model that has proved its worth on the local snow resource and changing to a model based on other local amenities and resources.

In comparison, the diversification actions projected throughout the Alps, several of which we know from experience will not succeed, amount to slightly less than 140 million euros.[7] However, and beyond this, it is the scope of the local repercussions from this diversification that is up for debate. For the elected officials and local actors, the stakes are real: what and how should we develop tourism diversification strategies capable of replacing the economic activity generated by winter sports? The lack of

[7] This sum corresponds to the total budget of the Valley Areas, and therefore does not take into account the investments made outside of public subsidies. The important role of public actors in the tourism development, specific to France, allows a precise monitoring of tourism diversification local choices, which may or may not benefit from financial support. In other countries however, investments are diffuse and therefore particularly difficult to capture, which does not mean that the dynamics are the opposite: quite the contrary.

consensus to this question emphasizes the need to change the assessment framework, and the economic model of diversification therefore has yet to be invented to its fullest diversity.

In addition, as a result of the latest elections and the changes in the executive powers in France at different territorial scales, there is a somewhat contradictory articulation between continued support for diversification and reaffirmed support for the snow economy. What can be expected of the future? What development choices will emerge over the medium and long terms, particularly given that the territorial reform, encouraging the creation of strong intermunicipality structures, will have consequences that will be even more difficult to measure on the local areas and the place allotted to tourism? In these new, vast project territories, what vision of tourism will the political actors have? Indirectly, what financing will they allocate to tourism, and most particularly diversification? Likewise, mountain planning and tourism development now have a century of history behind them. In this sense, the pioneering actors of the creation and expansion of resorts have known a very particular economic and political context, where climate change, sustainable development, and the problems of tourist attendance did not exist. Over the past few years, with the confirmation of these factors and their consequences, the frame of reference has been changing, as are practices, certainly progressively, even if some recoil effects are still possible. This is what is at stake in following resorts and tourism territories in the future, so that the effects of these diverse evolving factors on positioning the industry in an international and sustainable context can be assessed.

On the research side of things, this will undoubtedly require the ways in which tourism activities are organized to be re-qualified. While the Local Tourism Systems made it possible to accentuate the specialization of tourism carried out by local actors, united around the winter sports resort, the introduction of diversification entails adjustments. From now on, other economic sectors (notably agriculture and craft industries), as well as the growth in the creation of residential areas, confirm that the LTSs today are hybridizing and following the emergence of a new concept.

REFERENCES

Achin, C. (2015), *La gouvernance de la diversification comme enjeu de l'adaptation des stations de moyenne montagne: l'analyse des stations de la Bresse, du Dévoluy et du Sancy*, doctoral thesis, Grenoble: Université Grenoble-Alpes.

Achin, C. and George-Marcelpoil, E. (2016), "The tourism diversification in French ski resorts: what are effective drivers for sustainable tourism in mountain resorts?", paper presented at the International Conference on Global Tourism and Sustainability, 12–14 October, Lagos, Portugal.

Becattini, G. (1992), "Le district marshallien: une notion socio-économique", in Benko, G. and Lipietz, A. (eds), *Les régions qui gagnent. Districts et réseaux: les nouveaux paradigmes de la géographie économique.* Paris: PUF.

Bosello, F., Carraro, C. and De Cian, E. (2010), "Climate policy and the optimal balance between mitigation, adaptation and unavoided damage", *Climate Change Economics*, **1,** 71–92.

Comité de Massif des Alpes (2006), "Convention interrégionale d'aménagement pour le massif des Alpes".

Conseil Régional Rhône-Alpes (1994), *Charte "entreprise-station" 1995–2000*. Lyon.

Courlet, C. (2001), "Les systèmes productifs locaux: de la définition au modèle", in DATAR (ed.), *Réseaux d'entreprises et territoires: regards sur les systèmes productifs locaux.* Paris: La Documentation Française.

Cumin, G. (1970), "Les stations intégrées", *Urbanisme*, **116,** 50–53.

Dawson, J. and Scott, D. (2013), "Managing for climate change in the alpine ski sector", *Tourism Management*, **35,** 244–54.

Elsasser, H. and Bürki, R. (2002), "Climate change as a threat to tourism in the Alps", *Climate Research*, **20,** 253–7.

François, H. (2008), "Durabilité des ressources territoriales et tourisme durable: vers quelle convergence?", *Géographie, économie, société*, **10,** 133–52.

François, H., Hirczak, M. and Senil, N. (2006), "Territoire et patrimoine: la co-construction d'une dynamique et de ses ressources", *Revue d'Économie Régionale et Urbaine*, **5,** 683–700.

Gerbaux, F. and Marcelpoil, E. (2006), "Gouvernance des stations de montagne en France: les spécificités du partenariat public-privé", *Revue de Géographie Alpine*, **94,** 9–19.

GIEC (2007), "Bilan 2007 des changements climatiques: Rapport de synthèse", fourth assessment report of the Groupe d'experts intergouvernemental sur l'évolution du climat, OMM/PNUE.

Knafou, R. (1978), *Les stations intégrées de sports d'hiver des Alpes françaises l'aménagement de la montagne à la française*, Paris, France; New York, USA and Barcelona, Spain: Masson.

Marcelpoil, E. (2007), *L'ancrage territorial des stations de montagne: quelles trajectoires et marges de manoeuvre? Les sports d'hiver en mutation: crise ou révolution géoculturelle?* Paris: Lavoisier.

OMT (1995), "Charte du tourisme durable", Lanzarote Conference, 27–28 April.

Pasqua, C. (1995), *Loi n°95-115 du 4 février 1995 d'orientation pour l'aménagement et le développement du territoire*. Paris.

Pecqueur, B. (2001), "Qualité et développement territorial: l'hypothèse du panier de biens et de services territorialisés", *Économie Rurale*, **261,** 37–49.

Perroux, F. (1955), "Note sur la notion de pôle de croissance", *Economie Appliquée*, **8,** 307–20.

Reynaud, L. (2008), "Le tout-ski est peut-être fini, mais sans le ski, tout est fini!", *Dur'Alpes*, accessed 10 June 2019 at https://www.duralpes.com/le-tout-skiest-peut-etre-fini-mais-sans-le-ski-tout-est-fini/.

Scott, D. and McBoyle, G. (2007), "Climate change adpatation in the ski industry", *Mitigation and Adaptation Strategies for Global Change*, **12,** 1411–31.

SEATM (1993), "La diversification de l'offre de loisirs dans les stations de sports d'hiver françaises et étrangères: analyse et propositions", Chambéry: AFIT-SEATM.

Spandre, P., François, H., Morin, S. and George-Marcelpoil, E. (2015), "Snowmaking in the French Alps", *Journal of Alpine Research Revue de Géographie Alpine*, accessed 10 June 2019 at https://journals.openedition.org/rga/pdf/2913.

Voynet, D. (1999), *Loi n°99-533 du 25 juin 1999 d'orientation pour l'aménagement et le développement durable du territoire et portant modification de la loi n° 95-115 du 4 février 1995 d'orientation pour l'aménagement et le développement du territoire*. Paris.

7. Territorial energy transition strategies: new models for cooperation between actors and resource management?

Gilles Novarina and Natacha Seigneuret

7.1 INTRODUCTION

Since the beginning of the 2000s, territorial planning strategies in several European cities, for example urban project approaches, have included renewable energy production and energy-saving objectives more and more often. Some cities position their strategies around solar power, wind power or co-generation, while others focus on creating heating networks and recovering energy from waste, or saving energy in construction and managing energy distribution in an innovative way. The differences in approach are partly related to the resources that are available in the specific territory. But the term "resources" shouldn't bring to mind a purely economic conception of the term. From such a perspective, resources would constitute an initial endowment available to local actors. This idea is implied by the concept of a "*panier de biens*" (Hirczak et al., 2008), or basket of goods, in which goods and services that make up a stock of resources are placed side by side and can be mobilised as needed.

Imagining that local development processes depend exclusively on an endowment of diverse resources is rather simplistic. Any territorial context has both resources and constraints at the same time. To analyse the way in which actors influence the socio-spatial structures in order to foster development, two researchers studied the interaction between contextual factors (not only the totality of material and immaterial resources but also the constraints at the local level) and "*agenzia*" factors (the way in which actors mobilise these resources and act to counter the constraints) in order to gain a better understanding of the dynamics of the development processes (Buroni and Trigiglia, 2010). Players' actions run up against the inertia of at least one part of the contextual factors: besides the often colossal work, hilly areas and hydrography, just like road and other constructed networks, are constraints that have to be managed as well as possible in order to develop the territory. The search for sustainable development processes illustrates, if such proof were needed, that natural ecosystems grow dynamically, and if this is not taken into account, natural resources will be depleted, pollution will increase, and the climate will become warmer. Economic and social resources can be developed more easily, but work on the local anchoring of the economy (Veltz, 2005; Novarina, 2011) highlights the cultural and sociological dimensions that are the outcome of a long history and clarifies the (non-)structuring of local environments capable of fostering innovation and creating businesses (Becattini, 2009).

The crisis of the welfare state in the mid-1970s led to renewed interest at the local level. It is at this scale that new methods of "squaring" cultural, social and economic activities were being implemented (Bagnasco, 2003). This social organising in local societies where some "traces of communities" have persisted – for example, those of the "urbanised countryside" in north-eastern and central Italy – is informal and spontaneous (Bagnasco, 1999). In metropolitan areas, it takes on a more institutionalised character. One example in this regard is the emergence of strategic planning experiences based on the involvement of a diverse array of civil society actors and the joint action to work on developing orientations and objectives (Bagnasco et al., 2010). Starting in the 1990s, the new planning approaches – strategic and spatial planning (Albrechts, 2004; Healey, 2004) and territorial planning (Novarina and Zepf, 2009), according to the authors – have been based on both developing local economic resources (expanding the basket of goods and services) and generating intangible resources (increasing the level of education and training of inhabitants, developing entrepreneurship, creating an environment that is favourable to social relationships) with the goal of reviving the local economy and stimulating urban redevelopment. Since the beginning of the 2000s, in particular with climate-energy plans, local authorities have included climate change adaptation objectives in these approaches for the purpose of achieving an economic, social and ecological transition.

In this chapter we examine the new local strategies of energy transition and the modes of governance that underpin them. To this end, we present the results of a research programme focused on the development of energy transition strategies in three European cities (Bristol, Freiburg im Breisgau and Grenoble). First, after presenting our methodology, we start with an analysis of the specifics of the territorial context and identify the constraints and the resources linked to both the geographic framework and the forms that urban development can take. Second, we show how the local actors seize the opportunities offered by the development of new national and regional energy transition policies to come up with strategies for local resource mobilisation, and we analyse the relationships between territorial planning, local energy policies and new urban projects. Third, we identify the actors involved in these strategies and analyse the new modes of governance.

7.2 METHODOLOGY AND TERRITORIAL CONTEXTS

7.2.1 A Quantitative and Qualitative Research Methodology

This section draws on the results of research (Seigneuret et al., 2016), funded by the French Council of Energy and carried out by Enerdata (2016). This research was conducted on energy transition strategies and projects implemented in three European cities: Bristol (England), Freiburg im Breisgau (Germany) and Grenoble (France).[1]

First, we did a comparative analysis of 20 European cities. This analysis took into account the links and relations between the territorial characteristics (geographical framework, available natural resources, climate, compactness and the spread of urbanisation), these cities' socio-economic dynamics and the development of decentralised energy management strategies.

Second, we examined the issues of strategies and governance using three case studies. This work was done, on the one hand, by analysing documents on the national and regional energy policies and studying strategies of territorial planning and landmark urban projects at the local level and, on the other hand, by carrying out *in situ* investigations, conducting a series of interviews with elected officials, technicians, architects, urban planners, engineers, academics and residents and paying visits to architectural and urban operations. This approach enabled us to understand the drivers of urban ecosystems that foster the emergence of social and technological innovations in order to manage energy at the local level.

The analysis of urban projects and strategies was conducted with a funnelling approach to the three case studies: from the countries' current situation (political and administrative systems, energy policies and

---

[1] Research funded by the French Council of Energy and carried out by Enerdata, a research and consulting firm in the global energy industry, along with researchers from the PACTE Humanities and Social Sciences Research Centre, as well as the AE&CC Architecture and Urban Planning research unit and the G2Elab electrical engineering research centre.

national players) to regional energy planning and policies to the specific context of territorial communities, local urban planning and energy policies and landmark urban projects. The analysis may be close to what Yves Chalas calls a figurative analysis (Chalas, 2000), which is an approach that seeks to produce representations of an urban reality by giving equal weight to observation, description and analysis. The goal of this approach is to focus more on the similarities than the differences that may exist between metropolitan planning strategies and the implementation of local urban projects.

In this way, we show how the proliferation of actors – and especially of the relationships that are cultivated – reveals a process of cooperation aimed at reducing technological uncertainty and increasing the stakeholders' innovation skills. In particular, we have studied these relationships between political, economic and academic actors for the cities of Grenoble and Bristol as part of a comparative analysis of discourses of the "sustainable city" (Griggs et al., 2017).

7.2.2 The Territorial Contexts

7.2.2.1 Geographical framework and urban forms

The three European cities that were the focus of our research, whose common feature is that they are involved in innovative energy transition projects, are part of different territorial contexts.

Located in a hilly landscape in South West England, Bristol (440000 inhabitants) lies at the bottom of the Avon River Valley and is well connected to major international traffic routes. Bristol's geographical setting appears to favour growth, as the constraints resulting from the city's geographical positioning are of little significance. As for urban forms, Bristol grew by adopting a typology particular to English cities, namely terraced housing. This situation is confirmed by the analyses of Corine Land Cover: Bristol forms the main urban centre of a territory that is still predominantly agricultural, with a central urban zone that is relatively large given the number of inhabitants. The city's compactness index[2] is 1639 inhabitants per square kilometre, and its density[3] is 3900 inhabitants per square kilometre.

Freiburg im Breisgau is a medium-sized city located in the Rhine Valley, at the foot of the Black Forest. It lies in one of the main transport

[2] The compactness index is equal to the ratio of the population to the surface area of the community's central area.

[3] The density is equal to the ratio of the population to the total surface area of the community.

corridors in Europe. The city's terrain includes both a lowland area and hillsides. It is part of a string of medium-sized cities that dot the length of the valley. The urban form reflects a duality: The compactness index is 3558 inhabitants per square kilometre, while the density is 1400 inhabitants per square kilometre. Small buildings and houses have sprung up next to the historic centre, which itself has undergone redevelopment since the 1950s. Freiburg is "a slow-growing, organic city that, compared with the Ruhr metropolitan region, has faced few structural changes or sharp breaks" (Meyer, 2013).

Grenoble (405 156 inhabitants) is located far from major road, highway and railway routes. This isolated position has been presented as a constraint that local actors have had to deal with to grow their businesses (Blanchard, 1935). A valley floor situated at the confluence of the Isère and Drac rivers and surrounded by three mountain massifs has drawbacks (the narrowness of the plain prevents urbanisation from spreading, there is water in the subsurface, and the rivers create barriers) that have shaped the city's urban development. The lack of space explains the need to intensify urban development, which results in both a higher compactness index (3673 inhabitants per square kilometre) and especially a higher density (8500 inhabitants per square kilometre). The metropolitan area is characterised by contrasting urban features (historic centre, condominiums, individual homes, large complexes, business parks) that have made for a heterogeneous landscape.

7.2.2.2 Natural resources

A large part of the three urban areas' territory is still made up of natural, agricultural and forest space: agricultural land makes up 75.3 per cent of Bristol, 44.6 per cent of Freiburg and 37.2 per cent of Grenoble, while forest spaces comprise 9.4 per cent, 46.2 per cent and 57.2 per cent, respectively.[4] This differentiated division between agricultural land and forests means there are different ways of making use of the biomass.

The geographical location explains, at least in part, the existence or the non-existence of particular energy resources. Since the 19th century, Grenoble, situated at the foot of the mountains, has been at the forefront of harnessing the force of running water, and it is the adopted home of engineer Aristide Bergès, who discovered hydroelectricity in 1882. This resource enriched the city throughout the first half of the 20th century as numerous industries either manufacturing turbines or using this energy (paper mills, foundries, chemicals) started operating in Grenoble. The

---

4 Source: Corine Land Cover.

city of Bristol, located on England's Atlantic coast, has good wind exposure, which makes it possible to consider putting up wind farms. As for Freiburg, a little under half of its territory is covered by forest, and it also has the potential to utilise wind.

With regard to the possible use of solar energy, while cities in the south may have an advantage over those in the north, this advantage decreases when the number of heating degree days are calculated. While optimal irradiation in Grenoble is 4550 watts/m^2/day, it is only 3590 in Freiburg and 3460 in Bristol. The number of heating degree days is similar: 2252, 2780 and 2762, respectively. Natural resource endowments – and we will return to this point later on – do not seem to have had any decisive impact on the cities' commitment to energy transition, and taken on their own they do not explain why any particular type of renewable resource is favoured.

7.2.2.3 Economic and social resources

What the three cities have in common is that they have an industrial past and have had to confront economic change, which they have done with varying success. Bristol and Freiburg managed to take the wheel with respect to expanding the tertiary sector, and in this regard the two urban areas are very appealing: between 2008 and 2011, the annual growth rate in paid employment continued to be positive (around 1.5 per cent), with a migratory balance (2007–12) of 1.7 per cent and 5.9 per cent, respectively. By contrast, the indicators in Grenoble are more mixed: the rise in employment is negative (−0.27 per cent), and the migratory balance stands at only 0.8 per cent. While all three cities played the card of developing the tertiary sector (the so-called higher services' share of employment in 2011 was 16.8 per cent in Bristol, 14.5 per cent in Freiburg and 16.1 per cent in Grenoble), they had different development strategies.[5]

In Grenoble, the decision to focus on scientific and technological innovation led to a rise in employment in the design and research sectors but did not successfully counter the decline in industrial employment, which had already begun as far back as 1975 (Novarina and Seigneuret, 2015). Bristol highlights its residents' level of education (34.5 per cent have a graduate degree, compared with 29 per cent nationally), its university and the number of students (54000). Bristol also emphasises the ethnic and cultural diversity and its wealth of heritage, which make it a "brilliant city" (Bristol City Council, 2011). Freiburg, which also has a university and research centres, has become a place to visit in the Rhine

[5] The statistical data were compiled, as part of the Enerdata research, by Magali Talandier on the basis of Eurostat data.

Valley. The city first came to prominence because of the quality of the restoration work in its city centre. This policy resulted in maintaining the city's tram network, which has played a leading role in urban planning policy-making. This tourist appeal has continued ever since and has been strengthened by the eco-neighbourhoods of Vauban and Rieselfeld, which receive 25 000 visitors per year at present (Meyer, 2013).

The more or less strong dynamics of these three cities are linked less to so-called metropolitan functions[6] – foremost among which is higher education and research (the rate of employment in the higher services in each of them is close to 15 per cent) – than to their ability to link business creation and job creation in the production sector with the development of a residential economy, which is linked in particular to the quality of the city and a careful development of the places receiving it. While Bristol wants to be viewed as "brilliant" and Freiburg claims it has a "sweetness of life", Grenoble continues to define itself as a "city of scientific and technological innovation".

7.3 NATIONAL POLICIES AND LOCAL STRATEGIES

7.3.1 National Energy Policies

In France, despite the extension of the powers of local authorities, the State has retained control over major investment programmes (highways, TGV, nuclear power plants etc.). Investment in nuclear energy is an outlier, with one of the energy players, Electricité de France, playing a decisive role in shaping energy policy. This policy has resulted in nuclear energy having a predominant role in power generation (78 per cent). France had to wait for the implementation of the Grenelle Acts (2009 and 2010) and the law pertaining to the energy transition for green growth (2015) before it could reconvert its energy model.

The United Kingdom, which is also a centralised country, built its energy model on the development of its own resources by focusing on coal, as well as gas and petroleum from the North Sea. While these resources have contributed to its energy independence, they are running out, and since 2004, the United Kingdom has been a gas – and then, also,

[6] According to the National Institute for Statistics and Economic Studies, metropolitan functions are activities that have a strategic dimension and are preferably located in large urban areas. They include design, research, intellectual services, business-to-business trading, management, culture and recreation.

a petroleum – importer. "The United Kingdom is 42% dependent on imports (2012 data, Eurostat). Its energy production is close to those of France and Germany (in the order of between 110 million and 130 million tonnes of oil equivalent), but the British model is radically different". The share of nuclear energy in energy production "is only 13.5% in the United Kingdom, compared with 70% for hydrocarbons. While carbon and its derivatives (especially lignite) make up around 45% of the energy produced in Germany, they account for only 10% of British production" (Bailoni, 2014). Today, the United Kingdom has set itself a low carbon transition target, which calls for an energy mix to be established that would combine renewables, nuclear energy and shale gas. The early stages of nuclear recovery are perceptible, with Electricité de France's acquisition of British Energy in 2008 and the announcement in 2013 that a dozen new plants would be built.

In Germany, the electricity industry is built around regional companies – E.ON (Prussia and Bavaria), RWE (Rhineland and Westphalia) and EnBW (Baden-Württemberg) – that have developed territorial monopolies directly related to the partitioning of the German states (Länder). These are companies listed on the stock exchange but managed by the public regulations of their particular state, which is the main shareholder. In this context, the intermediate levels, namely the states, have a lot of flexibility to promote the use of renewable energy and energy savings. Germany's decision to halt nuclear power led to a turning point (*Energiewende*) that, in turn, issued a societal challenge and brought about an economic project. The search for energy efficiency has allowed the development of advanced technologies and the building and establishment of a business model. The energy transition has sought the societal acceptance of a policy based on the one hand on citizens' and industries' rising energy bills, with low-income households facing a double penalty, and on the other hand on the closing of all nuclear power plants by 2022, and consequently thermal power plants that pollute by using gas and coal.

National energy transition policies are being developed in the three surveyed countries, but they are proceeding at different tempos – in particular, because of the power wielded by the lobbies (nuclear lobby in France, hydrocarbon lobby in England) and of the social acceptability of the policies that are being undertaken. These policies are relayed via the Länder in Germany and to a lesser extent through the regions in France (Table 7.1). Freiburg gained support from the Land of Baden-Württemberg, and Grenoble took advantage of the Air Quality Regional Strategy that the Rhône-Alpes Region approved in 2014.

Table 7.1 Territorial and energy planning

National level	Regional level	Local level
France Principles and rules defined by law at the national level and control over the legality of municipal decisions. Successive laws: "Grenelle 1 and 2" laws (2009–10) and the law on "Energy Transition for Green Growth" (2015). A changing legislative context in 2015: The "Nouvelle Organisation Territoriale de la République" compels regions to adopt a "Regional sustainable development and territorial equality Strategy".	Auvergne–Rhône-Alpes Region This region has been reluctant to engage in territorial planning but has taken initiatives in terms of energy planning with the "Regional Climate Air Energy Strategy", approved in 2014.	Grenoble Urban Region, Metropolis Grenoble Urban region: 284 municipalities and 8 inter-municipalities. Its Territorial Coherence Plan, the "SCoT" (2012), attempts to regulate urban sprawl. Grenoble-Alpes Métropole: 49 municipalities An "Air Energy and Climate Plan" (2005). Since 2016, an inter-municipal local urban planning plan has been developed. Its objective is to combat climate change and engage in the energy transition.
United Kingdom Strategic framework: "National Planning Policy Statements and Regulations" and *a priori* control by the Department of Local Government and Communities of decisions by local authorities. Successive laws: "Climate Change Act" (2007) sets energy targets.	Western England With the adoption in 2011 of the "Localism Act", the abolition of Regional Assemblies, Regional Development Agencies and Regional Spatial Strategies. Abolition in 2013 of the "Regional Spatial Strategy" for the South-West.	Bristol City Council Its "Development Framework Core Strategy" constitutes the strategic part of the local plan (2011). In 2010, the Bristol Energy Network was created, and in 2013, the Community Strategy for Energy was published. Since 2018, the Bristol Local Plan has been under revision.

Table 7.1 (continued)

National level	Regional level	Local level
"Planning and Energy Act" (2008) allows local authorities to integrate energy-saving criteria in local plans. "UK Heat and Energy Saving Strategy" (2009) concerns heating networks and co-generation.	The Combined Authority, which includes Bristol, Bath, North Somerset and South Gloucestershire, launched a "Joint Strategic Planning Strategy" in 2014.	
Germany Principles of spatial planning with a framework law: "Raumordnungsgesetz" has combined federalism and local autonomy since 1991. A law to promote renewable energy: "Erneuerbare-Energien-Gesetz" (2010) and a National Action Plan, the "Nationaler aktionsplan energieeffizienz" (2014), which links societal challenges with an economic project.	Baden-Württemberg Land Land Development Plan: "Landesentwicklungsplan" (2002) describes a system of centralities, defines infrastructure programmes, establishes measures to protect open spaces and identifies high-, medium- and low-density areas. "E-Energy and E-mobility programmes", developed as part of the national MEREGIO programme. "Minimum Emission Regio" (2014) to limit greenhouse gas emissions.	Freiburg im Breisgau The "Flächennutzungsplan 2020" land use plan integrates landscape concerns for the first time in Germany (2002). The "Stadtentwicklungsplanung" (2006) urban development plan proposes a strategic vision, "Leitbild", based on urban development concepts. Introduction of the "Freiburger Effizienhausstandard" in 2009. Since 2014, the development of framework data for a climate-neutral city: "Klima neutrale kommune 2050".

Source: Authors, based on Seigneuret et al. (2016).

7.3.2 Territorial Energy Transition Strategies

The momentum of the energy systems in Grenoble, Bristol and Freiburg im Breisgau is driven by a move to increase the role of local authorities in controlling the energy resources and combating climate change, as well as a growing willingness on the part of the consumers (local authorities, businesses and households) to better control their consumption and to become local energy producers.

7.3.2.1 Spatial strategy and sustainable development in Bristol

South West England is considered a major contributor – second only to the Greater London area – to the country's economic growth. In 2004, following the adoption by Parliament of the Planning and Compulsory Purchase Act, this region embarked on developing a Regional Spatial Strategy. After the Conservative government voted to pass the Localism Act in 2011, which abolished regional planning, local authorities (Bristol City Council, Bath & North East Somerset, South Gloucestershire), in order to make up for the lack of a framework document, implemented a Joint Strategic Planning Strategy (2014) that focuses on a more limited territory: the West of England. They are now organised within the West of England Combined Authority.

In Bristol, the region's main urban centre, the Development Framework Core Strategy (2011), which forms a strategic part of the urban development plan, expects the rate of demographic growth (+26 per cent between 2006 and 2026) to remain stable and the city's population to reach 519 800 inhabitants. The City Council offers to support this development in order to prevent it from damaging the environment (rivers and canals), landscape (numerous parks and gardens) and cultural heritage (medieval centre, Georgian and Victorian quarters and the port and its industrial facilities). The quality of the places is considered as both part of the residents' quality of life and a factor of attractiveness. The city's goals are the sustainable development of its economy, the regeneration of its former industrial districts, the strengthening of local centres and the networking of its green infrastructure. In terms of mobility, the metropolitan area doesn't have a tram network, which explains why the share of people travelling by car (57 per cent) is higher than in the other two cities in the study (Bristol City Council, 2011). The aim of the proposed actions (introducing reserved corridors, improving frequency) is to ensure a better-functioning bus network.

The urban development plan is implemented through both sectoral strategies and a few major urban projects. In the field of energy, the strategies assess the available resources that may make it possible for an energy mix to be established (Smith, 2009). Three energy sources are to be favoured: wind; heat and power generation by burning waste; and biomass. This plan to diversify energies in order to generate power and heat is helped by the existence of a district heating network, which is projected to be extended. The functioning of this network supposes both the mobilisation of existing resources (exploiting forests, reclaiming wood, developing willow crops) and the use of non-local but non-polluting resources (gas, in particular). In terms of energy savings in construction, the strategy proposes an even more ambitious scenario than the national Building Regulations proposal: a further 28 per cent reduction in carbon emissions for a 7 per cent increase in construction costs.

Among the projects that are underway in the Greater Bristol area, the one that makes the most comprehensive use of the environmental and energy dimensions is without a doubt Avonmouth Severnside. This 1800-hectare enterprise area employs 14 200 people in the storage, distribution, wholesale and industrial sectors. The area, served by two highways, is located near the port, the main area where goods are unloaded to supply the southern part of England. The redevelopment project covers 650 hectares and prioritises activities related to renewable (wind) energies and waste treatment with an eye towards energy co-generation. The project, which meets the requirements of the energy transition, focuses on an area where logistics is of paramount importance. The stated objective is to reinforce this vocation with a view to strengthening the role of the port. Avonmouth Severnside's development role complements that of another enterprise area located near the main train station, Bristol Temple Quarter (70 hectares). The latter is intended to host research and technology activities in the media sector. Therefore, a balance is sought between welcoming new innovative companies and supporting the existing activities in industry and logistics.

7.3.2.2 Energiewende and the Klimaneutrale Kommune in Freiburg im Breisgau

Baden-Württemberg is one of the six pilot Länder of the E-Energy and E-Mobility programmes in Germany. The Minimum Emission Region (MEREGIO) programme aims to develop intelligent energy consumption, distribution and production in minimum emission regions. Located in the heart of the Land, Freiburg im Breisgau is one of the forerunners with regard to the development of the *Energiewende* energy policy. The economy and energy and environmental research play a particularly important role in Freiburg. With 12 000 jobs in 2000 businesses, this sector produces around 650 million euros in revenue and contributes to the region's positive image. In the solar economy sector alone, the number of jobs is three or even four times that of Germany's federal average (Interview with an elected official – Regional and local authorities, Freiburg 2015).

In Freiburg im Breisgau, the energy transition is the foundation for an overall energy equilibrium strategy that is supported by a shared vision (*Leitbild*). This vision is based on the following:

- An organisation of the urban framework aims to produce a city of short distances. Densification is preferable for industrial and military sites. Inner development (*inländische Entwicklung*) seeks to build the "city on top of the city" by implementing the concept of markets and centralities (*Märkte und Zentrenkonzept*), which favours local shops over supermarkets.
- The link between urban planning and transport is based on urban development along collective transport routes (65 per cent of the population lives close to a tram station), reserved lanes and secure parking areas for cycles, limited parking, reduced downtown access for cars and speed restrictions in residential areas. Thus, 90 per cent of the population in residential areas live in 30 km/h zones, and funding is reserved for residents committed to not using private transport.
- The principle of a shared and inclusive city implies that residents participate in designing projects, make the neighbourhood livelier and manage the sociability in public spaces. The Green City Cluster pools all the citizens' Green Ideas. The ideas, which are copyright-protected, can be accessed by everyone and range from realistic to utopian proposals to construct a sustainable city: Smart City and Living Lab, Mobility and hydrogen-based energy storage, renewable methane, sustainable bio-energy and sustainable plants, Green Hospital, Intelligent Green Tower.
- Respect for nature in the city requires that a green belt be maintained and that 46 per cent of the natural spaces be classified as protected areas. In addition, 500 hectares of green space are spread out from the periphery to the city centre with differentiated management. The air, water and soil are also subject to strict monitoring and protection in the Land Use Plan (Interview with a technician, Regional and local authorities, Freiburg 2015).

This urban planning policy is combined with multiple projects that reflect the development principles developed in the Vauban neighbourhood. This neighbourhood, which has been well publicised, is proof that the city can showcase a successful union between territorial and energy planning to visitors and residents. The know-how developed in this district has been applied to new construction and the redevelopment of residential areas and business parks on the basis of a specific energy benchmark in Freiburg, with more ambitious energy consumption criteria than the national requirements. This standard (*Freiburger Effizienzhausstandard*) applies to all public and private buildings, whatever their purpose. It is integrated into all urban planning documents and sales contracts. For new buildings, the orientation and placement of the buildings are defined for solar energy optimisation and passive standard construction, and a connection to a co-generation plant is mandatory. For existing buildings, during renovation, ways are being sought for buildings to be insulated and connected to a co-generation plant. Freiburg doesn't have one single urban heating network but rather a multitude of decentralised co-generation plants of various sizes that connect to the projects (Interview with a technician – Energy agency, Freiburg 2015).

The social acceptance of consumption reduction schemes has gained support from an energy agency that has developed and shared know-how with universities, businesses and construction professionals, as well as awareness campaigns. Longevity and the sharing of actions have made it possible in Freiburg to develop strategies collectively that go beyond individual interests and sectoral approaches. This community has the means to be an example in the fields of territorial planning, mobility management and construction, before being one in the energy field, too. There has been more development in the field of renewable energies in this city than in Bristol or Grenoble, with a very inclusive set of players and demonstration projects acting to come up with collective designs of topics that are usually tackled separately by the various parties.

The collective desire to have a climate-neutral community by 2050 (Freiburg-im-Breisgau, 2011) will require energy autonomy centred on renewable energy, ever more energy performance during the renovation of buildings that make up 80 per cent of constructed heritage and increased research into an efficient supply system.

7.3.2.3 Technological innovations and demonstration projects in Grenoble

The Grenoble metropolitan area has a strong potential for developing sustainable energy projects, and the public authorities are aware of this. Technological and innovation dynamism, along with wide availability for the decentralised implementation of energy projects, is found among the three major players: the local energy operator, Gaz Electricité de Grenoble; the public authorities, the City of Grenoble, Grenoble Alpes Métropole; and the public bodies that specialise in energy (the Agence Locale de l'Energie et du Climat and the Agence De l'Environnement et de la Maîtrise de l'Energie). In this favourable context, several small and medium-sized enterprises (SMEs), as well as start-ups, have sprung up. "The complementarity of Grenoble's players – between energy companies, state-of-the-art research centres and innovative SMEs – has created extremely favourable conditions for the advancement of new technologies, mainly in the fields of energy and electricity" (Rey, 2013).

Territorial planning was renewed around energy issues with localised demonstration projects. First, the demonstration was jointly carried out in a new neighbourhood, the De Bonne eco-neighbourhood, and so was a scheduled programme of thermal and energy improvements to buildings in an existing neighbourhood, the Grands Boulevards. A combination of technical interests and local policies then came to life in a full package based on the technological innovations obtained through these two initiatives, as well as a guide of recommendations for a High Quality Environmental Architectural and Urban standard, annexed to the Local Urbanism Plan. In addition, a policy of communicating about and enhancing demonstration projects resulted in a sustainable development biennale being organised in Grenoble (Interview with a technician – Regional and local authorities, Grenoble 2015).

Secondly, the demonstration focused on the Scientific Peninsula, where there is a focus on inserting technological activities into a broader urban project, a precursor to the "post-carbon city". This goal of urbanity is taking shape, first, through the innovation campus project, also called the "French MIT". As a result, it is being carried out with the elaboration of an urban project that links together the Grenoble Alpes Métropole, the City of Grenoble and scientists to position the metropolitan area for international scientific and university competitions (Grenoble-Alpes Métropole, 2011). This urban project is making it possible for the Scientific Peninsula to be turned into a demonstration of the Grenoble eco-city. This project has prioritised the development of technological innovations for an "efficient city" and a "peaceful city", with, on the level of integrated urban blocks, cooperative energy management (smart grids, smart metering) and a comprehensive approach to mobility (tram network, bike paths, ride-sharing, mobility pavilion) (Interview with a technician – Regional and local authorities, Grenoble 2015).

This technical orientation meets both the criteria set for the funding of eco-cities and the weight of the local scientific community, which seeks to pursue scientific and technological innovations in a territorial research centre with limited experimentation and a non-inclusive set of actors. However, beyond the construction of a technological showcase, the Peninsula project has made it possible to launch and carry out a metropolitan strategy that will need time to be assessed. The Grenoble metropolitan area is proposing to increase the number of projects across the entire territory, starting with successful demonstrations, for a Smart

City approach (Grenoble-Alpes Métropole, 2016), for a breathable, agile, collaborative and peaceful territory through:

- economic development by nurturing private initiatives and local know-how to develop renewable energies and more proactive choices so that consumers can better control their energy consumption and become local producers;
- the energy efficiency of buildings, with ever greater performance in the construction of new districts, as in the renovation of older districts (eco-renovation campaigns, extended to individual homes and to all condominiums, regardless of when they were built);
- networking natural spaces by creating ecological corridors and reintroducing nature in the metropolitan area.

The dynamics that we have studied in the energy field are based on proactive planning. And what distinguishes our three case studies from each other is the more or less integrated character of the territorial planning of sustainable urban development, the more or less proactive linking of territorial plans (territorial coherence plans) with energy policies (territorial climate-energy plans) and the more or less successful transition from strategies to projects (eco-neighbourhoods and eco-cities). Subsequently, the technological and social innovations that have been examined all tend to solve the difficult equation imposed by the paradigm of sustainable urban development: simultaneously strengthening economic efficiency, preserving natural resources and improving the social situation among populations, all within the context of a drop in public money.

7.4 THE ENERGY TRANSITION AND ITS GOVERNANCE

The study of territorial strategies of ecological transition in three cities, based in particular on a decentralised production of energy, makes it possible to identify the actors involved in this transition and the different roles they play.[7] What is the structure of the networks of actors involved in overseeing the transition? Of course, this analysis takes into account the way in which the local actors play with the constraints that the national policies have imposed on them and seize opportunities that these policies might offer them.

---

[7] This analysis is based on the work carried out by Oana Ionescu within the framework of research led by ENERDATA.

7.4.1 Bristol: Objective-based, Pragmatic Strategy

Bristol is known for its environmental initiatives, thanks to which the city has earned the title of *Green Capital*, which the European Union bestowed on it in 2015. The context of this recognition is that the British government favours business-led development strategies. One of the main features of the governance of policies is the existence of partnerships between a wide variety of actors from both the public and the private sectors and from the world of non-governmental organisations and foundations. These partnerships in fields ranging from territorial planning and sustainable development to renewable energy production are forged in collaboration with local authorities or replace them when it comes to managing particular projects.

Among the most active of these partnerships, the Local Enterprise Partnership is in charge of a West England-wide economic development strategy, and the Bristol Green Capital Partnership is working to make Bristol a sustainable city with a high quality of life. The latter partnership also played a major role when the city made an application to the European Union. In the first partnership mentioned, the actors involved, in addition to the local authorities, include businesses, financial companies and universities; in the second, the community interest company also involves foundations and environmental protection organisations. The City Council also has the Bristol Energy Network, founded in 2010 to support initiatives of Neighbourhood Community Energy Groups and that, with the mayor's support, coordinated the implementation of a city-wide energy strategy (2013).

These partnerships go hand in hand with the strengthening of local political leadership. Bristol is one of 15 British cities that, following the adoption of the Localism Act, opted to elect their mayor directly by universal suffrage. The first mayor elected in 2012 was an architect who had run as an independent candidate. His campaign slogan was: "my only purpose is to make Bristol, the city I love, a better city for all", and he emphasised urban regeneration. Despite his strong personality, he was beaten by a Labour Party politician in 2016. This leadership is further strengthened by the City Council's participation in a combined authority that also elected a mayor by direct universal suffrage. The partnerships, therefore, complement the actions of other powerful players, which include not only local political authorities but also private companies (especially those in charge of energy production and distribution across the West of England) and, to a lesser extent, residents' cooperatives or community-based organisations specialising in the energy field.

Thus, it is a local system in which the actors have an autonomous capacity for action and try to impose their views and choices within a competitive context. The strategy adopted in terms of energy transition does not require the prior development of a vision serving as a frame of reference for the actions undertaken but is built on the basis of sharing a few key issues, such as showcasing the city's heritage, networking green infrastructure, co-generation and wind power. This objective-based strategy is also characterised by its pragmatism; it identifies the energy resources available on the territory, mobilises private and public financial and enhances the quality of the places.

7.4.2 The City of Short Distances in Freiburg: An Integrated and Inclusive Strategy

Today, Freiburg and its eco-neighbourhoods are considered a benchmark of sustainable urban development in Europe. The exemplary nature of its achievements has enabled architectural and urban tourism and is the result of a strategy developed over time. This strategy focused first on promoting the city's historical heritage, then on developing a tram network and finally on creating eco-neighbourhoods.

The major stakeholder in this process is the City of Freiburg, which relies on the skills of municipal businesses, including *Badenova*, which is tasked with distributing energy and managing the networks. Over the years, the local authorities have also established a permanent dialogue with the residents, who are not considered simple users but are urged to take part in producing renewable and decentralised energy. The other stakeholders (universities, business groups, consulting firms and experts) are involved in *ad hoc* and specialised missions. As a stakeholder, the public plays a central role, but its actions are facilitated by the management flexibility of municipal urban service businesses (*Stadtwerke*).

The transition strategy adopted by the city appears to be well integrated. In concert with local actors, it starts by developing a strategic vision (*Leitbild*) that is visible in the willingness to build the "city on top of the city" by consolidating the existing centralities and reinforcing active mobility. The search for energy performance is one element among many that contribute to improving the living conditions. The strategy is also inclusive because it is based on an integration of sectoral actions and particular projects and built together with civil society.

While the development of such a strategy relies on heavy public involvement (including in terms of funding), there is know-how to seize the opportunities offered by the national policy and to utilise a range of available local resources. It also involves a mobilisation of a diverse set of actors, and residents' associations and cooperatives play an important role. Finally, it looks to strengthen the attractiveness of the city by highlighting the quality of its (heritage and contemporary) architecture and the "sweetness of life" that is the order of the day there.

7.4.3 The Eco-city in Grenoble: Technological Innovations and Demonstration Project

Grenoble has been recognised on the national stage, first of all for the quality of its first eco-neighbourhood, De Bonne. Its commitment to sustainable development has been recognised by the Ministry of Ecology, which in 2011 approved its candidacy as an eco-city. The latter's perimeter, which was initially supposed to cover the three secondary polarities (East, West, South) identified by the Conurbation Project that the Grenoble Alpes Métropole adopted in 2012, was, at the request of the ministry and of the Caisse des Dépôts et Consignations (Public Investment Fund) reduced to a single "neighbourhood", the Scientific Peninsula. This sector includes some of the research centres and businesses that make up what is called "the innovation ecosystem". The energy transition strategy featured in territorial planning, presented in Act II of the Metropolitan Project (Grenoble-Alpes Métropole, 2007), and sectoral planning documents (urban travel plans, climate-energy plan), which is the metropolitan area's responsibility, but there is a difference between these documents and the operational projects initiated by the City of Grenoble on the one hand and the scientific and technical community on the other hand.

This strategy has only a few stakeholders, and they are organised around three pillars: the local political authorities, the City of Grenoble, whose role is gradually taking a back seat to that of the Grenoble Alpes Métropole; energy suppliers, research laboratories and large companies (Schneider, Siemens etc.); and start-ups specialising in renewable energy. In this decision-making context, the experts, whose skills are in the fields of engineering, architecture, construction and, to a lesser extent, urban planning, take part in developing technical solutions whose innovative character is presented as the most effective way to meet the challenges of transitioning to a post-carbon city. Consultation is sought with the inhabitants, but the purpose is to inform the future occupants so that they appropriate the technologies installed in their housing.

The transition strategy adopted by the City of Grenoble can be described as incremental. It does not derive from general development guidelines defined in advance but seeks the best way to seize opportunities – such as the European Union's CONCERTO programme during the development of the De Bonne neighbourhood, or the Investment Plan for the Future when the eco-city's candidacy was being drafted. The strategy goes through a search for technological solutions (positive energy buildings, smart electricity meters, smart grids), whose effectiveness is assessed through the fastest possible implementation of innovative operational projects, which are thought of as demonstration projects. In such a perspective, the creation of a green and blue network and the re-vegetation of public spaces to reduce heat islands are perceived as being more in line with a classic environmental policy to preserve natural areas than the ecological transition strategy.

7.5 BY WAY OF CONCLUSION: RESOURCE MOBILISATION AND SOCIAL ORGANISING PROCESSES

Urban regime theory provides insight into the differences in strategy between the three cities that were the focus of the study. The "development regimes", which correspond to the management methods of the major urban projects underway at the beginning of the 1980s in many big cities in Europe or North America (Stone, 1993), continue in the strategy adopted today. In Grenoble, the development of the actions undertaken results from the search for a compromise between a small number of actors, namely the local authorities, representatives of large public companies and the heads of big research centres. They are based on immediately applicable technical solutions and do not require the prior development of a comprehensive reference framework. At least until recently, they have often been part of sectoral policies, and the selected urban projects are intended to demonstrate solutions that can be applied independently of the specificities of the territories comprising the conurbation.

The shift from a "development regime" to a "popular participation regime" entails an increase in the number of systems that enable the actors to participate (associations, community organisations etc.), less accustomed to the arcana of the power networks. The pragmatic strategy that the City of Bristol adopted, based on a proliferation of the number of partnerships, is similar to this type of regime. But in this city, initiatives tend to multiply and are often regulated by competition. The regulatory framework provided by the spatial strategies seems very flexible, and pragmatism prevails when energy solutions are selected.

The integrated and inclusive strategy developed in Freiburg im Breisgau is also based on the involvement of a wide range of local actors, foremost among whom are the city's residents. In this city, however, the actions carried out and the projects undertaken are part of an overall vision. Such a strategy involves substantial work to justify the choices because adherence to strategic orientations stems less from a convergence of interests than from shared values. The popular participation regime then takes on a "symbolic" dimension that appears to guarantee an enduring consensus among the actors (Stoker and Mossberger, 1994). The ecological transition strategies, adopted in Freiburg and to a lesser extent in Bristol, are based on social organising that is constantly seeking to increase interrelationships and promote intermediation. They are therefore based on the creation of this particular territorial resource, namely social capital, a resource that also has a renewable character. Furthermore, they are based on the creation of a "spatial capital" that brings together "the advantages resulting from a control of geographic layouts" (Lévy and Lussault, 2003) and that includes the organisation of the traffic networks, the morphology of the different clusters that the city is comprised of, the reservoirs of "naturalness" and the ecological corridors that structure the green and blue networks.

Thus, comparing the three cases with each other shows that the differences between the territorial energy strategies do not stem primarily from a differentiated endowment of resources. A mountainous area is, of course, more conducive to hydroelectric facilities than a coastal territory, which is more favourable to the installation of wind turbines. These resources are partly latent, and a mobilisation of local actors is necessary to make it possible to use them. The differences in strategy are rather related to the greater or lesser diversity of actors, their degree of mobilisation, the way in which they share or fail to share the same vision of the qualities of the territory they inhabit and the potential to transform it.

REFERENCES

Albrechts, L. (2004), "Strategic (spatial) planning reexamined", *Environment and Planning B*, **31** (5), 743–58.

Bagnasco, A. (1999), *Tracce di comunità*, Bologna: Il Mulino.

Bagnasco, A. (2003), *Società fuori squadra. Come cambia l'organizzazione sociale*, Bologna: Il Mulino.

Bagnasco, A., Courlet, C. and Novarina, G. (2010), *Société urbaine et nouvelle économie*, Paris: L'Harmattan, La Librairie des Humanités.

Bailoni, M. (2014), "Les évolutions du modèle énergétique britannique face aux enjeux géopolitiques internes", *Vertigo*, **12** (1).

Becattini, G. (2009), *Ritorno al territorio*, Bologna: Il Mulino, Fondazione Edison.

Blanchard, R. (1935), *Grenoble. Etude de géographie urbaine*, Grenoble: Didier et Richard.

Bristol City Council (2011), *Bristol Development Framework: Core Strategy*, Bristol.

Buronni, L. and Trigilia, C. (2010), "Le città dell'innovazione nell'alta tecnologia", Incontri di Artimino sullo Sviluppo Locale, IRIS, Università degli Studi di Firenze, Regione Toscana.
Centre for Sustainable Energy (2009), *Bristol Citywide Sustainable Energy Study*, Bristol.
Chalas, Y. (2000), *L'invention de la ville*, Paris: Anthropos.
Enerdata (2016), *Impact du développement de la décentralisation des énergies sur le système énergétique*, Grenoble and Paris: Conseil Français de l'Energie.
Freiburg-im-Breisgau (2011), *Freiburg klimaneutral bis 2050*, Freiburg.
Griggs, S., Hall, S., Howarth, D. and Seigneuret, N. (2017), "Characterizing and evaluating rival discourses of the 'sustainable city': Towards a politics of pragmatic adversarialism", *Political Geography*, **59**, 36–46.
Grenoble-Alpes Métropole (2007), *Projet d'agglomération, Acte II, 2007–2013*, Grenoble.
Grenoble-Alpes Métropole (2011), *Ecocité grenobloise. Vivre la ville post-carbone dans les Alpes*, Grenoble.
Grenoble-Alpes Métropole (2016), *Eléments pour un débat sur les orientations générales du Projet d'aménagement et de développement durable. Plan local d'urbanisme intercommunal*, Grenoble.
Healey, P. (2004), "The treatment of space and place in new strategic spatial planning", *International Journal of Urban and Regional Research*, **28** (1), 45–67.
Hirczak, M., Moalla, M., Mollard, A., Pecqueur, B., Rambonilaza, M. and Vollet, D. (2008), "From the model of 'basket of goods' to a broader model of territorialized goods: concepts, methodology elements and issues", *Canadian Journal of Regional Science*, **2** (31), 241–59.
Levy, J. and Lussault, M. (2003), *Dictionnaire de la géographie et de l'espace des sociétés*, Paris: Belin.
Meyer, A. (2013), *Les éco-quartiers de Fribourg. 20 ans d'urbanisme durable*, Paris: Le Moniteur.
Novarina, G. (2011), "L'ancrage territorial de l'économie. Du district industriel à la métropole", *L'Economie Politique*, **53**, 16–25.
Novarina, G. and Seigneuret, N. (2015), *De la technopole à la métropole? L'exemple de Grenoble*, Paris: Le Moniteur.
Novarina, G. and Zepf, M. (2009), "Territorial planning in Europe. News concepts, new experiences", *DISP, The Planning Review*, **179** (4), 18–27.
Rey, M. (2013), "Grenoble fait le pari des énergies vertes", *L'Entreprise*, **319**, 64–7.
Seigneuret, N., Talandier, M. and Novarina, G. (2016), "Les villes post-carbone: un écosystème favorable à l'émergence de nouvelles formes de gestion décentralisée de l'énergie", in Enerdata, *Impact du développement de la décentralisation des énergies sur le système énergétique*, Grenoble and Paris: Conseil Français de l'Energie.
Smith, A. (2009), "Civil society in sustainable energy transitions" in Verbong, G. and D. Loorbach (eds) (2012), *Governing the energy transition: reality, illusion, or necessity*, New York: Routledge.
Stoker, G. and Mossberger, K. (1994), "Urban regime theory in a comparative perspective", *Environment and Planning C: Government and Policy*, **12** (2), 195–212.
Stone, C.N. (1993), "Urban regime and the capacity to govern: a political economy approach", *Journal of Urban Affairs*, **15** (1), 1–28.
Veltz, P. (2005), *Mondialisation, villes et territoires*, Paris: Quadrige, PUF.

PART II

Multifaceted well-being

8. Beyond monetary well-being: can sociabilities offset the effects of low income? A case study in the Grenoble metropolitan area

Anne Le Roy and Fiona Ottaviani

8.1 INTRODUCTION

Economic literature contains many debates around the issue of well-being, and monetary well-being in particular. This theme is at the heart of numerous publications and has produced a variety of approaches over time.

In the 1970s, Easterlin (1974) brought to light the lack of correlation between income per capita and long-term happiness, even if there is an observable correlation in many countries in the short term. Such works have sharpened the debates instead of shutting them down since the number of studies aiming to assess the existence of a correlation between income per capita and self-reported happiness has soared. In this respect, the overview seeking to test the "size of the coefficient of correlation between the income per capita and self-reported happiness", which Claudia Senik delivered at the Collège de France on 13 March 2013, made clear that it is not possible to settle the debate definitively since some research has found a positive but weak correlation while other works have shown a positive but weak and non-systematic correlation or even no correlation at all.

The alternative social and environmental indicators of development give new insight into this debate. Indeed, they reveal a lack of agreement between economic growth and the observed evolution in inequality, social and environmental health and well-being in all Western countries since the 1980s. Whether it is described through the indicators of well-being, the French Barometer of Inequalities and Poverty (BIP 40) or the Index of Social Health (ISH), the situations in France and the United States systematically appear to be less favourable than the countries' gross domestic product might suggest. The existence of such a gap points to the problem of merging the notions of GDP, prosperity and well-being, especially as doubt remains regarding the potential of Western economies to return to growth (Gadrey, 2010).

The debate on the relation between financial prosperity and well-being remains open. Furthermore, there is a growing consensus that people's well-being relies non-exclusively on economic characteristics (Stiglitz et al., 2009). Therefore, apprehending well-being makes us confront the analytical difficulties of analysing a multifaceted reality with only an economic and/or monetary (and often mono-disciplinary) approach. Social relations, our bonds with other people and with society in general, are central to numerous works devoted to understanding the various socio-economic "realities" that underpin well-being. Scientific literature on this topic, beyond the plurality of their theoretical positions, underlines the crucial role that social relations play in people's well-being.

Even if sociabilities are at the root of well-being in these works, only a few of them analyse their various aspects at a local level.[1] The deficit of knowledge on sociabilities is the cornerstone of the wealth-focused research that has been done in the Grenoble metropolitan area since 2012 thanks to urban policy professionals. This led to the collective construction of alternative indicators of well-being (*Indicateurs de Bien-Être Soutenable Territorialisés* – IBEST) with the help of academics, urban policy professionals, elected representatives, local associations and citizens.

Urban policy professionals made the following observation in 2002: if qualitative studies[2] at the neighbourhood scale show the importance of the social fabric to people's individual self-realisation, a generalisation of these results on the scale of a territorial unit and a precise characterisation of the social situation of the different socio-economic groups is not possible. The study could not assess whether the resource deficit (especially the monetary resource deficit) had a negative impact on people's sociabilities or whether their integration into the social fabric improved their financial situation. Thus, two questions require further examination and will be at the heart of this chapter: first, is the lack of monetary and relational resources cumulative, as some of the scientific literature suggests? And

---

[1] This is particularly true in the case of French studies, even though the 1983 Dubedout Report, entitled *Together, Remaking the City*, had already emphasised the importance of taking local sociabilities into account and had led to Neighbourhood Social Development operations (*Développement Social des Quartiers* or DSQ in French) and to the creation of the DSQ National Board for sensitive neighbourhoods.

[2] We refer here to the Neighbourhood barometer, which is an observation system that has existed for 15 years in the Grenoble metropolitan area and whose purpose is to collect the opinions of the locals (Duarte et al., 2012).

second, what is the relationship between interpersonal sociabilities, institutional sociabilities and income?

The variables examined in this research are specifically created at their particular geographic scale and form part of a broader consideration of sustainable well-being. We will start by elaborating on the theoretical position and methods adopted in order to understand the different kinds of sociabilities and answer our questions. Next, we will demonstrate how a thorough examination of the different types of sociabilities suggests that there is very little connection between people's income and their sociability resources, whether interpersonal or institutional. This will allow us to emphasise that the importance of sociabilities in people's self-realisation and their impact on their territory over time should expand the perception of inequalities beyond their financial aspects to the broader notion of inequalities in capabilities (Sen, 1992). It will also allow us to highlight that there is no single way in which to approach self-realisation and that it is necessary to make a detailed analysis of the different sociabilities in order to take into account their positive or detrimental effects regarding the development of public policies that support well-being.

8.2 THEORETICAL POSITION AND METHODS

To assess the different sociabilities and the role they play in well-being, the IBEST experimentation was informed by the following principles.

First, *it regards sociabilities not only as a means to an end* (access to status, higher income etc.) *but also as a purpose in itself*. Therefore, it is considered that relationships engender personal fulfilment but are also intermediate means (Meadows, 1998) that facilitate people's lives (for example, when it comes to access to housing, health care and financial or material resources).

Second, *it cross-references data on people's perception of their living conditions*. The goal is not to adopt a normative position on sociabilities; the IBEST position is that there is no ideal standard of sociability.[3]

Third, *its approach to sustainable well-being is based on capabilities* (Sen, 2008). This holistic vision of individuals is not restricted to assessing the effects of public policies (on employment, housing, health etc.) by only using sectoral indicators or subjective evaluations of well-being. It also uses thorough examinations that include transversal indicators of these

[3] The position expressed here should be distinguished from the approach by Putnam (1995), who draws a distinction between activities that are supposedly good for the community (like being involved in an association) and those that are bad (like watching television).

policies' positive or detrimental effects on people's real opportunities for self-realisation. It also takes the locals' different objectives and positions into consideration by expanding the informational basis for judgements (Sen, 1993).[4]

Fourth, *it accounts for individuals being socially embedded in institutional environments* that determine their ability to act. Such a theoretical position is also in accordance with the institutional dimension of sociabilities. The partition between individual and collective resources is often porous, which leads to the examination of "social interactions and their implications" on every level as a continuum (Andrew, 2005, p. 134). People's social resources are conditioned by the institutional structure of the territory they live in. Therefore, these non-monetary resources are not only the result of individual choices and characteristics but also constructs created by political and social environments promoting their development, notably by helping to strengthen informal links. Non-monetary resources are "unconventional resources" (Max-Neef, 1991), which means they are seldom taken into account by the commonly used definition of territorial wealth. It is easier to give an extended definition of the notion of non-monetary resources than to apprehend it in all its complexity. However, it is possible to list the material assets and skills that it can include: "social awareness, organizational know-how and managerial ability, popular creativity, solidarity and ability to provide mutual help, the expertise and training provided by training agencies, and dedication and commitment from internal and external agents" (Max-Neef, 1991, p. 79).

These theoretical positions resulted in the elaboration of a survey that was co-constructed with local actors (academics, elected representatives and field professionals) and was subsequently tested in two neighbourhoods: an "average" one and a "priority" one. The construction of the survey was based on identifying existing deficiencies in the assessment methods of relational and institutional sociabilities and, more broadly, identifying elements that could contribute to the locals' well-being. The survey was then circulated among people living in the Grenoble metropolitan area to produce information that had not yet been recorded in local administrative data registers or in local public statistics. This is important because it is essential to shed new light on and enhance the statistical categories currently used by the public administrations in order to build sustainable indicators of well-being or of the quality of life.

4 We will not spend much time elaborating on this aspect in this chapter because the purpose is rather to focus on the quantitative investigation's results. However, the combination of quantitative and participatory methods in the IBEST experiment largely conditions the way in which the quantitative data are processed (cf. Ottaviani, 2015).

Public administrations are "encapsulated" in the analytical categories of the statistical systems that already exist (Desrosières, 2007) and must be reconsidered.

The November 2012 survey targeted the Grenoble metropolitan area's inhabitants and was based on a questionnaire that included 86 questions and had a time for completion of 25 minutes. The quantitative survey relies on a statistical inference method with significant attention given to the quality of the sample selection. The purpose is to (1) legitimise the survey in the eyes of the different participants and (2) validate the operationalisation of this new approach from a scientific viewpoint by creating precise conditions in which to reproduce the experiment. The sample was stratified by eight urban districts of the Grenoble metropolitan area and is representative in terms of gender, age, profession and social class (PSC) at each district level. To stay on topic, we will not introduce the entire set of variables in the database[5] but will present the ones at the heart of this analysis (sociabilities and monetary resources).

To assess relational and institutional sociabilities, the survey data give us indications on:

- People's actions (diverse forms of participation, voting, given and received assistance etc.)
- Their appreciation of:
  - their personal situations (sense of being involved, satisfaction regarding their relationships)
  - the opportunities they are given (the opportunity to ask someone for help)
  - the importance accorded to some parts of their lives (family, friends)
  - their environment (their trust in others and in the institutions)
- Their aspirations (willingness to spend time with their families, willingness to be engaged in the community).

Through these three survey inputs, it is possible to examine people's interpersonal relationships,[6] their involvement in diverse institutions and the density, diversity and quality of the ties in their network all at once. In short, the purpose is to assess the variety of different modes of sociability.

---

[5] See final report: http://lametro.avantagemedia.com/info.php.

[6] It can be difficult to differentiate between interpersonal and institutional relationships. For example, it is frequent to see that "institutional" relationships established in local associations become friendships ("interpersonal" relationships).

This set of data feeds the review of sociabilities through two types of indicators: "raw" variables and scores (Table 8.1).

Table 8.1 Indicators of sociability

Raw variables	Scores
• Satisfaction with one's own sociability	• Institutional trust
• Frequency of interactions (friends, family, colleagues, neighbours)	• Diversity of mutual self-help
• Assistance provided and received	• Social involvement
• Possibility to rely on someone	• Intensity of relationships
• Sense of involvement	
• Participation in an association	
• Participation in a collective action	
• Trust in others	
• Importance given to family and friends	

The raw variables result from a full survey data processing and include different forms of answers. The scores are pools of answers on various questions. For example, the score for institutional trust is produced as follows: a person is said to be rather confident regarding institutions if that person has answered being "rather confident" to more than 5 out of 10 questions concerning those institutions.

When it comes to income, the main variable that is used in the survey is the disposable income per consumption unit (CU) because it allows an estimate of the standard of living while the composition of people's households is also taken into account. We used the OECD consumption unit calculation system, which assigns 1 consumption unit to the households' first adult, 0.5 units to every other household member aged 14 or older and 0.3 units to members younger than 14. The remaining income, the average income and the poverty line are all calculated on the basis of the disposable income per CU. We will occasionally employ these variables to refine our analysis.

Last but not least, we can add that the data processing is grounded in a descriptive analysis, a logistic regression, multicomponent-based analyses, a cluster analysis and bivariate correlations analyses that are carried out by applying Kendall's tau coefficient to some ordinal variables. The diversification of the statistical treatments prevents false correlation and brings to light the connection between sociabilities and the income of Grenoble's inhabitants.

8.3 RESULTS

The complexity and the equivocality of the relationship between monetary resources and sociabilities lead us to examine each variable that can link them to each other. If monetary resources are not attached to some of sociability's key variables, notably those linked to relational intensity (section 8.3.1), then the link with the variables related to the quality of relationships, such as trust in others or the opportunity to reach out to someone for help, is ambiguous (8.3.2). The study reveals that people's socio-economic situation is relatively independent from mutual self-help and their monetary resources (8.3.3).

8.3.1 Satisfaction with Regard to One's Own Sociability and Relational Intensity: Money Does Not Create Bonds

Is relational intensity related to monetary income, and is it a self-reported factor of satisfaction in people's sociability?

When it comes to relational sociabilities, income is not related to perceived satisfaction with one's sociability, to the relational intensity in or the composition of one's social circle (family, friends, colleagues or neighbours) or to the possibility of receiving or providing help in the six months prior to the survey. In other words, having a higher monetary income is not related to having more intensity in or greater satisfaction with one's social relationships. This raises the following question: what is the basis for satisfaction with one's sociability?

Relying on a descriptive analysis and a logistic regression, we can pinpoint three factors that have a predominant impact on satisfaction with one's sociability.[7] These are the levels of: (1) satisfaction with one's life; (2) socialising with family and friends; and (3) health. We can see that it is mainly non-monetary resources that influence how someone views his or her relationship with others, particularly with respect to the variables of satisfaction with housing, neighbourhood and health. Therefore, we can say that money does not create bonds.

Concerning institutional sociabilities, people's sense of involvement in their neighbourhood or in their city or their involvement in collective action are also relatively independent from their income level. We use the word "relatively" because a close examination of the link between income

---

[7] These results are found repeatedly in the descriptive analysis, the logistic regression on people's satisfaction with regard to their relationships and the multinomial component. The binary logistic regression model that was used allows for the correct classification of 96.5 per cent of the participants, and these three variables explain 24 per cent of the variance.

and involvement in associations (in particular, bodies such as AMAP or SEL[8]) reveals that people with a higher income are involved in those kinds of structure.[9] However, this is not observable for other types of association such as sports associations, charities, political associations and so on.

Thus, people's behaviour in terms of sociability appears to be weakly related to their income (Appendix Table A8.1). If social relationships with family essentially depend on demographic characteristics such as age or health, criteria such as length of residence, PSC and gender affect people's institutional involvement and generate distinct institutional sociabilities.

In short, having monetary wealth does not equal having a personal and institutional sociability that feels dense and is very satisfying. But we can ask ourselves, if money does not create bonds, does it enable people to create relationships that are favourable to creating trust?

8.3.2 Trust in Others and having the Possibility to rely on Someone: Perceptions of the Quality of Relationships Vary According to Income

Along with the quantity or the intensity of relationships, our study of people's well-being highlights the importance of the quality of relationships, which is based on one's trust in others and having someone to rely on.

The first raw variable is found at the intersection between "interpersonal" and "institutional" sociability and is key to appreciating the relationship fabric's contribution to well-being. It relates to:

- trusting institutions;
- socialising with acquaintances;
- being involved in the community in various ways;
- having different types of reliance on other people (in case of difficulty, being able to ask one's family, colleagues, neighbours, friends or others for help). The diversity is defined by being able to rely on different categories of people. For example, being able to rely simultaneously on neighbours and family.

In the scientific literature, trust is conceived either as the product of repeated relationships or as the premise for their existence. This makes

---

8 AMAP (*Associations pour le maintien d'une agriculture paysanne*) and SEL (*Systèmes d'Echange Local*) are associations that promote and implement short and alternative exchange circuits.

9 Seven percent of the people whose income is below 1000 euros per CU, compared with 19 per cent of the people whose income is above 3500 euros, are involved in SEL or AMAP (the average being 10 per cent across the whole metropolitan area).

the definition of trust equivocal and difficult to interpret. However, it is possible to assert that there is a strong link between one's appreciation of one's social sphere and one's social environment (either relational or institutional). Therefore, the notion of trust can be used to understand how people conceive of their relationship with others regardless of the direction in which there is causality. Thus, even if, as McKnight and Chervany (2001) do, we can identify several categories and conceptual levels for the notion of trust, it is at its core a result of the social and institutional structure of society. And even if trust is an attribute of people's personality, and interpersonal trust is an attitude, a feeling and/or a behaviour, it is nevertheless the result of the entanglement of the individuals and their environment and expresses people's perception of the world. In order to analyse both aspects of the notion of trust, we will analyse trust in others and trust in institutions separately.

Trust in others is clearly linked to people's disposable income per CU.[10] In this regard, two income categories stand out: whereas 78 per cent of people with a disposable income per CU above 3500 euros declare having a fair amount of trust in others, this percentage drops to only about 50 per cent for people with an income lower than 1500 euros (Figure 8.1).

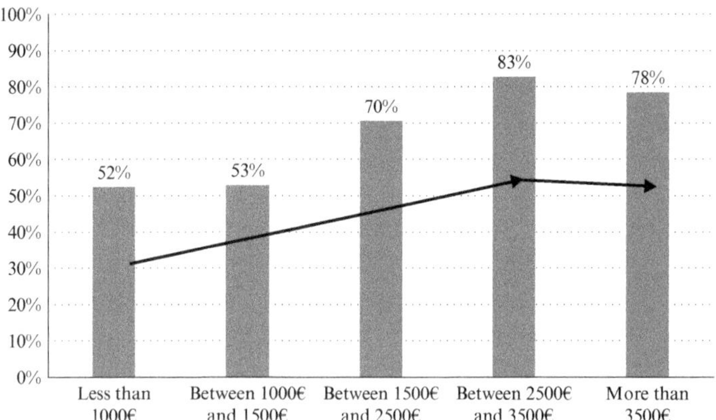

Source: Authors.

Figure 8.1 Percentage of people declaring having a fair amount of trust in others based on their disposable income per CU

[10] The association is significant (P: 0.000) and Cramer's V is 0.235. The Cramer's V test allows a comparison of the intensity of the link between two variables. The closer V is to 0, the less the variables are co-dependent. By contrast, V equals 1 when two variables are completely co-dependent. Thus, the closer V is to 1, the stronger the link between the two variables is.

Broadly speaking, distrust of others is associated with a general dissatisfaction with one's life. This can be explained by a perceived lack of prospects in life linked to either a lack of cultural resources (diplomas), monetary resources (modest income) or a poor state of health (a quarter of the people expressing distrust of others also report being in mediocre or bad health). These results consolidate an observation made by the OECD in 2011, according to which the most important factor in trusting others is the level of education. Whereas trustfulness is the prevalent attitude for people with a post-secondary school degree, distrust prevails for people with a diploma below secondary education (i.e. baccalaureate) level or without a diploma at all. Generally, this lower level of diploma goes together with being in lower socio-professional categories and a sense of belonging to a lower social class with no prospects of improvement.

This feeling of being in a hostile environment can lead to social withdrawal. Indeed, this distrust of others is associated with a lack of trust in institutions. This can be both the cause and the result of people's limited involvement in the community and in public life.

Trust in institutions is also linked to the level of income (Figure 8.2).[11] Indeed, those with a disposable income per CU below 1000 euros are the most defiant towards institutions.

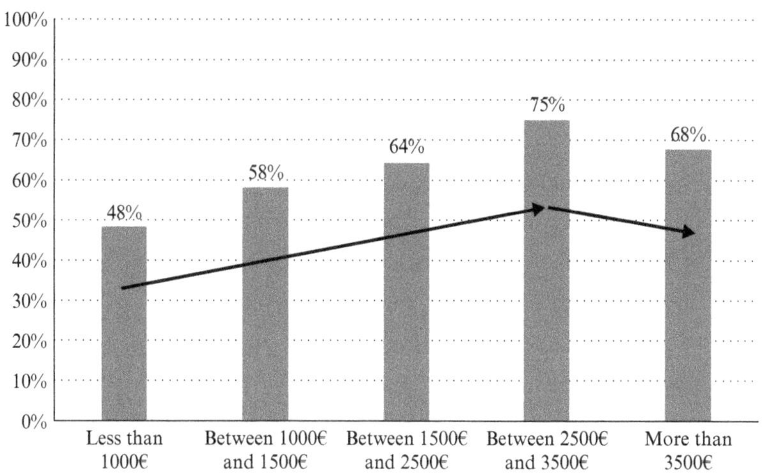

Source: Authors.

Figure 8.2 Percentage of people declaring having a fair amount of trust in institutions based on their disposable income per CU

11 The significance is good (P: 0.000) with a Cramer's V of 0.163.

Why are people who are less well-off more defiant towards institutions? We can formulate the following hypothesis: it is possible that people in lower socio-economic conditions have been confronted more frequently with harsh public services at times they needed help. Thus, they faced difficulties in putting their rights into effect or expressing their opinion, which can explain their level of distrust. Furthermore, because of the link between trust in institutions and people's feeling of involvement, it can be worsened by a sense of social exclusion. This statement is corroborated by the fact that 8.6 per cent of people with an income below 1000 euros declare that they belong to "the underclass, the excluded", whereas this is the case, on average, for only 2.1 per cent of the population surveyed in the metropolitan area.

However, having a high income level does not have a univocal effect on sociabilities. Indeed, regarding trust in others or in institutions, *the possibility of requesting assistance* is low for people with a low income and also for people with the highest income. The rates are the lowest for people who identify with the upper class, the working class or the lower class, the excluded. If we go into the details of the analysis, two categories stand out:

- On the one hand, 35 per cent of the households whose income is above 3500 euros per CU declare that they cannot rely on anyone for help.
- On the other hand, 42.9 per cent of active households comprising people in their 40s and living in a social neighbourhood declare that they cannot rely on anyone for help.

Thus, the statistical data treatment reveals that two factors predominate in the appreciation of one's ability to rely on someone for help.

First, if someone has received help, and especially if that person has received several types of help in the past six months, he or she would be more likely to believe that it is possible to rely on others.

Second, the older people are, the more they tend to say that they cannot rely on others. The indicator that measures the possibility to request assistance facilitates an analysis of isolation without restricting it to the type of household. Rather, it includes factors like the ageing process, health deterioration, unemployment, divorce and so on. These factors can lead to people having a smaller family and circle of friends and, therefore, to their feeling isolated. The results of the analysis, produced by combining these factors with the possibility to rely on others, point to new ways of apprehending isolation and are close to the conclusions of some works of the INSEE (Pan Ké Shon, 2003). They are also closely related to studies on isolation and solitude (Avramov, 2003 and Klinenberg, 2013) that point out that residential isolation (living alone) is not systematically congruent with relational isolation (having little to no contact with other people) or even a feeling of solitude (feeling lonely).

Having social relationships based on trust, whether in others or in institutions, and having the opportunity to rely on others are two dynamics that are facilitated by people's access to monetary resources, but to what extent? And what about the relation between assistance and one's income?

8.3.3 Mutual Help: a Resource that can Offset the Lack of Income?

Whereas the scientific literature tends to focus on the accumulation of monetary and relational resource deficiencies, our analysis reveals an unexpected link between the diversity of mutual help[12] and people's income.

At first glance, it appears that mutual help does not offset the lack of monetary resources: it is relatively independent from people's socio-economic situations (Appendix Table A8.1).

However, while people with a low income per CU are no different in their appreciation of the possibility of giving or receiving help, people with less than 1000 euros of income receive more help than those whose income is between 1000 and 3500 euros per CU.

If we focus our analysis on people living below the poverty line who are effectively included in community support networks, we find that these people receive and/or give more diversified material and immaterial support than other categories of people (loans and donations, lending or giving objects, tools, instruments, domestic help, help with handwork, child care and school support, help for administrative procedures, housing and access to leisure or any other type of help).

Half the people living below the poverty line receive more diversified material and immaterial help, which means that the percentage of people giving or receiving help at least once is not determined by their level of income. If we distinguish between those households living below the poverty line who receive public assistance and those who do not, we can see that receiving public assistance is not associated with receiving more

---

[12] The analysis of this relationship is complex because there are methodological difficulties. People's assessment of the help available to them can depend on either their real ability to reach out for help or the perception of this possibility based on past experience. Studies have shown how these elements combine with and influence each other (Cohen, 1992, in Henly et al., 2005). People will perceive that they lack the opportunity to find help if they have received little help in the past.

interpersonal assistance. Therefore, there is no compensatory mechanism between private and public assistance.

Overall, the links between mutual help and monetary resources are relatively independent from people's socio-economic situations. However, a closer analysis reveals the following paradox: when people with low incomes are engaged in dense community support networks, they have people around them who can help them. Therefore, we can say that, under certain conditions related to people's relational network, mutual help becomes a resource that can offset the lack of income.

8.4 DISCUSSION

We have proved that while monetary wealth does not necessarily go hand in hand with a dense social network and personal satisfaction, it does influence the existence of relationships based on trust and the ability to reach for help (up to an income per CU of 2500 euros). And while at first glance mutual help does not appear to be linked to the level of income, a closer look shows that people who receive an income below the poverty line and who are surrounded by people who can provide them with help can receive a greater diversity of assistance. Therefore, in some cases, mutual help is a resource that can improve the living conditions of the least well-off. It also means that the lack of monetary resources and relational resources is not always cumulative.

Therefore, it appears that people's assessment of their own situation cannot be explained solely by their financial conditions.

It is the result of a particular combination of monetary and non-monetary factors: whatever the aspect that is considered (health, housing, work, etc.), it is clear that sociabilities are very important to people's satisfaction with their life. Satisfaction with one's relationships is a good example of this complex combination since it is the product of all the other variables of satisfaction that we have studied (Appendix Table A8.2).

Furthermore, our analysis reveals that the absence of monetary resources mostly has an impact on people's perception of their environment and social situations, on their social involvement and on their perception of their institutional and relational environments. The accumulation of monetary and relational resource deficiencies is not inevitable, however, as evidenced by the independent relation between the mutual help factor and people's socio-economic situation. However, this does not mean that there is not a compensatory mechanism between monetary and non-monetary resources revolving around sociabilities, especially for people with very low incomes.

The results of our work echo other quantitative research that shows that the relation between monetary resources and non-monetary resources is not univocal. While sociabilities can offset some of the lack of monetary resources (Scott and Carrington, 2011) by working as a safety net for people with a low income, they cannot completely compensate for their absence. In a study on people with a low income in the Michigan area, Henly and colleagues (2005) shed light on the fact that social relations, and particularly mutual help, allowed people to cope with precarious socio-economic circumstances but did not affect people's economic mobility. Therefore, while social links can make life easier for people in precarious life situations, they cannot provide a sufficient dynamic impulse for their economic integration.

Monetary resources remain a decisive factor in the quality of life of the Grenoble metropolitan area's inhabitants. This is true even if they do not guarantee the existence of social relations to satisfy them. In other words, the inhabitants' economic integration is a precondition for a good quality of life but is not the only condition. A public policy whose purpose would be to achieve well-being for local citizens cannot be based solely on increasing monetary resources and purchasing power. Neither can it be based on a univocal vision of sociabilities that will establish one "good" way to interact socially. Instead, it should integrate multiple representations of satisfying relationships and social self-realisation.

8.5 CONCLUSION

Our analysis of social bonds cautions against a simplistic approach to sociabilities and the relationships between monetary and non-monetary resources. Like previous studies on national or international levels, it demonstrates the impossibility of limiting well-being and sociabilities to monetary resources. It also shows the ambivalence of all the variables included in the notion of well-being, as well as the complexity of their relations.

This complexity, at work in constructing social bonds and maintaining trust, hampers the possibility to delineate clearly the cause-and-effect relationship between interpersonal and institutional sociability. The limits of the analysis are related both to the lack of data on the causes of defiance (discrimination, psychological data etc.) in the IBEST study and to its experimental nature, which confined its participants to a cross-sectional analysis; a longitudinal analysis could have been beneficial. In addition, the specificities of the Grenoble metropolitan area, for which the study was specially tailored, prevent any systematic generalisation of the results, even if some of the findings are observable on other territorial scales.

In spite of these analytical limits, the data analysis relating to the different modes of sociability reveals a complex relationship between the quantity and diversity of people's available resources and the way they experience their sociability. Whether the issue is social interactions or living conditions, "more" is not always "better" for people. Consequently, the acknowledgement of these matters compels us to rethink the categories and levers of public action. In conclusion, we suggest three lines of reflection on these topics.

First, the existence of social bonds and mutual help – often ignored in most socio-economic analyses – can lead to a debate on territorial development public policies. Since the working classes draw their resources from the local level, we can question the impacts that those policies seeking socially mixed areas and urban regeneration policies have on the resources. The pressure put on people to be mobile and find a job in order to earn a wage and be socially and economically "integrated" ignores the importance of social interpersonal networks. It also ignores the importance that people give to their political and institutional involvement. By only conceiving of social integration through a market perspective, there is a risk of further exacerbating the tendency to develop weak social bonds[13] by depending only on the job status at the expense of other institutions that have, in Perret's words (2003), "an important activity of symbolic production".

Second, the IBEST experiment as a whole brings to light the fact that sociabilities cannot be summarised as a monetarily valued social capital and that it is necessary to provide synergetic responses to social needs and hence apprehend the complexity and diversity of social relations. This means switching from sectoral policies to more transversal policies conceived to answer social needs in their complexity and globality.

Lastly, people's low income has an impact on their sociability and more broadly on their ability to achieve personal growth. Therefore, even if approaches in terms of well-being question the range of social inequalities, they should not discard the issue of income inequalities, which still play a decisive role in people's self-fulfilment.

BIBLIOGRAPHY

Andrew, M.K. (2005), "Le capital social et la santé des personnes âgées", *Retraite et société*, **46**, 131–45.

[13] People with fixed-term contracts socialise more on a daily or weekly basis with their co-workers outside their working hours than independent workers and open-ended contract workers.

Avramov, D. (2003), "Démographie et exclusion sociale", *Etudes Démographiques*, **37**, 180.
Bacqué, M.H. and Fol, S. (2007), "L'inégalité face à la mobilité: du constat à l'injonction", *Swiss Journal of Sociology*, **33**(1), 89–104.
Costanza, R., Hart, M., Posner, S. and Talberth, J. (2009), "Beyond GDP: the need for new measures of progress", *The Pardee Papers*, **4**, accessed 6 October 2017 at https://www.bu.edu/pardee/files/documents/PP-004-GDP.pdf.
Council of Europe (2005), *Concerted Development of Social Cohesion Indicators – Methodological Guide*, Strasbourg: Council of Europe Publishing.
Desrosières, A. (2007), "Surveys versus administrative records: reflections on the duality of statistical sources", *Courrier des Statistiques, English Series*, **13**, accessed 6 October 2017 at http://citeseerx.ist.psu.edu/viewdoc/download?doi=10.1.1.490.3806&rep=rep1&type=pdf.
Diener, E. and Seligman, E.P. (2004), "Beyond money: toward an economy of well-being", *Psychological Science in the Public Interest*, **5**(1), 1–31.
Duarte, P., Léard, F., Boulanger, E. and Michel, B. (2012), "Le quartier des Ruires à Eybens", *Baromètre des Quartiers*, accessed 6 October 2017 at https://halshs.archives-ouvertes.fr/halshs-00807480/document.
Dubedout, H. (1983), *Ensemble Refaire la Ville, Rapport au Premier Ministre du Président de la Commission Nationale pour le Développement Social des Quartiers*, Paris: La Documentation Française.
Easterlin, A.R. (1974), "Does economic growth improve the human lot?" in David, P.A. and Reder, M.W. (eds), *Nations and Households in Economic Growth: Essays in Honour of Moses Abanovitz*, New York: Academic Press.
Fol, S. (2010), "Mobilité et ancrage dans les quartiers pauvres: les ressources de proximité", *Regards Sociologiques*, **40**, 27–43.
Gadrey, J. (2010), *Adieu à la Croissance: Bien Vivre dans un Monde Solidaire*, Paris: Les Petits Matins.
Henly, J.R., Danziger, S.K. and Offer, S. (2005), "The contribution of social support to the material well-being of low-income families", *Journal of Marriage and Family*, **67**, 122–40.
Klinenberg, E. (2013), "Vivre seul, mais pas solitaire", *Le Monde Diplomatique*, **708**.
Layard, R. (2011), *Happiness – Lessons from a New Science*, London: Penguin Group.
Le Roy, A., Offredi, C. and Ottaviani, F. (2015), "The challenges of participatory construction of social indicators of well-being", *Social Indicators Research*, **120**(3), 689–700.
Max-Neef, M.A. (1991), *Human Scale Development*, New York: Apew Press.
McKnight, D.H. and Chervany, N.L. (2001), "Trust and distrust definitions: one bite at a time", in Falcone, R., Singh, M. and Tan, Y.-H. (eds), *Trust in Cyber-societies*, Berlin: Springer-Verlag, pp. 27–54.
Meadows, D. (1998), "Indicators and information systems for sustainable development – a report to the Balaton Group", *The Sustainable Institute*, accessed 6 October 2017 at https://www.iisd.org/pdf/s_ind_2.pdf.
Miringoff, M. and Miringoff, M.-L. (1999), *The Social Health of the Nation: How America is Really Doing*, New York: Oxford University Press.
Nordhaus, W.D. and Tobin, J. (1973), "Is growth obsolete?", in Moss M. (ed.), *The Measurement of Economic and Social Performance*, Cambridge, MA:

National Bureau of Economic Research, pp. 509–64, accessed 21 June 2017 at http://www.nber.org/chapters/c3621.
OECD (2011), *How's Life? Measuring Well-being*, Paris: OECD Publishing, accessed 14 June 2019 at http://dx.doi.org/10.1787/9789264121164-en.
Ottaviani, F. (2015), "Performativité des indicateurs: indicateurs alternatifs et transformation des modes de rationalisation", thesis in Economics, Grenoble Alpes University.
Pan Ké Shon, J.-L. (2003), "Isolement relationnel et mal-être", *INSEE Première*, **931**.
Perret, B. (2003), "De la société comme monde commun", Paris, Desclée de Brouwer.
Putnam, R.D. (1995), "Tuning in, tuning out: the strange disappearance of social capital in America", *Political Science and Politics*, **28**(4), 664–83.
Putnam, R.D. (2000), *Bowling Alone: The Collapse and Revival of American Community*, New York: Simon & Schuster.
Requena, F. (1995), "Friendship and subjective well-being in Spain: a cross-national comparison with United States", *Social Indicators Research*, **35**, 271–88.
Scott, J. and Carrington, P.J. (2011), *The SAGE Handbook of Social Network Analysis*, London, UK, Thousand Oaks, CA, USA, New Delhi, India and Singapore: SAGE Publications.
Sen, A. (1992), *Inequality Re-examined*, Cambridge, MA: Harvard University Press.
Sen, A. (1993), "Positional objectivity", *Philosophy & Public Affairs*, **22**(2), 126–45.
Sen, A. (2008), "The economics of happiness and capability", in Bruni, L., Comim, F. and Pugno, M. (eds), *Capabilities and Happiness*, New York: Oxford University Press, pp. 16–27.
Stiglitz, E., Sen, A. and Fitoussi, J.P. (2009), *Report by the Commission on the Measurement of Economic Performance and Social Progress*, Commission on the Measurement, accessed 6 October 2017 at http://www.stiglitz-sen-fitoussi.fr/documents/rapport_anglais.pdf .
Vignal, C. (2005), "Injonctions à la mobilité, arbitrages résidentiels et délocalisation de l'emploi", *Cahiers Internationaux de Sociologie*, **118**(1), 101–17.

APPENDIX

Table A8.1 Links between interpersonal sociability and institutional sociability and income per consumption unit

	Income per consumption unit
Interpersonal sociability	
Satisfaction with the sociability	No link
Intensity of relationships	P: 0.083; V: 0.088
Have received help in the past six months	P: 0.056; V: 0.106
Have helped in the past six months	P: 0.725; V: 0.050
Institutional sociability	
Feeling of involvement in the neighbourhood	P: 0.324; V: 0.074
Feeling of involvement in the town	P: 0.356; V: 0.073
Participation in an association	P: 0.004; P: 0.137
Collective mobilisation	P: 0.044; V: 0.109
Participation in local exchange trading systems or community-supported agriculture	P: 0.35; V: 0.112

Note: The table shows the significance (P) and V of Cramer (V) for each association.

Source: Authors according to IBEST 2012 data.

Table A8.2 Relationship between satisfaction with relationships and other types of satisfaction

	Satisfaction with their sociability
Life satisfaction	P: 0.000 and V: 0.214
Satisfaction with their house	P: 0.000 and V: 0.131
Satisfaction with their neighbourhood	P: 0.000 and V: 0.127
Satisfaction with their town	P: 0.007 and V: 0.103
Satisfaction with their work	P: 0.001 and V: 0.154
Satisfaction with their conditions of employment	P: 0.001 and V: 0.154
Positive perception of one's state of health	P: 0.000 and V: 0.180

Note: The table shows the significance (P) and V of Cramer (V) for each association.

Source: Authors according to IBEST 2012 data.

9. Accessibility of urban public space: considering the diversity of ordinary pedestrian practices

Rachel Thomas

9.1 INTRODUCTION

Over the past 30 years in France, different approaches have evolved concerning urban public space's accessibility to pedestrians. Its position in the fields of architecture and town planning continues to improve, and accessibility is now regarded as one of the qualities of urban life (Talen, 2002) and an element of the "politics of conviviality" (Hinchliffe and Whatmore, 2006). Two reasons explain this evolution. The first is that the ageing French population and its associated disorders (walking difficulties, memory impairment, vision and/or hearing loss etc.) compel city planners to adapt urban public places to their needs. They express the same needs as other city-dwellers – autonomy, recognition, hospitality, user-friendliness and the ability to make more of a contribution to the community (Katz et al., 2011). With the issue of disability, the ageing population has become a major point of interest for city planning policies. The second reason that explains this renewal of thought about accessibility in France is that on 11 February 2005, the government enacted Law no. 2005-102 "for the equality of the rights and the chances, the participation and the citizenship of the disabled people". This legislation addresses accessibility in terms of user comfort, establishes new design rules and sets financial penalties for those who fail to meet the standards.

This chapter provides background and a review of assistive devices to conceptualise those urban public places that have been adapted. It offers a critically argued look at these evolutions by showing that a technical approach to accessibility – centred on the disabled individual – is favoured. Developed from the field of architectural and urban ambience research, which promotes a sensitive approach to the built environment, this critical perspective adopts the opposite stance to the concepts advanced until now on accessibility by defending two ideas.

The first idea is that pedestrian access to the city is the result of a practical and perceptual process of taking root. It is never predetermined by the spatial qualities but is constructed during the walk. Such an assertion has an empirical basis. In the field of architectural and urban ambiences, we consider the understanding of the links between the city-dweller and his or her environment as one that requires situated and multisensory approaches. Rather than spatialist and normative approaches, which are often based on an "above ground", decontextualised hypothesis, we favour the field survey. In each of our approaches, we pay attention to pedestrians' perceptual activity, their sensations and the (physical and sensory) qualities of space. In this work on accessibility, our field surveys take the form of walking trips with various groups of people (disabled, elderly, accompanied by children, suffering from vascular problems, pregnant etc.) and observations of ordinary walking situations. These excursions and observations took place in Grenoble (France), Athens (Greece), Prague (Czech Republic) and Copenhagen (Denmark) between 1997 and 2005. A researcher accompanied a pedestrian on a daily journey (lasting approximately one hour) or discreetly tailed them. The aim of this survey was to understand the different tactics used by pedestrians on their journey and how they adapt themselves to difficult situations, such as the presence of physical obstacles or crowds, certain intense events, orientation problems and so on. In other words, not only do we focus on architectural barriers but we broaden our questions to the role that sounds, light, floor coverings and so on play in the comfort of mobility.

The theme of mobility is still central to the debate about pedestrian access in the city. But, in this line of thought, mobility often continues to be viewed in terms of a succession of physical mechanisms: moving or being mobile is a matter of demonstrating one's capacity to change position in space. From this perspective, thinking about the city's accessibility to pedestrians boils down to the conditions under which it is possible to achieve movement. In practice, recent town planning schemes have sought to reduce the number of physical barriers to movement, increase the legibility of space (in particular, by harmonising signage) and encourage connections between the various means of transportation. We have a slightly different point of view: mobility, we would suggest, cannot only be seen in its physical dimension. Because walking also plays a part in chance encounters between strangers, it constitutes a form of urbanity (Goffman, 1963, 1971; Whyte, 1980; Solnit, 2001; Augoyard, 2007; Holland et al., 2007) and "an aesthetic practice" (Careri, 2002). This is based on compliance with the rules of civility in public, the physical and sensory qualities of the built environment, the pedestrian's motor and perceptual skills and, lastly, the specificities of the social milieu in which he or she is integrated.

Consequently, we are required to think about and reveal the permanent process of adjustment between the pedestrian's perception and how the (physical, social and sensory) resources of both the environment and the ongoing action are used. From this perspective, pedestrian access to the city is not so much a matter of architectural barriers to movement or various individual disabilities but rather a question of the poor match between the resources available in a given place and the pedestrian's perception and action.

The second hypothesis that we recommend to develop concerns the way of thinking about disability. The question of disabilities, and more specifically of how to alleviate physical disabilities, is still uppermost in the current debate about accessibility. However, only partial allowance is made for sensory deficiency, particularly for hearing; the allowance made for mental disabilities is marginal (Blackman et al., 2003). But it is seen in terms of organic deficiency: the "disabled" are often defined as people whose physical or mental integrity has been gradually or permanently diminished, either congenitally or because of ageing, illness or accident, with the result that their autonomy – their ability to go to school or do a job – is compromised. For the disabled, depending on their disability, access to the city is conditional on its being alleviated or the physical barriers in its way being removed.

We hold that it is no longer sustainable to conceptualise urban accessibility in terms of disabilities. The limitations of this approach, with regard to both urban design and the perception of the disabled, are manifest. It is time to question not so much the shortcoming itself as the skills required of pedestrians and what they reveal about the city. The experience of the physically disabled as they make their way shows that the design and surface of streets encourage the development of motive potentialities; as drivers or pedestrians, the experience of the blind and visually impaired is testimony to the help provided by the city's sonic environment and sometimes by contrasting colours and lights (Coulter and Parsons, 1990; Bordreuil, 2005; Thomas, 2005, 2010). Policymakers and city planners have neglected these intrinsic qualities of the urban space for too long or at best treated them as minor details (Imrie and Kumar, 1998; Van der Linden et al., 2016), even though they are essential to a politics of urban public spaces (Low and Smith, 2006). By contrast, our purpose is to draw attention to them and highlight their role in affording access to the city for all pedestrians, ultimately making explicit the conceptual and empiric issues our position raises. We also think that a detour via the experience of disabled people as they travel from A to B offers a heuristic tool to conceptualise urban public space's accessibility to everyone.

9.2 DISABLING URBAN SITUATIONS

Thinking about the accessibility of urban public space and the adoption of a regulatory framework started in France in the 1970s as a result of social unrest – in particular, the revolt of the motor-disabled against architectural barriers to their movement. There were numerous such obstacles: raised platforms or steps at the entrance to many public buildings, steeply sloping streets, a profusion of often badly placed street furniture, pavements that were too high to be accessed by wheelchairs, and so on. The revolt gathered strength when the motor-disabled were joined by the sight-impaired and then by a host of other people experiencing difficulties getting about. The list of material constraints on movement grew longer, focusing attention on issues with urban signage and legibility. At the same time, the disabled gained greater visibility as they questioned a society that had kept them out of the public eye and cloistered inside special institutions. Furthermore, for an urban world, they raised the question of how to obtain autonomy and social recognition and develop their well-being by gaining access to the city.

The response to this social and regulatory pressure by urban design professionals has come in two stages. Starting in the mid-1980s, minimalist application of the new regulations prompted them to try to alleviate physical and/or sensory disabilities. In practice, this policy entailed the creation and installation of "architectural prostheses" in cities to assist the disabled with their movements. These physical or conceptual devices were added to an existing space where an architectural barrier or defective signage had imposed limits on the movements on those with disabilities. Their primary characteristic was their specialisation, with a specific device to alleviate each type of disability. In this way, "*bateaux*", or dropped kerbs, and "*oreilles*", or kerb build-outs at junctions, became widespread and assisted the movement of people in wheelchairs: by lowering the edge of the pavement and/or reducing the width of the road, designers made it easier to cross (Figure 9.1). They also sought to increase safety for the sight-impaired or the blind by making it easier for them to find their way by laying tactile tiles on the pavement for hazard warning and directional guidance. Such tiles differed in their form and purpose. Hazard warning strips generally consisted of a rectangle, with a rough surface marked by grooves or bumps. They were placed before dropped kerbs, the start of an escalator or staircase and on the platforms of tram, subway or train stations. Detectable by foot or stick, they warn of a potential hazard. Such warning strips in France must comply with the NF P98-351 standard. Since 2007, the presence of these devices has been compulsory at pedestrian crossings and along urban transportation platforms.

Source: © Rachel Thomas.

Figure 9.1 Example of "bateaux" *and hazard warning strips at pedestrian crossings*

Directional strips are marked by hollowed-out or raised grooves or elastomer adhesive tape. They provide directional guidance for the sight-impaired, who can keep track of them with a stick as they make their way from A to B (Figure 9.2). Since 2014, they have had to comply with the NF P98-352.

At road crossings, these devices were generally supplemented by audible signals coinciding with pedestrian lights: a loudspeaker or transmitters informed pedestrians that they could step out onto the pedestrian crossing and cross safely. For example, the EO guidance system, designed by the French society Études et Développement de Produits et Services, operates as follows: a microchip receiver is built into pedestrian cues, and sight-impaired pedestrians carry a remote control that can trigger the receiver. Once activated, the system produces two types of audible messages: the name of the street being crossed and the colour of the pedestrian light.

The use of this technology has now become widespread, particularly to assist in dealing with difficulties finding one's way because of a sight

Source: © Rachel Thomas.

Figure 9.2 Directional strips at pedestrian crossings

disability. It is part of a new approach adopted by designers that involves erasing any urban situation likely to constitute a handicap and improving the quality of life. This means identifying, understanding and eliminating those features of the surroundings that hinder the continuity of movement and prevent people from finding their way. So, the handicap concept is still present, but in a different form. The concern now is to highlight such "situational" handicaps posed by a given space to those using it. In practical terms, this determination to achieve accessibility for all results in the "smoothing" of space: the ground is flattened out, visual and sound signage is enhanced, the placing of street furniture must comply with strict standards regarding alignment and number, and pedestrian routes are secured.

The proliferation of these isolated technical devices has remedied the most common problems impeding movement. But this trend has also affected the design of cities and thinking on handicaps. First, the problem of competition between the senses remains unresolved, and competition between individual items of street furniture seems to have been exacerbated. Numerous works (Imrie and Kumar, 1998; Thomas, 2005;

Lauria, 2017) have shown that dropped kerbs have had a positive impact on movement by people with limited mobility but have disoriented the sight-impaired. Reducing the rise on a dropped kerb avoids the risk of an accident for wheelchair users but deprives the sight-impaired of cues on the ground. On complex road crossings (with a large number of traffic flows and sound signals), this "blandisation" of the podo-tactile space forces the sight-impaired (due to the loss of cues it entails) to venture across the road unassisted. Secondly, these tools single out disabled persons with regard to their particular disability and distinguish them from a "normalised" framework of locomotion. By drawing a distinction between various forms of disability and differentiating locomotion by the disabled from that of ordinary pedestrians, the new approach to street design suggests that there are marginal walking practices (Kitchin, 1998; Lauria, 2017).

These practices would necessitate the creation of specific technical spaces, passages and/or systems. This sort of design approach is surely open to debate. With longer life expectancy and the incidents inherent in human life, we are all confronted with situations of disability. For example, similar to wheelchair users, people pushing a child's pushchair have difficulty getting onto a pavement or into a means of transportation and entering public buildings.

Lastly, by creating set routes, all these devices functionalise urban travel: the routes made accessible in this way generally lead those taking them to carry out useful tasks (shopping, administrative formalities, health care etc.). In this sense, pedestrian journeys are reduced to their practical finality. Surely, we may imagine other purposes and timeframes for walking in the city? For example, what about aimless strolling through the city during which pedestrians may sometimes search out its least-known spaces? What about the hordes of shoppers packing the streets when the sales are on? How do these many ordinary ways of moving about and gaining access to the city co-exist? Which features of the environment and which skills do they bring into play on the part of the pedestrian?

9.3 RESOURCES DESIGNED TO RESPOND TO MOVEMENT

Having focused on public sociability (Goffman, 1963, 1971) for many years, social scientists are now taking an interest in the issue of urban mobility. Two main schools of thought have emerged, which has sparked some controversy. The advocates of an ecology of perception have turned to a notion originally developed by Gibson (1979) as part of his analysis of visual perception, addressing the subject in terms of "action affordances": from their position in space, any perceiving subject extracts the information needed to accomplish their action. The work of Levy (1994) and Sanchez and Velche (1996) on stations and Mehta's work on walkable streets (2008) demonstrate the part played by surroundings in the direction and continuity of movement: every device (ticket office or machine), service (toilets, telephones, bar) and sensory input (sign, public address) in a given space may aid in or obstruct a pedestrian's locomotion and information. Their nature depends on their position in space, their connection to the current action and the pedestrian's ability to make use of them in a set space–time framework.

The study of transport hubs reveals three typical situations that appear to exist and occur in exactly the same way in urban public space and discusses the notion of "affordance".

In the first situation, the environment provides pedestrians with the resource they require: a public address announcement and/or visual display reassures hurrying travellers by confirming their train's time of arrival and platform number. In this case, movement is continuous.

In the second situation, there is a hiatus between the information required and the resource afforded by the surroundings. For example, the public address announcement does not concern the train the hurrying travellers want to take. Movement is consequently slowed, and the travellers are obliged to seek guidance from some other medium.

The third and final situation is subject to constraint, the environment failing to respond to the travellers' demands. Neither the public address announcement nor the visual display tells them anything about their train. As a result, the travellers must find another source of information and run the risk of missing their train.

In each of these cases, the notion of a disability disappears, driven out by a disabling urban situation. This refers less to the idea of an organic deficiency in the individual and more to the built environment being ill-suited to the action. Thus, a disabling situation may occur in two circumstances: when the design of spaces is totally unsuited to the demands of users or when the latter have difficulty mobilising and appropriating a place's facilities. From this point of view, the idea of action affordances changes to take on an ambivalent character: space as it is built and objects that play a part in the design of a place can assist in or obstruct pedestrians' movement. They "do not exist [. . .] as such in reality; it is when they are mobilised, at the point in time when they are contextualised, that they make sense" (Levy, 1994). Furthermore, a resource only exists as a function of the perceiving subject, of his or her action and position in space.

Approaches of this sort enable us to refocus the debate on urban accessibility on the environment and design of space. Architecture, as well as street furniture, road surface and some visual and audible signals help to create disabling situations or, conversely, to facilitate elements. However, these approaches do leave some questions unanswered.

The first relates to the sensory nature of movement. According to theorists of the ecology of perception, the sensory modality may be reduced to its environmental dimension. Accordingly, the surface qualities of objects (texture, colour, etc.) or space constitute resources or obstacles for action (Mehta, 2008; Jenkins et al., 2015). Although we are told that these resources are built in a dynamic of movement, no information is forthcoming on the type of perceptual activity that underpins efforts to find them. Do pedestrians anticipate the presence of potential resources in a space and memorise their position, or do they go about selecting such resources? Is the process of looking for resources linked to a particular type of motor activity, or is it common to all forms of locomotion? In other words, can one go further in specifying the links between the environment, the perceptual activity of pedestrians and locomotion?

The second problem posed by this type of approach relates to its restrictive conception of the role and nature of sensory modality. The latter only seems to act as a vector for information to pedestrians, for use in the immediate control of their action. In addition, this information-seeking role is largely dependent on the visual modality. But what about sonic, tactile, thermal, olfactory and "atmospheric" material? Do these forms of material engage pedestrians' perceptual and motor activity? If so, in what way? Does the specificity of each of the senses also play a role in the way space is grasped on a journey?

Lastly, this type of analysis leads to a technocratic approach to urban accessibility, as travel is reduced to a physical, material relation to the environment. Yet surely any movement through urban public space also involves meeting other city-dwellers and communicating through speech and body language? It must therefore be plausible to posit the idea of public sociability linked to urban wayfaring.

Work on ethnomethodology and urban sociology attest to the collective dimension of mobility (Ryave and Schenken, 1975; De Certeau, 1984; Livingston, 1987; Coulter and Parsons, 1990; Lee and Watson, 1993; Bordreuil, 2005). Whether it takes the form of a stroll, a trip to the shops or just passing movement, travel brings city-dwellers into relation with one another. However, such situations of co-presence run the risk of having bodies collide, and everyone is exposed to the others' gaze. But public order is very rarely disturbed by situations of bodily and visual accessibility. Why is this the case? The work of Goffman (1963, 1971), along with that of Whyte (1980) and Lee and Watson (1993), reveals the existence of rituals governing social life. With regard to pedestrian traffic, a range of procedures are in place to reduce the risk of shocks, keep movement fluid and allow overtaking. The "sliding step" technique is widely used in crowds. It entails "a slight inclination of the body, rotation of the shoulder and an almost imperceptible sidestep" (Goffman, 1971: 14). Such manoeuvres go hand in hand with visual orientation strategies, the purpose of which is to limit public encounters to a fairly superficial plane and allow all parties to keep up appearances. Thus, a civil lack of attention prevails (Goffman, 1971): each person anticipates the action of others from a distance and takes care in the stream of unfocused interaction (not requiring any engagement) not to catch their eye. This particular mode of observation enables everyone to understand and anticipate the other's trajectory, adjust their own course and action and categorise the individuals present in any space. According to Lee and Watson (1993), such visual orientation strategies take various forms: pedestrians may choose to see but also to scrutinise or simply glance at others. Furthermore, such behaviour seems to be directly connected to motor action: a pedestrian's route is organised by the direction of his or her gaze, while at the same time the direction in which they walk determines the focus of their gaze. In some cases, this visual organisation of pedestrians' conduct may give rise to social formats (Lee and Watson, 1993): objects or devices that, on account of their visual configuration, organise motion. For example, spotted at a distance, a queue obliges pedestrians to wait behind the last person and not to try to squeeze in further along. In this respect, such visibility of the urban public space is not to be taken as an instrument for the normalisation or control of social life. In a much broader sense, it constitutes a resource from which city-dwellers may draw to move around in compliance with the rules of civility in public.

This approach has the advantage of updating the accomplished, situated and collective character of urban travel: the public conduct of people, regardless of its nature, is reciprocally adjusted to suit the place where it occurs and what pedestrians mutually opt to display. This perceptual organisation of social life modifies courses of action and shapes the environment to form multiple perceptual milieus (Coulter and Parsons, 1990; Mehta, 2008; Thomas, 2010). In this sense, urban accessibility cannot be conceived as something pre-defined; it organises itself through the action of city-dwellers. Here again, can one assume that urban accessibility is only dependent on the visual modality? Can one reduce the role of pedestrians' perceptual activity simply to one of framing their actions?

9.4 THE EFFECTIVENESS OF ARCHITECTURAL AND URBAN AMBIENCES

Our analysis seeks to provide answers to these questions. It takes its cue from the work in social science while also adopting an ecological approach. Two hypotheses underpin our thinking. The first concerns the commonly established connection between urban accessibility and mobility. From our point of view, access to urban public space depends more on the motivity of pedestrians than on their mobility. By "motivity" we mean the primal, immediate human act by which we inhabit space and time. So, unlike mobility, motivity does not necessarily require movement in space, nor does it always fulfil a practical purpose. Motivity engages the senses, body and attention of the pedestrian more than mobility does. *De facto*, it requires that various perceptual, bodily and social attitudes be actualised. Our second hypothesis concerns the nature of and role played by the sensory modality in this access to the city: urban accessibility involves a dynamic process that needs to be revealed and depends just as much on the resources of the sensory environment as on the perceptual activity of the pedestrian.

In the past few years, research works from the field of the architectural and urban ambiences have highlighted the effectiveness of architectural and urban ambiences. An ambience results from perceptual (both sensory and cognitive) organisation or an expert production and/or a technical device. In practice, it exists when an assembly of knowledge and know-how is perceived in a characterised space–time, social, cultural context inscribed in an objectifiable given (Augoyard, 1998). These works show that individuals' (visual and/or sonic, tactile, thermal. . .) surroundings contribute to positioning them in space and to their action. More specifically, ambience organises their perceptual activity, contextualises practice and supplies a potential for use. The effectiveness of ambience is apparent both in the social practices of pedestrians and in their motor actions. However, it is uneven: each ambience, in so far as it brings into play one or more sensory modalities in combination with each other, plays a specific part in each of these practices.

Furthermore, their operationality often depends on the context in which city-dwellers act and use them. As part of an acousmatic experience of the world (in other words, hearing a sound without seeing its source), sound may, for instance, be taken as a vector for verbal communication: it enables individuals to communicate with one another despite the fact that the surroundings do not allow them to make themselves mutually accessible by sight. Sound also plays a part in re-composing urban territories. Through an analysis of the soundscape, Augoyard (2006) shows how the manipulation of surroundings or sonic objects makes it possible to play on the distance (or proximity) between people and redefine the spatial limits of a place:

> The distribution of the sonic forms of a place does not necessarily correspond to what the visual organization suggests [. . .] The sonic map of a town, in the mind of a city-dweller, is a here-and-there based on a qualitative rationale; people associate or categorize places according to their sound quality: an area with noisy places, another with tranquil spots (Augoyard, 2006: 18).

In a different register, work on underground spaces (Chelkoff and Thibaud, 1997) reveals the part that the sensory environment plays in movement. According to these authors, visual perception has a motor component: as much as other sensory modalities, any visual and/or lighting configuration brings pedestrians' perceptual activity, their ability to act and their relation to others into play. For example, some lighting configurations challenge the visual acuity of pedestrians, upsetting their stride: a ceiling light reflecting on the ground causes the visual space to dilate vertically, leading to ambiguity regarding the nature of the material on which pedestrians are supposed to be walking. By contrast, other configurations exaggerate the legibility of space and the direction of pedestrians.

> The blind subway corridors connecting to the Grand Louvre [museum in Paris] are almost an injunction to keep moving, due to the powerful directionality of the space produced by the narrow passage and the line of light on the ceiling, with no eye-catching objects or inscriptions, or obstacles on the ground and opaque surfaces delimiting a very restricted field of vision (Chelkoff and Thibaud, 1997: 82).

From this point of view, the accessibility of urban public space relates simultaneously to:

- a principle of physically opening the place to city-dwellers. This is a reminder of an early definition of the term: accessibility, from *accedere*, to approach, where one can accede, which is open or sensible to something, which does not present any hindrance and is within the grasp of someone (Dictionnaire Larousse, 2017);
- a regulatory principle for pedestrian traffic;
- an organising principle for the modes of co-presence in public.

But our analysis goes further. From our point of view, urban accessibility represents a perceptual accomplishment: over and above motor and civic skills, it brings into play pedestrians' senses and engages multiple perceptual procedures. Accordingly, when crossing a street without the help of a crossing with lights, pedestrians' hearing plays as important a role as their visual acuity and/or ability to accelerate their pace, because hearing tells them about the possible presence of vehicles and their speed. In the same way, in a crowd, pedestrians actualise visual and/or kinaesthetic skills: anticipating at a distance and with a single glance the trajectory of others; avoiding collisions, sometimes without even looking, while paying attention to air turbulence caused by others' movement. These kinaesthetic skills displayed by pedestrians were brought to light following a study of obstacle-detection modes deployed during urban trips by people who have been blind from birth (Supa et al., 1944). The aforementioned study revealed that they have the ability to "perceive facially" bulky, immobile obstacles in their way: the sensation of slight pressure on the forehead, likely caused by air turbulence, provides clues as to the presence and location of such obstacles. With sighted pedestrians, the supremacy of sight overrides this facial perception. Furthermore, this perceptual accomplishment seems to be situated in time and space: it is contextualised in so far as pedestrians act as a function of their social surroundings and the (sensory, built and conceptual) qualities of the setting; it also has a temporal framework given that the perceptual, social and motor skills are actualised in the dynamic of the journey and depend on its sequentiality.

In practice, this perceptual accomplishment is formalised by pedestrians' configuration activity. The term "configuration" is used here as originally defined, abstracting itself from the many meanings it has been given in disciplinary fields as varied as poetry, psychology or sociology. The notion of configuration refers to the process by which any city-dweller, in the course of a journey, shapes his or her environment. It does not relate to the idea that stable data exist somewhere in the space but rather that the space is in a state of constant creation. Three steps, inherent to the sequentiality of an urban journey, organise this configuration activity:

- In the first step, upon entering a site, pedestrians select one or more noticeable sensory phenomena. This is also an opportunity to allocate a particular identity to each of the places through which they pass. Each place will stand out to a pedestrian's ear and subsequently in their memory because of the force and special nature of the sonic environment; it will thus remain designated as a marketplace, for instance, not so much because of the trading that actually occurs there in the morning but rather because of the mixture of voices and noises that seems to characterise it.
- In the second step, in this work of configuration pedestrians can combine a site's sensory qualities. In practice, this involves

highlighting the most operative sensory modality (or modalities) to access both the particular space and others. The second step occurs as pedestrians immerse themselves in the space. In this case, their perceptual activity has nothing to do with registering psychic content; it is much more a way of grasping the space as an object, depending on specific situations. For example, pedestrians in a hurry will probably prefer a smooth road surface, so that they can accelerate their pace without the risk of tripping. Similarly, young children will probably take advantage of a street with an echo, which preserves the intelligibility of their words and enables them to play at a distance while trading insults.

- The third and final step involves a process of incorporating in movement and exchanging the potential for action afforded by the sensory environment. In this respect, the third step bears out the relation of co-determination between the perceptual construction of the relation to place and urban practices. In other words, this "sensory shaping" of the urban public space is embodied in the conduct of pedestrians: in the dynamic of the urban journey itself, affecting both the motor action of pedestrians, their modes of perceptual attention, gestures and posture in space. For example, places perceived as overcrowded often give rise to conflicting behaviour: the crowd forms a mass, the physical proximity of bodies forces each person to contract inwards, only moving their upper limbs, their feet barely moving, with increasingly frequent glances right and left, and (visual and sonic) attention scanning all round to anticipate the reaction of others at a distance. By contrast, less crowded places produce a sense of well-being: the pace of walking slows, bodies seem relaxed and supple, and attention drifts.

From this point of view, pedestrians' access to urban public space is subject to this configuration process. The (partial or total) failure of this process will give produce a disabling situation. For example, the proliferation of sensory stimuli in a single place seems to upset the configuration process in pedestrians: the selection and composition steps are impeded, and perceptual powers focus on the need to avoid obstacles and adjust behaviour to the surroundings. By contrast, a successful configuration process gives rise to an "enabling" situation. In this case, the sensory environment of the urban public space represents a wealth of resources for pedestrians, facilitating the three steps in the configuration process. Pedestrians can easily focus their attention and organise their practices and the contexts in which they take place.

9.5 CONCLUSION

This chapter tests the thinking about pedestrian access to urban public space against ordinary situations encountered by city-dwellers. Our purpose is to reverse the direction taken by current thinking in order to centre it on the particular experience of the disabled as they travel from one point to another. We also seek to refocus the debate on the issue of pedestrian mobility, its diversity, the skills it brings into play, the links it necessarily makes with the surroundings and the community at large. This line of reasoning leads to two conclusions that make the subject more complex.

First, in practical terms, we question the idea of accessibility as something unique and pre-defined by the urban space's physical and conceptual qualities. Similarly, our study casts doubt on the normalisation of design rules and the rigid solutions they sometimes impose. It shows, on the contrary, the extent to which pedestrian access to the city is the result of an ongoing process of creation: depending on time and place and the presence or absence of a crowd, pedestrians will adjust their actions to suit the characteristics of their surroundings. This way of "acting" out (and on the environment) is the result of a dynamic configuration process carried out over the course of each urban journey. It engages both the senses of the passer-by and the potentialities afforded by the sensory environment. In other words, pedestrian access to the city results from permanent adjustment between these potentialities and conducts. The sensory process remains variable: for each sense, there is a corresponding manner of apprehending space and giving shape to the contexts of action. In this sense, there cannot be an ideal or model design solution suited to each situation.

In the field of design, receiving this type of result upsets acquired knowledge and habits. By proposing, finally, a matrix for reading and assessing space perceived in motion, we question first the basis for thinking that focuses essentially on the techniques by which passers-by move around. The accessibility of a place is as much the result of its capacity to facilitate physical movement by humans as its propensity to allow the co-existence of various modes of inhabiting and configuring space. More than just physical access to urban public space by the pedestrian, what matters is to take into account his or her perceptual access and the capacity of the surroundings to "connect" them. Similarly, by emphasising the three steps in the configuration process, we address an oft-neglected aspect of pedestrian access to the city, namely its temporal dimension. The space of perception in motion definitely seems to be a shifting space, its form recomposed, its qualities re-appraised with each succeeding step. Therefore, urban planners face practical questions, like how best to design and lay out the space–time of urban travel.

Secondly, in conceptual terms, our study highlights the practical dimension of situated perception: the configuration activity of passers-by enables them to decipher their surroundings, to find their way, to move onwards and comply with the rules of civility commonly accepted in public.

In this sense, perception is limited neither to a role of information nor to one of framing ordinary activities: it orchestrates pedestrian access to the city and even organises the contexts of action. The pedestrian's physical and perceptual accessibility does not only concern urban mobility: perception acts on pedestrian progress just as much as it does on the modalities of their meeting or co-existence with others. At the same time, our study draws attention to the (motor and social) efficacy of the sensory environment, the latter being both the medium and the matrix of urban practices. In other words, the sensory environment of urban public space exerts a spatialising and socialising power over the pedestrian's ordinary practices. Earlier works in the field of the architectural and urban ambiences revealed the potentialities of the sonic or visual environment; the present study supplements them by highlighting, in particular, the role of certain audiovisual configurations in the passer-by's onward movement and the shaping of his or her relationship with others. It also prompts new thinking on the importance of the tactile modality (podo-tactile but also kinaesthetic, haptic and proprioceptive) in pedestrian access to the city. In each case, the quality of these sensitive configurations promotes the comfort of the pedestrian: it increases the clarity of the space, facilitates its orientation and makes it possible to catch the best "affordance".

Finally, in terms of methodology, there is heuristic merit in the detour via a disabled person's experience of moving from A to B in order to conceptualise urban accessibility for all. By questioning the validity of a specific feature of disabled movement, we are able to draw attention to the diversity of modes for accessing space. From this standpoint, "the handicap" (every bit as much as empowerment) constitutes one degree among others of urban accessibility. In ageing societies such as ours, it is a universal experience that needs to be taken into account in order to improve the quality of our urban public spaces and thus, the well-being of users. Encouraging thought about situations in which perception is problematic raises the question of the right to be different and the necessary re-specification of the language of accessibility.

REFERENCES

Augoyard, J.-F. (1998), "Eléments pour une théorie des ambiances architecturales et urbaines", *Les cahiers de la recherche architecturale*, **42/43**, 13–23.

Augoyard, J.-F. (2006), *Sonic experience: a guide to everyday sounds*, Montreal: McGill Queen's University Press.
Augoyard, J.-F. (2007), *Step by step: everyday walks in a French urban housing project*, Minneapolis, MN: University of Minnesota.
Blackman, T., Mitchell, L., Burton, E., Jenks, M., Parsons, M., Raman, S. and Williams, K. (2003), "The accessibility of public spaces for people with dementia. A new priority for the open city", *Disability and Society*, **18**, 357–71.
Bordreuil, J.S. (2005), "Culture, attentions visuelles et orchestrations des mobilités", in Allemand, S., Ascher, F. and Lévy, J. (eds), *Les sens du mouvement*, Paris: Belin, pp. 207–15.
Careri, F. (2002), *Walkscapes: walking as an aesthetic practice*, Barcelona: Gustavo Gili.
Chelkoff, G. and Thibaud, J.-P. (1997), *Ambiances sous la ville: une approche écologique des espaces publics souterrains*, Grenoble: Cresson.
Coulter, J. and Parsons, E.D. (1990), "The praxiology of perception: visual orientations and practical action", *Inquiry. An Interdisciplinary Journal of Philosophy*, **33**, 251–72.
De Certeau, M. (1984), "Walking in the city", Chapter VII in *The Practice of Everyday Life*, Berkeley, CA: University of California Press.
Dictionnaire Larousse (2017), Paris: Larousse.
Gibson, J.J. (1979), *The ecological approach to visual perception*, Boston, MA: Houghton Mifflin.
Goffman, E. (1963), *Behavior in public places: notes on the social organisation of gatherings*, New York: The Free Press.
Goffman, E. (1971), *Relations in public: microstudies of the public order*, New York: Basic Books.
Hinchliffe, S. and Whatmore, S. (2006), "Living cities: towards a politics of conviviality", *Science as Culture*, **15**, 123–38.
Holland, C., Clark, A., Katz, J. and Peace, S. (2007), *Social interactions in urban public places*, Bristol: Policy Press.
Imrie, R. and Kumar, M. (1998), "Focusing on disability and access in the built environment", *Disability and Society*, **13**, 357–74.
Jenkins, G.R., Yuen, H.K. and Vogtle, L.K. (2015), "Experience of multisensory environments in public space among people with visual impairment", *International Journal of Environmental Research and Public Health*, **12**(8), 8644–57.
Katz, J., Holland, C., Peace, S. and Taylor, E. (2011), *A better life – what older people with high support needs value*, New York: Joseph Rowntree Foundation.
Kitchin, R. (1998), "Out of place, knowing one's place: space, power and the exclusion of disabled people", *Disability and Society*, **13**(3), 343–56.
Lauria, A. (2017), "Tactile pavings and urban places of cultural interest: a study on detectability of contrasting walking surface materials", *Journal of Urban Technology*, **24**(2), 3–33.
Lee, J.R.E. and Watson, R. (1993), *Interaction in public space: final report to the Plan Urbain*, Paris: Plan Urbain.
Levy, E. (1994), "L'accessibilité à l'épreuve", in Joseph, I. (ed.), *Gare du Nord: mode d'emploi*, Paris: Plan Urbain, RATP, SNCF, pp. 181–240.
Livingston, E. (1987), *Making sense of ethnomethodology*, London: Routledge.
Low, S. and Smith, N. (2006), *The politics of public space*, New York: Routledge.
Mehta, V. (2008), "Walkable streets: pedestrian behavior, perceptions and atti-

tudes", *Journal of Urbanism: International Research on Placemaking and Urban Sustainability*, **1**(3), 217–45.

Ryave, A.L. and Schenken, J.N. (1975), "Notes on the art of walking", in Turner, R. (ed.), *Ethnomethodology, Selected Readings*, New York: Penguin, pp. 265–74.

Sanchez, J. and Velche, D. (1996), *Vécus et usages de la gare de Lyon par des personnes handicapées*, Paris: CTNERHI.

Solnit, R. (2001), *Wanderlust: a history of walking*, New York: Penguin.

Supa, M., Kotzin, M. and Dallenbach, K. (1944), "Facial vision: the perception of obstacles by the blind", *The American Journal of Psychology*, **53**(2), 133–83.

Talen, E. (2002), "Pedestrian access as a measure of urban quality", *Planning Practice and Research*, **17**(3), 257–78.

Thomas, R. (2005), *Les trajectoires de l'accessibilité*, Bernin: A la Croisée.

Thomas, R. (2010), "Architectural and urban atmospheres: shaping the way we walk in town", in Methorst, R., Monterde i Bort, H., Risser, R., Sauter, D., Tight, M. and Walker, J. (eds), *PQN final report: pedestrians' quality needs*, European Science Foundation: COST, pp. 54–68.

Van der Linden, V., Dong, H. and Heylighen, A. (2016), "From accessibility to experience: opportunities for inclusive design in architectural practice", *Nordic Journal of Architectural Research*, **2**, 33–58.

Whyte, W.H. (1980), *The social life of small urban spaces*, New York: Project for Public Space Inc.

10. The British "Healthy New Towns" initiative: a step towards reuniting planning and health?

Stéphane Sadoux and Cecilia Di Marco

10.1 PUBLIC HEALTH AND TOWN PLANNING

In most countries, in Europe, the rise of town planning as a discipline and profession was intrinsically linked to public health. This close relationship has been well documented in a number of works that show how concerns stemming from epidemiological studies led to the first public health acts (for example Moughtin et al., 2009). These laws aimed to set up appropriate institutional frameworks to tackle health-related issues in industrial cities, but they also led to health being approached from a spatial perspective. In Great Britain, for example, successive acts led to dramatic alterations in the morphology of working class neighbourhoods, as various rules were set out to reduce density and overcrowding. However, action was not taken by public authorities alone. A number of "utopian" architectural and urban experiments were carried out by philanthropists in the 19th century: Robert Owen in New Lanark (1800–1810), Titus Salt in Saltaire (1853–63), George Cadbury in Bourneville (1879–95), William Hesketh Lever in Port Sunlight (1888) and, at the beginning of the 20th century, Ebenezer Howard and the Garden Cities Association in the garden cities of Letchworth (1903) and Welwyn (1920). All these new settlements aimed to combine working and living in a healthy environment (Hall, 2002), with a range of innovative design solutions. These pioneering experiments undoubtedly contributed to putting health at the centre of town planning in its early years and, as a result, to dramatically improving urban living conditions in the first half of the 20th century.

Later, however, particularly in the post-war years, attention shifted away from public health, which, although still identifiable as an objective of planning, was somewhat overshadowed by other pressing issues such as laying down new infrastructure, renewing and later regenerating inner cities and stimulating economic development. As a result, the contemporary city is somewhat of a paradox. On the one hand, the considerable progress made at the end of the 19th century, through major works aiming to sanitise the industrial city, dramatically improved health and reduced the risk of epidemics. On the other hand, the urban and architectural design theories and practices that prevailed during much of the 20th century appear to have contributed to generating a new type of unhealthy city, although the types of health issues it created are naturally very different from those to which the industrial cities' population was exposed. Today, the risk in cities of developed countries is no longer cholera or the plague: concern is related to a range of problems that include obesity, respiratory diseases and stress.

According to the *Journal of Pediatrics*, in 2011, almost 12 per cent of US children were obese, and "although some argue that this obesity epidemic is attributable to genetic factors, others believe that rapid change in rates of children obesity are related to changes in and characteristics of the environment, whether home, school or neighbourhood" (Halloran, 2011, p. 3). In Britain, studies have shown that over one-third of children are overweight; they also suggest that by 2030, 48 per cent of adult men and 43 per cent of adult women will be obese (Health and Social Care Information Centre, 2016). A recent paper by Townshend and Lake (2017) summarises some of the main debates and research questions related to the forces that are believed to influence levels of obesity and remind us that land use patterns contributing to shaping so-called walkable neighbourhoods are believed to support physical activity. Some studies have concluded that factors such as access to shops and services, high residential densities, pavements and public transport stops are associated with residents meeting activity guidelines (Adams et al., 2013). The role of green spaces has also been subject to research, with studies pointing to the influence that high-quality parks near homes have on active recreation (Giles-Corti and Donovan, 2002); however, some other academic research has produced contradictory results (Limstrand, 2008). Food environments have also been closely examined. These include both food prepared at home and out-of-home sources. Here, Townshend and Lake (2017) note that moderate evidence was found to support an association between neighbourhood food environments, consumption and health. They provide evidence showing that outlets selling fast food have tended to cluster around areas of deprivation in the United Kingdom, and they remind us of the links between fast food outlet density and weight in children and adolescents. These trends have led to what Townshend and Lake refer to as a move to reunite town planning and public health.

Health problems, obesity, in particular, are also good indicators of social and spatial disparities (Marmot, 2010). A major report jointly published by the World Health Organization and UN Habitat in 2016 shows that in London, people living in Westminster will most likely live 17 years longer than others who live just a few underground stations away (World Health Organization & UN-Habitat, 2016).

As a result, it comes as no surprise that health has regained momentum across the disciplinary spectrum. A brief survey of academic literature published over the past ten years clearly illustrates this trend. A number of publications highlight the links between climate change and public health and point to heat-related disorders; allergic and respiratory issues; vector-borne, waterborne and food-borne infectious diseases; health impacts due to food insecurity; and mental health impacts (Woodward and MacMillan, 2015). The health impact of population growth, urbanisation, sprawl (Verderber, 2012) and industrialisation on the environment due to the emission of a range of pollutants into different ecological compartments (air, water and soil) is also a major concern and has prompted the need for ecological restoration (Wong, 2012). In other words, the environmental determinants of human health are under scrutiny and have led to a reappraisal of environmental policy in the light of public health (Rom, 2012), as well as to a number of actions, such as the EU Environment and Health Action Plan (Pacyna and Pacyna, 2016).

Additionally and more specifically, academic research has recently sought to provide in-depth analyses of the relationships between the built environment and health. Studies have acknowledged that "the built environment in general and healthcare infrastructure in particular have a very important role to play in terms of supporting health and well-being, encouraging healthy lifestyles, improving quality of life and increasing efficiency and effectiveness". As a result, "the increasing awareness of the role of the built environment for health and well-being resulted in it being at the heart of many public sector initiatives [. . .]" (Kagioglou and Tzortzopoulos, 2010, p. 1). In this chapter, and as part of this book focusing on well-being, we assume that, as suggested by the seminal definition provided by the World Health Organization (1948), health is inclusive of well-being: "Health is a state of complete physical, mental and social well-being and not merely the absence of disease of infirmity" (World Health Organization, 1948).

As a result of this renewed interest in these issues, health has gradually regained a central role in architectural and urban design theory – a trend that is reflected by the publication of a wide range of general and theoretical material (for example Barton et al., 2015; Otgaar et al., 2011), but also of some more practice-oriented works that offer analyses of the impact of design on health and provide diagnosis methods and design toolkits to shape healthy places and spaces in which to live, work and engage in recreation (Dannenberg et al., 2011). A number of works have also sought to provide an insight into specific interdisciplinary research approaches and methods to look at urban health (Freudenberg et al., 2009). In addition, specific issues, such as the dramatic impact of mobility on health, have been subject to research (Gatrell, 2011), since health cannot solely be addressed by examining "fixed" geographical locations.

The place of health in academic urban studies has also been reflected by the publication of special issues of journals,[1] as well the ongoing publication of dedicated journals, such as *Health and Place* and *the Journal of Urban Health* and, more recently, the launch of *City & Health*. This topic is also the focus of a number of cross-disciplinary international conferences, including the first *Healthy City Design* event, which took place in October 2017 at the Royal College of Physicians in London.

It is in this context of increasing concern over the environmental determinants of health that a number of actions have been taken in Britain over the past ten years. This chapter first looks back at the rise – or rather, the return – of health in public policy. In particular, it draws on the review of major publications issued by the central government over the past decade and shows some of the ways in which the aims set out in this guidance have been translated into urban policy, in particular through the 2008 Healthy Towns programme.

The second part of the chapter focuses more specifically on the Healthy New Towns programme that the National Health Service (NHS) launched in 2015. The aims and the process underpinning this initiative are summarised, and a brief case study of one of the pilot projects (Barton in Oxford) is provided. More specifically, we aim to summarise the various approaches to fostering a healthy place by providing a typology of actions taken in Barton, which are classified according to the "Behaviour Change Wheel" set out by Michie et al. (2011).

Although the Healthy New Towns programme is too recent for us to assess its success, the chapter concludes with a discussion of possible successes and shortcomings, based on a discussion of available literature (project briefs, masterplans) and on formal and informal interviews with a number of stakeholders.

10.2 PROMOTING HEALTHY LIFESTYLES AND FIGHTING OBESITY: A NATIONAL CHALLENGE

In 2007, the Government Office for Science published the "Tackling Obesities: Future Choices" project report. This report suggested that over

---

1 See for example issue no.142 of *Urban Design* published by the Urban Design Group.

half of the UK population could be obese by 2050. It noted that the economic costs would be substantial, and suggested that the National Health Service costs attributable to overweight and obesity were projected to double to £10 billion per year by 2050. The Foresight programme was designed to identify the range of factors influencing obesity; create an understanding of the relationships between the key factors and their relative importance; identify effective interventions to fight obesity; analyse how future levels of obesity might change and identify the most effective future responses. The report made it clear that these issues must be addressed holistically since obesity is caused by both biological and social factors. The key determinants of obesity identified were primary appetite control in the brain, dietary habits, levels of physical activity and the psychological ambivalence experienced by individuals in making lifestyle choices. It was indicated that policies and actions focusing heavily on one element of this system were unlikely to be successful.

Changing the environment is one key aspect. However, the Foresight report (Government Office for Science, 2007) suggested that such actions, including alterations in transport infrastructure and urban design, can actually be more difficult and costly to carry out than targeting intervention at the group, family or individual scale. By contrast, the report suggested that they are more likely "to affect multiple pathways within the obesity system in a sustainable way" (Government Office for Science, 2007, p. 11): whilst in the short term, such change may involve aligning the benefits with those arising from pollution or traffic congestion, in the long term, actions taken to fight obesity may produce a "generally healthier and more environmentally sustainable society" (Government Office for Science, 2007, p. 11).

The Foresight report suggested that the promotion of "active transport" can contribute to increasing physical activity. However, it also pointed out that complementary measures are required, such as tackling commuting distances. The report suggested that measures must not only deal with the city or neighbourhood scale, but also pay heed to buildings' architecture, for example, by designing prominent and appealing staircases to discourage the use of lifts. In addition, this publication reported that there is as yet limited evidence on the impact of the built environment on food choices, although such evidence may be available in the future.

10.3 THE 2008 HEALTHY TOWNS PROGRAMME: A FIRST STEP IN DEVELOPING A COMPREHENSIVE APPROACH

In January 2008, the government published "Healthy Weight, Healthy Lives" (Department of Health, 2008). In his introduction to this document, the UK's then-Prime Minister Gordon Brown claimed that, despite improvements in care and quality of life, the British population was increasingly exposed to "a growing problem of the so-called 'lifestyle disease'". He cited obesity as the primary concern and highlighted the risk of "rising chronic disease and long-term ill-health". At the time when this report was published, almost one-fifth of children between the age of two and five were obese, and an additional 14 per cent were overweight. Whilst Brown claimed that maintaining a healthy weight may be individuals' responsibility, he argued that "the responsibility of Government, and wider society, is to make sure that individuals have access to the opportunities they want and the information they need in order to make choices and exercise greater control over their health and their lives" (Department of Health, 2008, p. iii).

As part of this strategy, government, business, local communities and other organisations were encouraged to create "urban and rural environments where walking, cycling and other forms of physical activity exercise and sport are accessible, safe and the norm" (Department of Health, 2008, p. xiii). The document quotes a report by the Royal Commission on Environmental Pollution (Royal Commission on Environmental Pollution, 2007) that suggests that modern urban systems can serve to discourage activity, thereby promoting weight gain and other health risks. As an illustration, the report refers to statistics produced by the Department for Transport, which show a dramatic change in passenger transport by mode between 1952 and 2006: the percentage of kilometres travelled by cars, vans and taxis skyrocketed (from under 30 per cent to nearly 90 per cent) whilst travel by buses and coaches, motor cycles, pedal cycles and rail plummeted. Combined, they accounted for just over 10 per cent in 2006. The report also pointed out that, in addition to contributing to excess weight, a lack of physical activity increases the risk of Type 2 diabetes. This is of particular concern as children are increasingly inactive.

It is against this background that the Department of Health and the Department for Children, Schools and Families set up the Healthy Community Challenge Fund in 2008 to test and assess a range of different approaches to fighting obesity by making physical activity and healthy food choices easier for local communities. Overall, the programme was intended to "test and validate holistic approaches to promoting physical activity" (Department of Health, 2008, p. 22). A call for expressions of interest was launched, which invited local authorities to submit bids in partnership with Primary Care Trusts. In recognition of their commitment to promoting health on the local level, successful applicants would be designated as "Healthy Towns". Up to £5 million would be available for each of these local areas over a three-year period, from 2009 to 2011, although successful authorities were required to provide 50 per cent matching funds, 25 per cent of which could be in kind. Successful applicants were expected to "invest in infrastructure improvements that implement the lessons of a variety of programmes", such as Homezones and Cycling Demonstration Towns (Department of Health, 2008, p. 22). Additionally, these improvements were to be combined with actions aiming to alter food and activity habits, following the example of the EPODE[2] model. Over 160 expressions of interest were received, of which 22 were subsequently invited to submit a more detailed application; 12 were selected as part of stage two.

Over 300 interventions were developed in the nine designated Healthy Towns over the five-year funding period. In Dudley, the "Let's go outside" programme encouraged families to use outdoor areas, by turning parks and play areas into so-called "family health hubs". Activities included connecting homes to parks through "active travel corridors", and offering a range of programmes, activities and events. Community safety, the provision of public toilets, signage and adequate lighting were also addressed. In Middlesbrough, an urban farming programme was initiated to promote fitness and healthy eating. Halifax set up a grow-your-own fruit and vegetable scheme for social housing tenants. In Manchester, the action plan included a points-based reward scheme for residents. An award scheme was proposed in Tower Hamlets for fast food outlets offering healthy alternatives. Amongst other actions, Sheffield promoted breastfeeding.

The 2008 Healthy Towns programme was of course subject to evaluation. A team of academics led by Steven Cummins of the London School of Hygiene and Tropical Medicine published a report in October 2016. From a methodological point of view, this piece of work relied in part on the "Behaviour Change Wheel" produced by Michie et al. (2011) (Figure 10.1), who defined behaviour change interventions as "coordinated sets of activities designed to change specified behaviour patterns" (Michie et al., 2011). This research stems from the fact that, although there have been many cases of successful actions aiming to change behaviour, there are also many examples of interventions that have not achieved their intended goals, hence the "need to develop the science and technology of

---

[2] The French programme "Ensemble prévenons l'obésité des enfants" is defined as a "community-based, family-oriented nutrition and lifestyle education programme" designed to "prevent child obesity by bringing together influential individuals and groups in the community including education and health professionals, retailers and the media in a campaign of local activity and healthy eating initiatives aimed at both children and their parents" (Department of Health, 2008, p. 22). This programme drew from previous programmes, in particular the French "Fleurbaix-Laventie Ville Santé" study, a nutritional and physical activity programme set up in Northern France, running from 1999 to 2007.

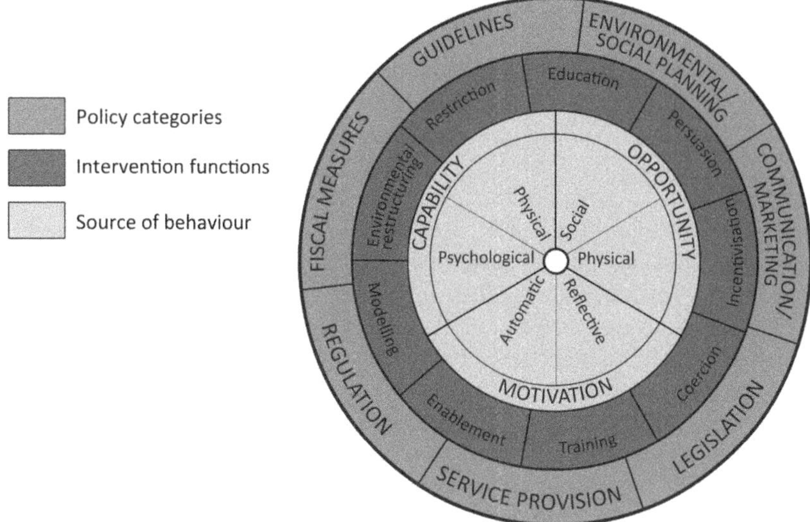

Source: Michie et al. (2011).

Figure 10.1 The Behaviour Change Wheel

behaviour change and make it useful to those designing interventions and planning policy" (Michie et al., 2011).

The evaluation carried out by Cummins et al. (2016) was based on the various categories of the Behaviour Change Wheel. In the following paragraph, definitions in inverted commas are direct quotations from Michie et al. (2011).

The most frequently used method appears to have been enablement (21.2 per cent), defined as "increasing means and reducing barriers to increase capability or opportunity beyond education and training; opportunity beyond environmental restructuring". This included the employment of a healthy urban planner to contribute to the design of an environment that would support a healthy lifestyle, and to carry out training; this amounted to 20.2 per cent of actions. Measures included free cycle training courses for secondary pupils. The second-most widely used method was environmental restructuring, defined as "changing the physical or social context", with 72 actions (17.8 per cent). These included the provision of more allotment spaces and shared growing spaces following a mapping of existing allotment spaces. Actions falling into the "education" category amounted to 13.6 per cent. These included the running of sessions on healthy lifestyle choices, including cooking sessions focused on cooking on a budget and preparing healthy lunch-boxes. Such education measures are defined as "increasing knowledge or understanding". They were accompanied by "persuasion" methods, defined as "using communication to induce positive or negative feelings or stimulate action". These represented 10.3 per cent of actions and included the use of social marketing techniques to improve health and encourage people to engage in health-related activities. In total, these measures amount to over 83 per cent of the actions. Interestingly, incentivisation, defined as "creating the expectation of reward", which was used in Manchester by allowing people to receive points for buying healthy food, using leisure facilities and taking part in physical activity, only represented 4.2 per cent of measures. Modelling, defined as "providing an example for people to aspire or to imitate", only made up 1.2 per cent of measures. Such actions were based on "positive peer influence" and included the training of 96 young people aged 16 to 19 to become "local health champions" and model a positive and healthy lifestyle, advocate healthy diets, lead active lifestyles and advise their peers of obesity risks. Restriction measures, defined as "using rules to reduce the opportunity to engage in the target behaviour", and coercion measures, defined as "creating an expectation of punishment", amounted to 0.5 per cent and 0 per cent, respectively, of the measures. The remaining 11.1 per cent of actions did not fall into one of the predefined categories since they were incompatible with the Behaviour Change Wheel model. These included partnerships with organisations such as Sustrans Link to School, Living Street and the development of active travel corridors. The most widespread types of policies used to implement these various actions were "service provision" (49.4 per cent) and "environmental and social planning" (22.8 per cent). Much less used were "communication and marketing" policies (8.4 per cent), "guidelines" (2.7 per cent) and "regulation" (3.6 per cent). No fiscal policies were used. Unclassifiable policies, including the involvement of local communities in the identification of barriers to active lifestyles, amounted to 13.2 per cent of policies. The research carried out by Cummins et al. (2016) highlights that although the amount of funding allocated to each of the designated Healthy Towns is known, "no cost-effective data is available making any additional assessment of the funding very difficult" (Cummins et al., 2016, p. 30).

The other main published source of evaluation of the Healthy Towns programme was produced by Goodwin et al. (2012). This research relied on qualitative interviews with 20 local programme stakeholders and national policy actors. It shows that the people involved in designing and delivering the programme essentially relied on local anecdotal and observational evidence to guide the programme's development. Whilst this study lists a number of successes, it draws attention to the relative lack of guidance made available to local communities engaging in the programme, which is reflected in comments by one interviewee:

> I remember going through various relevant NICE guidance reports and I was thinking "well it's all very interesting, but at the end of the day it doesn't really amount to much". It says like well walking's a good thing, so we've got quite a big emphasis on walking in our programme. It doesn't really take you much further in terms of how to do it. So we felt we had to work that out pretty much ourselves. (Goodwin et al., 2012, p. 106).

10.4 THE HEALTHY NEW TOWNS PROGRAMME

The next major step in reuniting health and planning was taken in 2012 with the publication of the National Planning Policy Framework, which stated that the planning system can play an important role in facilitating social interaction and creating healthy, inclusive communities (Department for Communities and Local Government, 2012). An information note published in 2012 by the NHS London Healthy Urban Development Unit (NHS, 2012) showed how health issues are picked up by the National Planning Policy Framework. Two years later, the National Planning Guidance for Health published in 2014 suggested that local planning authorities should ensure that health and well-being, as well as health infrastructure, are considered in local and neighbourhood plans and when planning decision-making. Kevin Fenton, the National Director of Health and Wellbeing at Public Health England, pointed out that "for the first time, the need for new developments to consider wider public health issues is recognised through the inclusion of such a section in guidance provided by the Department for Communities and Local Government".[3] A guide to town planning for health organisation was published in order to help health organisations and public health teams to understand how the town planning process works and to explain how and why they should engage with their local planning authority (Department of Health, 2015). Other publications provided additional advice, such as the Health Urban Planning Checklist, which the NHS London Healthy Urban Development Unit published in 2014 (Table 10.1) (NHS, 2014b).

---

[3] Public Health England (2014) "New national planning policy and guidance aims to promote health and reduce inequalities", Press Release, 13 March 2014.

Table 10.1 Summary table to healthy urban planning checklist

Theme	Planning issue	Health and well-being issue
1. Healthy housing	• Housing design • Accessible housing • Healthy living • Housing mix and affordability	• Lack of living space – overcrowding • Unhealthy living environment – daylight, ventilation, noise • Excess deaths due to cold / overheating • Injuries in the home • Mental illness
2. Active travel	• Promoting walking and cycling • Safety • Connectivity • Minimising car use	• Physical inactivity, cardiovascular disease and obesity • Road and traffic injuries • Mental illness from social isolation • Noise and air pollution from traffic
3. Healthy environment	• Construction • Air quality • Noise • Contaminated land • Open space • Play space • Biodiversity • Local food growing • Flood risk • Overheating	• Disturbance and stress caused by construction activity • Poor air quality – lung and heart disease • Disturbance from noisy activities and uses • Health risks from toxicity of contaminated land • Physical inactivity, cardiovascular disease and obesity • Mental health benefits from access to nature and green space and water • Opportunities for food growing – active lifestyles, healthy diet and tackling food poverty • Excess summer deaths due to overheating
4. Vibrant neighbourhoods	• Healthcare services • Education • Access to social infrastructure • Local employment and healthy workplaces • Access to local food shops • Public buildings and spaces	• Access to services and health inequalities • Mental illness and poor self-esteem associated with unemployment and poverty • Limited access to healthy food linked to obesity and related diseases • Poor environment leading to physical inactivity • Ill-health exacerbated through isolation, lack of social contact and fear of crime

Source: NHS (2014b) Healthy Urban Planning Checklist.

The *Five Year Forward* report published by the NHS in 2014 identified three main – and widening – gaps to address. First, the "health and well-being gap", which means that health inequalities will widen and that funding may well have to be spent on treating avoidable illnesses. Second, the "care and quality gap", which requires the reshaping of care delivery, harnessing technology and driving down variations in quality and safety of care. Third, the "funding and efficiency gap", which may result in worse services, fewer staff, and continuing deficits and restrictions on new treatment (NHS, 2014a, p. 7).

In order to address these challenges, a set of strategies was put forward. One of them relates to the "acceleration of useful health innovation" (NHS, 2014a, p. 32). The report rightly points out that Britain has a track record of discovery and innovation. Therefore, it is suggested that speeding up innovation in new treatments and diagnostics will make a major contribution to achieving the objectives; so, too, will finding new ways of delivering care, for example, through the combination of different technologies that may allow the remote monitoring of patients. One of the measures, however, is of particular relevance for town planning: the NHS recommends that the development of health and care "new towns" should be explored since they "offer the opportunity to design modern services from scratch, with fewer legacy constraints – integrating not only health and social care, but also other public services such as welfare, education and affordable housing" (NHS, 2014a, p. 35). These would take the form of actual new towns or the refurbishment of some existing urban areas.

A call for expressions of interest was launched in July 2015 (NHS, 2015), pointing to the fact that building strong communities and healthy places can contribute to addressing the three gaps identified in the *Five Year Forward Report.* The call clearly aimed to go beyond existing good practice and to drive closer collaboration between local authorities, planners, developers and the NHS. The three main aims were to develop new and more effective ways of shaping new towns, show what is possible when the ways in which health and care services are delivered are radically rethought, and accomplish these objectives in a way that can be replicated elsewhere. Several new approaches were suggested, including: building of healthier homes and environments that support independence at all stages of life; tackling unhealthy and so-called "obesogenic" environments by creating walkable neighbourhoods, encouraging safe active travel and providing more accessible public transport, as well as providing easy access to healthy and affordable food locally; creating connected neighbourhoods and inclusive public spaces that allow populations of all ages, abilities and backgrounds to mix, including "dementia-friendly" design; designing healthy workplaces, schools and leisure facilities to encourage physical activity, healthy eating and positive mental health and well-being; and implementing a new "operating system" for health that integrates primary and secondary care, mental and physical health, and health and social care. The call also highlighted the fact that this programme potentially stretches beyond the health and care sector, which points to the possible contribution of "digitally-enabled 'smart towns'".

Initially, the NHS intended to establish up to five long-term partnerships with local areas in which healthier neighbourhoods and towns could be developed. Provision was made for a range of possible projects to be undertaken. These could include larger sites for up to 10000 homes, including transport infrastructure, housing and open spaces, as well as smaller sites and neighbourhoods of approximately 250 homes for which the focus would be meeting the needs of particular groups with a particular design and the use of so-called "behavioural nudges"[4] to encourage healthy behaviours. According to the NHS, over 76000 affordable homes are expected to be built across England to address the country's "obesity crisis" and to shape dementia-friendly environments.

In a short paper published in *Perspectives in Public Health*, Holly Norman and Daniel McDonnell[5] (Norman and McDonnell, 2017, p. 29), both involved in the NHS Healthy New Towns programme, explain that the ambition was initially "concerned in terms of opportunities to accelerate development of integrated care models and design modern services from scratch", and add that these ambitions have "evolved rapidly, with equal emphasis now being placed on shaping new towns, neighbourhood and strong communities that promote health and well-being, prevent illness and keep people independent". In other words, the programme now intends to "bridge public health and planning" and to bring together disciplines and partners. Interestingly Norman and McDonnell suggest that applications share a common appetite to make the most of the opportunities offered by new developments, since, they argue, these are expected to be less constrained than other places by existing infrastructure that "lock-in established behaviours and traditional service models" (Norman and McDonnell, 2017, p. 29).

---

4 The term "nudge" used by the NHS in this document is not further defined, but existing academic literature provides useful definitions. In a seminal book, Richard Thaler and Cass Sunstein explain that a nudge is "any aspect of choice architecture that alters people's behaviour in a predictable way without forbidding any options of significantly changing their economic incentives". They add "to count as a mere nudge, the intervention must be easy and cheap to avoid. Nudges are not mandates. Putting the fruit at eye level counts as a nudge. Banning junk food doesn't." (Thaler and Sunstein, 2008, p. 6).

5 Daniel McDonnell is a Strategy Programme Manager with NHS England and leads on engagement and spread for the Healthy New Towns programme.

Given the housing crisis, or housing challenge as it has recently been called, the NHS expected proposals to emerge from areas identified for future population growth in regional or local plans. Developments could be located in urban or rural areas and could be of different types, such as urban extensions or regeneration. It was also expected that projects be in the pre-application, pre-master planning or master planning phase and that they include at least 250 homes, although no upper limit was set for the size of developments. It was expected that projects be backed by local authorities.

The first stage of the process was deliberately limited to the submission of a two-page expression of interest, due a couple of months after the call was launched. Ten projects (Table 10.2) were selected from the 114 applications received from local authorities, housing associations, NHS organisations and housing developers. These ten demonstrator projects will eventually accommodate over 170 000 residents. Speaking at a conference at the King's Fund in London on 1 March 2016, NHS England Chief Executive Simon Stevens said "the much-needed push to kick-start affordable housing across England creates a golden opportunity for the NHS to help promote health and keep people independent" and added that "we'll kick ourselves if in 10 years' time we look back having missed the opportunity to 'design out' the obesogenic environment [. . .] and 'design in' health and well-being" (quoted in Siddique, 2016).

Table 10.2 The ten "Healthy New Towns" demonstrator sites selected by the NHS

Project name	Location	Number of homes
Barking Riverside	London	10 800
Barton Park	Oxford	885
Eco-Bicester (Elmsbrook project)	Oxon	393 of the 13 000 planned for the entire development
Ebsfleet Garden City	Kent	Up to 15 000 homes
Cranbrook	Devon	8000
Darlington	County Durham	2500
Halton Lea	Runcorn	800
Northstowe	Cambridgeshire	10 000
Whitehill and Bordon	Hampshire	3350
Whyndyke Farm in Fylde	Lancashire	1400

10.5 THE BARTON PROJECT, OXFORD

One of the ten NHS Healthy New Towns demonstrator sites is Barton Park, a 36-hectare urban extension located to the north-east of Oxford and adjoining the existing deprived neighbourhood of Barton. The main aim of the development is to foster "one Barton" and ensure that the new development contributes to regenerating the existing neighbourhood by establishing social and physical connections between residents, promoting inclusion and improving the quality of life. The project is led by the Barton Healthy New Town (BHNT) steering group, which is composed of public authorities (Oxford City Council and Oxfordshire County Council), the housing developer Grosvenor and the Oxfordshire Clinical Commissioning Group (the local representation of the National Health Service).

The new settlement is part of the Oxford City Council's strategy to address the dramatic housing shortage in the urban area, in particular of affordable and social units. This garden suburb will provide 885 housing units with a range of types and sizes, including semi-detached and detached houses, town houses and apartments, a primary school, retail units, services and a hotel, as well as formal and informal recreational spaces and landscape areas. The project is expected to provide high-quality houses in a well-connected, sustainable and green environment, inspiring a healthy lifestyle.

Numerous operations are currently underway in the British Healthy New Towns. As the process is ongoing, the insight we provide here should be considered as a work in progress. A summary of the main actions taken as part of the Barton redevelopment is provided in Table 10.3, which presents them in a matrix based on the previously mentioned Behaviour Wheel Change tool. To date, this theoretical framework has not yet been applied to assess the current Healthy New Towns initiative – therefore, this chapter aims to provide a first account of the various ways in which health planning is being tackled in Oxford.

10.6 CONCLUSION

Although it is too early to assess the effectiveness of the Healthy New Towns programme, a few preliminary conclusions can be drawn.

First and foremost, and whatever the outcome may be, we are certainly witnessing a reuniting of health and planning, at least in terms of discourse and processes. Through its Healthy New Towns programme, the NHS is engaging in planning for the first time in its history and this is occurring at

Table 10.3 Barton actions matrix

Intervention	Description	Leader	Intervention areas	BCW source of behaviour	BCW intervention functions	BCW Policy
Health walks	Free 12-week short walks programme, for inactive people to walk for one hour	Oxford City Council	Healthy lifestyle Physical activity	Physical capability	Training	Service provision
Mental health drop-in	Awareness raising and discussion about mental health and mental health services	Mind for better mental health (charity)	Healthy lifestyle	Psychological capability	Education	Service provision
Barton mural	Joint intervention between a professional artist and the local population to create a mural behind the sports hall	Barton community centre	Urban planning	Automatic motivation	Environmental restructuring	Communication/ marketing
Cooking up a Feast cookery course	Cook and share meals, recipes book to be delivered to new Barton Park homes	Barton community centre	Food system	Psychological capability	Education	Service provision
Free sport session	Free sport session	Barton community centre	Physical activity	Physical capability	Training	Service provision
Accessing fuel poverty related services in Oxford	Information events: supporting vulnerable Oxford residents to keep warm and healthy	Oxford City Council	Healthy lifestyle	Social opportunity	Enablement	Guideline
Sports hall refurbishment	Sports hall refurbishment	Oxford City Council	Urban planning	Physical capability	Enablement	Environmental/ Social planning
Affordable home		Oxford City Council	Urban planning	Reflective motivation	Incentive	Regulation

Table 10.3 (continued)

Intervention	Description	Leader	Intervention areas	BCW source of behaviour	BCW intervention functions	BCW Policy
Food store	Open new food store in New Barton	Oxford City Council and Grosvenor Developments	Food system	Automatic motivation	Enablement	Guidelines
Space for community uses		Oxford City Council and Grosvenor Developments	Urban planning	Social opportunity	Environmental restructuring	Environmental/ social planning
New sports facilities	Sports pavilion, sports pitches and a 3G sports pitch	Oxford City Council and Grosvenor Developments	Urban planning Physical activity	Physical capability	Environmental restructuring	Environmental/ social planning
Improved allotment		Oxford City Council and Grosvenor Developments	Urban planning Physical activity	Social opportunity	Environmental restructuring	Environmental/ Social planning
Healthy Urban Mobility (HUM) research project	Understand the impact of everyday (im)mobility on health and well-being with a variety of social groups. Explore the potential for participatory mobilities planning with local communities to support and develop solutions for healthy urban mobility	Oxford Brookes University	Urban planning	Unclassifiable	Unclassifiable	Unclassifiable

Fettiplace Recreation Ground	Installation of a fitness trail	Oxford City Council, in partnership with WREN (Waste Recycling Environmental)	Urban planning Physical activity	Physical capability	Environmental restructuring	Environmental/ social planning
Barton Neighbourhood Centre Refurbishment		Oxford City Council	Urban planning	Social opportunity	Environmental restructuring	Environmental/ Social planning
Health Impact Assessment (HIA)		Ove Arup & Partners Ltd	Urban planning	Physical opportunity	Coercion	Legislation
Social prescribing	Mean of enabling GPs, nurses and other primary care professionals to refer people to a range of local, non-clinical services. Development of Barton Healthy Living Centre	Hedena Health surgery, Bury Knowle Health Centre, Oxford Clinical Commissioning	Healthy lifestyle	Social opportunity	Enablement	Service provision
Barton LLP	Recommendations on the design of the new development, infrastructure and services	Oxford City Council	Urban planning	Social opportunity	Restriction	Environmental/ Social planning
Food poverty report	Evaluation of food need in Barton	Good Food Oxford	Food system	Unclassifiable	Unclassifiable	Unclassifiable
Healthy Start vouchers	Vouchers for fruit, vegetables, milk and formula for parents and carers who have young children and are receiving benefits	Oxford City Council and Good Food Oxford	Food system	Reflective motivation	Incantation	Communication/ marketing

Table 10.3 (continued)

Intervention	Description	Leader	Intervention areas	BCW source of behaviour	BCW intervention functions	BCW Policy
Barton community cupboard food bank	Storage and distribution of food, market-style provision	Good Food Oxford	Food system	Social opportunity	Environmental restructuring	Environmental/ social planning
Training session	Training session on food poverty for frontline service providers, to identify and discuss food poverty and share best practices	Good Food Oxford	Food system	Psychological capability	Training	Guidelines
Barton older people day	Opportunity for older people to free advice and information	Oxford 50 + Network	Healthy lifestyle	Psychological capability	Education	Communication/ marketing
Football club	Activities targeting local people who wouldn't normally get involved in sport	Barton unite football Club	Physical activity	Automatic motivation	Persuasion	Communication/ marketing
Future food kids	5 workshops to Barton schoolchildren. The programme focuses on healthy food and food sustainability	Fusion Arts	Food system	Reflective motivation	Education	Communication/ marketing
Appointment buddies	Appointment buddy services for elderly residents to help ensure they make health appointments and can engage more with health professionals	Getting Heard	Healthy lifestyle	Reflective motivation	Education	Communication/ marketing
Workshop and outreach visits	Performance about health and social care, encourage to make connection with other people	Oxford concert party	Healthy lifestyle	Automatic motivation	Persuasion	Communication/ marketing

Youth ambition girls sport	Physical activity and health & well-being sessions for inactive girls aged 10-17	Youth Ambition Oxford City Council	Healthy lifestyle Physical activity	Physical capability	Training	Service provision
IBA training overview: alcohol & smoking brief intervention		Tenancy Management & Sustainment Officer for Barton, Health Care Assistant and Cardiac Rehabilitation Specialist nurse	Healthy lifestyle	Psychological capability	Training	Service provision

a large scale. There appears to be a real potential for joint activity: whereas previous initiatives, such as the Healthy Town programme, essentially provided funding for laudable but piecemeal actions initiated at the local level, the NHS Healthy New Towns programme offers a unique opportunity to plan for health in a rather rare context: one in which a number of medium- and large-scale human settlements are planned from scratch.

Second, the current Healthy New Towns programme appears to focus on partnerships. According to Daniel McDonnell, there is a clear shift in the approach if we compare the NHS programme with the 2008 Healthy Towns:

> The Healthy New Towns programme is only going to be around for a few years. One of our primary concerns is therefore its legacy. We are operating in the world of the built environment, planning and development, all of which take years. What also takes years is measuring the health outcomes.[6]

The Healthy New Towns programme is, therefore, focusing on building strong links at the local level in order to allow actions to be pursued and monitoring to take place after the programme itself has been wound up:

> From the start we encouraged each of the sites to build strong academic links because programmes such as the NSH Healthy New Towns are around for a couple of years. Academics, however, will be around longer. They will therefore be able to contribute to measure the outcomes. This is particularly true if we build partnerships with local universities whose research staff focuses on these issues. We have therefore tried to connect people up in the right areas. Academics were enthusiastic about being part of something which is potentially quite big.[7]

Some lessons from previous initiatives appear to have been learned but the new programme does also come with its fair share of uncertainty and possible shortcomings. The call for expressions of interest published in 2015 did invite local authorities to come forward with projects that would involve retrofitting existing urban areas. Although a number of the selected pilot projects do cover some existing urban areas, it is fair to say that most of them – if not all – are new settlements (garden suburbs, urban extensions etc.). According to Daniel McDonnell, this is because "new housing development is a driver for improving existing areas". Arguably, this is the case. However, little if anything seems to be on the cards in terms of retrofitting existing urban areas – in particular the suburbs. What

---

6 Interview 16 October 2017.
7 Interview 16 October 2017.

is clearly needed now as an extension of the NHS Healthy New Towns programme is a "Healthy suburbs and new towns" initiative – in which "New Towns" would refer to post-war planned settlements rather than new communities.

ACKNOWLEDGEMENTS

This research work has been supported by:

- The French National Research Agency's "Investissements d'avenir" programme, through LabEx AE&CC and the CDP LIFE project (ANR-15-IDEX-02).
- Fondation Braillard Architectes through the Eco-Century research programme.
- Région Auvergne Rhône Alpes through the SCUSI international cooperation programme.

REFERENCES

Adams, M.A., Ding, D., Sallis, J.F., Bowles, H.R., Ainsworth, B.R., Bergman, P., Bull, F.C. et al. (2013), "Patterns of neighborhood environment attributes related to physical activity across 11 countries: a latent class analysis", *International Journal of Behavioral Nutrition and Physical Activity*, **10** (1), 34.

Barton, H., Thompson, S., Burgess, S. and Grant, M. (2015), *The Routledge handbook of planning for health and well-being: shaping a sustainable and healthy future*, London: Routledge.

Cummins, S., Ogilvie, D., White, M., Petticrew, M., Jones, A., Goodwin, D., Sautkina, E. et al. (2016), *National evaluation of the healthy communities challenge fund: the Healthy Towns Programme in England*, Final Report to the Department of Health, London: London School of Health and Tropical Medicine.

Dannenberg, A., Frumkin, H. and Jackson, R. (2011), *Making healthy places: designing and building for health, well-being, and sustainability*, Washington, DC: Island Press.

Department for Communities and Local Government (2012), *National planning policy framework*, London: HMSO.

Department of Health (2008), *Healthy weight, healthy lives: a cross-government strategy for England*, London.

Department of Health (2015), Health Building Note 00-08 Addendum 2 – A guide to town planning for health organisations, London.

Freudenberg, N., Klitzman, S. and Saegert, S. (2009), *Urban health and society: interdisciplinary approaches to research and practice*, San Francisco, CA: Jossey-Bass.

Gatrell, A.C. (2011), *Mobilities and health*, Farnham: Ashgate Publishing.

Giles-Corti, B. and Donovan, R.J. (2002), "The relative influence of individual, social and physical environment determinants of physical activity", *Social Science & Medicine*, **54** (12), 1793–812.

Goodwin, D.M., Cummins, S., Sautkina, E., Ogilvie, D., Petticrew, M., Jones, A., Wheeler, K. et al. (2012), "The role and status of evidence and innovation in the healthy towns programme in England: a qualitative stakeholder interview study", *Journal of Epidemiology and Community Health*, **67** (1), 106–12.

Government Office for Science (2007), *Tackling obesities: future choices*, London: HMSO.

Hall, P. (2002), *Urban and regional planning*, 4th edn, London: Routledge.

Halloran, D.R. (2011), "Home environment, asthma, and obesity: how are they related?", *The Journal of Pediatrics*, **159** (1), 3–4.

Health and Social Care Information Centre (2016), *Statistics on obesity, physical activity and diet*, London: HSCIS.

Kagioglou, M. and Tzortzopoulos, P. (2010), *Improving healthcare through built environment infrastructure*, Chichester: Wiley-Blackwell, John Wiley & Sons.

Limstrand, T. (2008), "Environmental characteristics relevant to young people's use of sports facilities: a review", *Scandinavian Journal of Medicine & Science in Sports*, **18** (3), 275–87.

Marmot, M.G. (2010), "Fair society, healthy lives: strategic review of health inequalities in England post-2010", London: The Marmot Review.

Michie, S., Van Stralen, M.M. and West, R. (2011), "The behaviour change wheel: a new method for characterising and designing behaviour change interventions", *Implementation Science*, **6** (42), doi:10.1186/1748-5908-6-42.

Moughtin, C., Moughtin, K.M. and Signoretta, P. (2009), *Urban design: health and the therapeutic environment*, Oxford: Architectural Press.

NHS (2012), *The National Planning Policy Framework and Health*, HUDU Planning for Health Information Note No.2, London: NHS London Healthy Urban Development Unit.

NHS (2014a), *Five year forward view*, London: NHS.

NHS (2014b), *Healthy urban planning checklist*, NHS London Healthy Urban Development Unit, London: NHS.

NHS (2015), *The forward view into action: registering interest to join the Healthy New Towns programme*. London: NHS.

Norman, H. and McDonnell, D. (2017), "The NHS Healthy New Towns programme", *Perspectives in Public Health*, **137** (1), 29–30.

Otgaar, A.H., Klijs, J. and Van den Berg, L. (2011), *Towards healthy cities: comparing conditions for change*, Farnham: Ashgate Publishing.

Pacyna, J.M. and Pacyna, E.G. (2016), *Environmental determinants of human health*, Cham: Springer.

Rom, W.N. (2012), *Environmental policy and public health: air pollution, global climate change, and wilderness*, San Francisco, CA: Jossey-Bass.

Royal Commission on Environmental Pollution (2007), *The urban environment: twenty-sixth report*, London: Royal Commission on Environmental Pollution.

Siddique, H. (2016), "Ten new 'healthy' towns to be built in England", *The Guardian*, 1 March, London.

Thaler, R.H. and Sunstein, C.R. (2008), *Nudge: improving decisions about health, wealth, and happiness*, New Haven, CT: Yale University Press.

Townshend, T. and Lake, A. (2017), "Obesogenic environments: current evidence of the built and food environments", *Perspectives in Public Health*, **137** (1), 38–44.

Verderber, S. (2012), *Sprawling cities and our endangered public health*, London: Routledge.
Wong, M.H. (2012), *Environmental contamination: health risks and ecological restoration*, Boca Raton, FL: CRC Press.
Woodward, A. and MacMillan, A. (2015), "The environment and climate change: determinants of health and disease", in Detels, R. and Gulliford, M. (eds), *Oxford Textbook of Global Public Health*, 6th edn, Oxford: Oxford University Press, pp. 201–18.
World Health Organization (1948), "Preamble to the Constitution of WHO", as adopted by the International Health Conference, Geneva: World Health Organization.
World Health Organization & UN-Habitat (2016), *Global report on urban health: equitable healthier cities for sustainable development*, Geneva: World Health Organization.

11. A framework for describing and analysing life course trajectories: taking a step towards studying residential migration factors

Marlène Villanova-Oliver, David Noël, Jérôme Gensel and Pierre Le Quéau

11.1 BACKGROUND AND KEY ISSUES

The topic of attaching to and detaching from urban space has pervaded the work of writers and poets since at least the 19th century, but sociologists have, since the beginning of the 20th century, taken up this inquiry, too. Simmel's interest lies in the new kinds of connections that inevitably result from the development of the big modern cities (Simmel, 1989). Weber ponders the development of cities by looking at a combination of determining factors for each civilisation, as well as the political aspects that are required for different social strata to cohabitate within the same space (Weber, 1982). In this regard, following this initial investigation, the "tradition of the Chicago School of Sociology" will find a "social laboratory" and fertile ground not only for questioning the external (political, economic etc.) factors constraining its form but also for digging into its "state of mind" (Park, 1990): the urban man develops lifestyles that sociologists have sought to understand by crafting a programme of "urban ecology".

From the outset, the manner in which the urban issue is formulated within the tradition of the Chicago School of Sociology also gives rise to questions pertaining to migration and mobility: not only those that lead to "outside" populations increasing in numbers but also those that weave the urban fabric. The work of Park (1990) and Wirth (1980) on intra-metropolitan migrations laid the foundation for this exploration of the moves that constitute urban complexity. However, we would be ill-served by limiting our approach to the urban man to that of "uprooting" (Duvignaud, 1977) – the atom fired into the masses from some "multitudinous machine" (Beauchard, 1985) – especially because of his continued attachment to the places where he lives.

This theme of a connection with space will be developed, in particular by studying modes of appropriating space that becomes a "practised place" (De Certeau, 1980). Neighbourhood relations are another ever-present dimension of that which creates an attachment to the place (Haumont and Morel, 2005). Man deals with the city: while sometimes opposing his objectivity (Simmel, 1989; Halbwachs, 1994), it also allows him to be fulfilled. A sensitive, dreamlike, poetic relationship with the city (Sansot, 1984) can be born from this double movement of resistance and appropriation. Thus, for a sociology that strives to account for how the link between man and the city is formed, there has to be a return to a "microsociology" and a grasping of public space through all the thrills and excesses that comprise and organise its fabric (Joseph, 1984): the deviances, the apparent rupture and the multiplicity of lifestyles bear witness to the city men's strategies of adaptation to, sociability with and appropriation of the space.

The analysis of intra-urban migration reveals what is playing out in the stories of individuals and groups. Their movements inside the metropolis cannot be understood without referring to life phases and cycles (composition/recomposition of households), the shared aspirations of the moment and even the modes concerning the living environment, notwithstanding other more directly economic elements (Lelévrier, 2007; Bonvalet and Bringé, 2012).

Our aim is to gain a more detailed understanding of the reasons that lead households to make choices regarding where to live. A sequence of such choices eventually forms a residential trajectory. The use of the term "residential trajectory" (Authier et al., 2010) refers not only to the spatio-temporal aspect of individuals' residential life. For sociologists Yves Grafmeyer and Jean-Yves Authier (Grafmeyer and Authier, 2011), using the word "trajectory" is more specific than describing a simple evolution in time and space: "the use of the term 'trajectory' rather than 'itinerary' or 'mobility' is tantamount to suggesting that a given series of successive positions is not mere coincidence but, on the contrary, linked according to an intelligible order".

Our work strives to give meaning to the processes of urban migration by studying residential trajectories. Our aim is to understand the underlying reasons that push people to change their residence, at what point in their life and in exchange for what (other) space. But the reasons for making a residential choice can only be apprehended within the context of a global approach to individuals' *lifelines*, that is, by taking into account family and professional aspects, as well as the ones that relate to the sphere of leisure and all aspects of life that play a decisive role in the choice a particular individual or household makes. One of the applications that this work targets is the collection and analysis of elements that seem to contribute, for different profiles, to a better (especially residential) quality of life.

The notion of a trajectory, which underpins the concept of urban migration, has been the subject of many works in computer science, especially since the boom in technologies based on the GPS location of all kinds of moving objects (vehicles, humans, animals etc.) (Güting and Schneider, 2005). In addition to the storage of GPS data in dedicated databases, many works have been oriented towards expressing the semantics associated with traces of trajectories in order to explore movement. When people are the moving objects that are being studied, one of the main issues is to know or to recognise their activities. Most of the time, the point of interest is the notion of displacement, most often carried out over a short period of time – for example, on a daily or a weekly basis (Christophe et al., 2010). The work of Hägerstrand (1970), and more broadly that of *Time Geography*, on the representation of the evolution of activities, is devoted to it. Following a complementary and dual approach, the detection of activities (Laube and Purves, 2006) involves the implementation of statistical methods or spatial analysis, as well as scientific visualisation, to extract activity patterns from the analysed traces.

When the time scale is larger, which is the case that interests us here, we can observe what are called "lifelines". In this respect, the work of Thériault et al. (2002) is a precursor in geomatics. Describing migrations and residential trajectories can be a major tool in urban planning. In the background, apart from imposed displacements, we hope to better understand why individuals or households leave a place or, on the contrary, join it, while taking into account the personal, professional, socio-economic and cultural context elements. The approach aims to elicit all knowledge that might be useful to make an informed decision, for example, by better adapting the housing supply or promoting the development of a particular local service. In this way, collected data will make it possible to test different hypotheses regarding the reasons behind changing residence and, in turn, to inform policy decisions. For example, it could be confirmed that the exodus to the suburbs is explained by the (lived, expressed, quantified) lack of adapted housing in the city centre but also – why not? – by any other cause that has not been explained to date. Such results could allow decision making or even action (reorienting the housing supply) in relation to phenomena (peri-urban exodus) with major repercussions (the pollution effect linked to commuting).

Thus, by working on the description and spatial analysis of the inhabitants' migrations within a metropolitan area, the aim is to make a contribution in terms of methodology and the tools to identify the logic behind residence and displacement and highlight the metropolitan dynamics. The goal of this multidisciplinary research is to design and develop a computer tool to support the observation approach to urban and/or peri-urban migration and decision aids in the areas of urban planning and territorial development. The work presented here concerns the initial fruits of this research.

The following section presents a state of the art relating to the modelling of lifelines and residential choice. Section 11.3 presents the concepts that we deemed important to consider in order to represent multi-dimensional lifelines; these concepts also incorporate explanatory factors. Section 11.4 describes how our approach is implemented in the proposal of models and an approach equipped with an *ad hoc* software solution. This work's conclusions and perspectives are given in section 11.5.

11.2 STATE OF THE ART

11.2.1 Modelling Trajectories

For the purpose of observing urban and/or peri-urban migrations, the central concept that has to be modelled is the "*residential trajectory*", in the sense of the sequence of places where an individual has lived throughout his/her life. Such a trajectory is a spatio-temporal object that can be described by taking inspiration from work on the modelling of moving objects,[1] which leads, for example, to the trajectories of vessels in the maritime domain (Fournier et al., 2007). These spatio-temporal trajectories usually take the form of a sequence of triplets (latitude, longitude, time). The aim of semantic trajectory modelling (Alvares et al., 2007) is to enrich such "raw" mobility data with information that can help to make sense out of them. Most semantic approaches consist in annotating the different parts of the proposed division of spatio-temporal trajectories. Thus, drawing on "time geography" (Hägerstrand, 1970), researchers have modelled spatio-temporal trajectories by using periods of displacement and periods of activity (Zheni et al., 2009) or movements and stops (see, for example, Spaccapietra et al., 2008; Hu et al., 2013; Krisnadhi and Hitzler, 2016). This first level of structuring is subsequently used to combine information such as the mode of transport during a displacement or the nature of an activity during a period labelled as such.

---

[1] Here, the term "moving object" also refers to objects such as parcels, ships, animals or people tracked by dedicated devices.

11.2.2 Lifeline Modelling

In our context, the represented trajectory is the life of an individual: the provided semantics aims to understand what this trajectory comprises. The work initiated by Marius Thériault is often referred to in the field of lifeline modelling. The spatio-temporal model for analysing lifelines (Thériault et al., 1999) is based on three different trajectories: residential, family and professional. Each of these trajectories is conceptually modelled with episodes – stable statuses for a period of time – and events that alter one or more of these statuses. The conceptual model is rooted in a relational approach. Later, the model will be modified to determine the probability that an event will occur under certain conditions on a lifeline (Thériault et al., 2002). The conditions of residential choice are also addressed by Vandermissen et al. (2009), who place particular emphasis on the role played by job changes in the working lives of individuals. The models that are proposed in this work focus on the temporal aspect of residential choices: the reasons why individuals will move at a particular moment (depending on their circumstances) are of greater interest than the reasons why they leave a place and choose a new one.

11.2.3 Residential Choice Modelling

The conditions for residential choice have been well documented in recent decades, particularly by sociologists and demographers. The use of a biographical perspective (in other words, considering the connection between the residential choice and the life course) has greatly contributed to enriching the modelling of this notion (Clark and Whiters, 2008). Residential choices are considered an integral part of individuals' biographies in order to better put them into perspective and to analyse the relationships between the different aspects of the individuals' lives (Willekens, 1991).

The first studies on residential choices from a biographical perspective seek in particular to highlight the relationships between the different events punctuating individuals' lives. In many cases, the principle is to model the imbalance caused by the events that have occurred in people's lives (change of job, birth of a child etc.) and to consider that this imbalance pushes them to move when it crosses a certain threshold (Mulder and Hooimeijer, 1999). Other studies have focused specifically on events that occur simultaneously (Mulder and Wagner, 1993).

More recently, some authors have pointed out that – although individuals' biographies are often considered as a series of interrelated events – the importance of periods of residential stability must not be underestimated (Coulter and Van Ham, 2013) because individuals' lives ultimately contain relatively few moves, whether actual or even just considered. The authors' logical conclusion is that if a better understanding of residential choices comes from answering the question "Why do people move?", one should not underestimate the importance of another question, "Why do they *not* move?" To answer these questions, researchers emphasise the importance of considering individuals' aspirations, in order to relate an effective (or proven) trajectory with a projection towards the individual's future (Coulter and Van Ham, 2013).

The aforementioned approaches, which come from different fields (geomatics, geography, sociology, demography), have clearly laid the conceptual foundations to represent the lifelines. The goal of our work is to enrich this representation with a semantic trajectories model that allows for multiple perspectives to be taken into account and the different explanatory factors of a trajectory to be integrated. To this end, we want to provide a generic model for representing lifelines, whatever the field of application, and the themes on which to focus. In the same way, beyond re-transcribing proven observations, we aim for the model to represent individuals' projects with respect to their lifelines. In the following section, we present the key concepts that should be considered for the representation and study of the lifelines.

11.3 KEY CONCEPTS FOR THE REPRESENTATION AND STUDY OF THE LIFELINES

11.3.1 Introductory Example

Figure 11.1 represents an extract from the lifeline of an individual and is inspired by the work presented in Thériault et al. (1999).

The left side of the figure enumerates a set, which here is not exhaustive because it is only used for the purpose of illustration, of attributes[2] that exemplify the situation of an individual: the number of children in the household, the position occupied, the type of housing and so on. The right part shows the values that the different attributes have taken over time (for example, after a period without a child, the household including one child, then two children). The shift in the value of the attribute *number of children at home* to another is marked by an *event* (symbolised by a labelled pellet, like E5), which, here, can correspond to a birth. Before and after an event (or between two events), there is a period of stability during which

[2] Thériault et al. (1999) calls the values taken by these attributes "statuses".

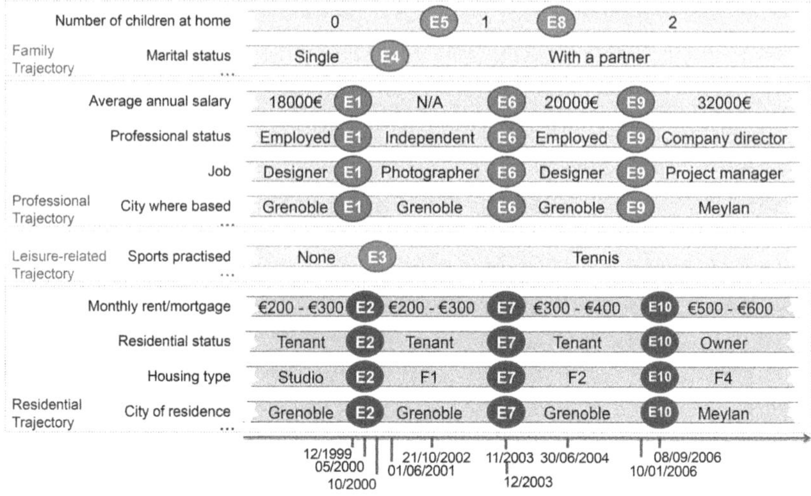

Source: Representation inspired by Thériault et al. (1999).

Figure 11.1 Extract of a lifeline

the attribute's value does not change. In our example, we can distinguish three periods in the life of the individual, only with respect to the number of children in the household. These periods of stability are called *episodes*.

To define an episode, several attributes can be grouped together according to whether they contribute to describing the same "aspect" that one wishes to observe in the life of a person (e.g. the residential, family, professional, leisure-related aspect).[3] The grouping of attributes on the basis of this criterion can thus be seen as a "thematic" focus on the lifeline. For this reason, we posit as a principle that the lifeline is multi-dimensional, with each dimension corresponding to a point of view according to which one "observes" the life of the individual. In other words, a lifeline consists of different *thematic trajectories*. For example, the family trajectory here corresponds to the grouping of the *Number of children at home* and *Marital status* attributes; the residential trajectory is represented by the grouping of the *Monthly rent/mortgage*, *Residential status*, *Housing type* and *City of residence* attributes (see Figure 11.1). Quite naturally, events and episodes can also be described as *thematic* because they are linked to attributes, which, in turn, are attached to a theme. For example, E2 in Figure 11.1

---

[3] In Thériault et al. (1999), only three different aspects are considered: residential, family and professional.

stands for a so-called *residential* event because it has an impact on the attributes of the residential trajectory. A new thematic episode, defined from all the attributes of the associated trajectory, appears as soon as at least one of its attributes has undergone a change in value (resulting from an event). Thus, for the family trajectory illustrated in Figure 11.1, four episodes are observed:

- an episode before E4: the individual is single and has no children;
- an episode between E4 and E5: the individual is in a relationship and has no children at home;
- an episode between E5 and E8: the individual is in a relationship and has one child at home;
- an episode since E8: the individual is in a relationship and has two children at home.

11.3.2 Interest of the Approach for an Understanding of Residential Migration

The lifeline can be considered according to a particular theme of interest: a point of view is adopted to describe (and, subsequently, to explore, to analyse) the lifeline and the episodes and events included in it. For example, it makes sense to take an interest in people's lifelines so as to better understand their residential choices. Thus, the lifeline of an individual will be described/explored/analysed from a residential point of view. We will then talk about a *residential trajectory* in order to emphasise the succession of residential choices that have been made over time. Here, a residential choice takes the form of an episode in the lifeline of the individual and the events that led to this episode. In this context, a (residential) episode can be described on the basis of location, housing characteristics and so forth, and an event will be defined by its type (for example, a move), a date and so on.

A residential trajectory is strongly linked to other elements of an individual's lifeline. Thus, in order to study an individual's residential trajectory (that is, to identify and understand their successive residential choices in time and space), it should be viewed as an integrated part (i.e. a thematic trajectory) of a broader vision (the individual's lifeline). Consider the following simple illustration: a move (residential point of view) can be explained by a professional transfer (professional point of view). The opposite can capture another reality just as well – one that is just as plausible (professional change is the cause of the move). Beyond this trivial example, there is an issue in the representation of various kinds of explanatory factors, possibly in combination with one another and intervening at different levels (a professional transfer may have made a move necessary; a growing feeling of insecurity may have initiated it). Therefore, our approach is to represent episodes and events attached to different thematic points of view and to establish connections between them, as some play the role of explanatory factors for other events in an individual's lifeline. In this section, we have illustrated the interest of the approach to understanding residential migrations; genericity is our goal. The approach that considers multiple and interconnected points of view and thanks to which it is possible to observe the lifeline of an individual is inspired by the work of Thériault et al. (1999). However, we propose a generic model capable of supporting the complexity related to the protean character of a lifeline (and to the explanatory factors that each of the thematic points of view can have to explain the evolution of another point of view, as we will see in section 11.3.5). The work on lifelines is applicable to many fields (sociology, town planning, medical sector etc.), and our model is generic in that it does not predict the represented study themes.

11.3.3 Representing Episodes and Events

We consider a lifeline as the structured transcription of the *episodes* and *events* that can be observed in the life of an individual. Noël et al. (2017) present formal definitions of these concepts.

An episode is the stable state of a person observed from a thematic point of view at a certain point in time. A thematic point of view is concretely translated by a set of attributes that make sense to describe the theme. A state is considered stable when all the values of the descriptive attributes remain unchanged. This choice of modelling requires careful choice of the information that will be represented (the relevant attributes) but it is also necessary to determine the relevant degree of precision. For example, concerning the rent, it is not the exact amount that we are interested in but rather a range of values. A categorisation of information (moderate/high. . . rent) has the advantage of providing some stability to observe the phenomena. It is indeed useless for the general objective (better to apprehend the residential trajectories) to record a new episode simply because there has been a slight increase in rent.

In a lifeline, there are also *events* corresponding to something that occurs and is observable (Abler et al., 1971). An event sparks a transition between two episodes (of an individual's trajectory) that belong to the same theme. The event, which is also associated with the theme, marks the transition from one stable state to another in a point of view and, therefore, a change of at least one attribute value (for example, a birth leads to the modification of the attribute indicating the number of children in the household).

All the episodes and events, and consequently the trajectories, are intrinsically temporal because they are linked to a timeline according to which they can be ordered. Dating the events makes it possible to limit the episodes on the trajectories. Time will naturally play a role as a common point of reference for all thematic trajectories to allow the cross-exploitation of information from them.

Space can also play a role as a common point of reference in the representation and study of trajectories (these objects that we described as spatio-temporal in the introduction). Nevertheless, unlike time, the spatial dimension (in the geographical sense of the term) is not intrinsic to any information: while all kinds of information are valid over a period of time, not all of them have an obviously spatial character. Of course, some thematic trajectories can be qualified as spatial in the sense that they incorporate attributes whose values are information of a geographical nature (for example, the location of successive homes). In other cases, however, the term *trajectory* is used as a metaphor: to characterise evolution in an *abstract space* (for example, the different positions occupied over the course of a career can be expressed in an abstract space thanks to the nomenclature of the INSEE's CSP[4]). Thus, our model makes it possible to characterise any evolution in a generic way, whether it is part of an abstract or a geographical space.

11.3.4 Granularity of the Information

The granularity levels on which the information is represented determine which phenomena will be revealed. In line with works such as those of Hornsby and Egenhofer (2002), the importance of temporal granularity levels cannot be ignored with respect to the representation of moving objects. A first challenge is to define the temporal granularity adapted to the modelling of the lifeline. For Jensen et al. (1998), a *chronon* is the minimum amount of time – the smallest time unit that is considered in order to temporally mark an event. In the case of the lifeline, a relevant chronon may be the day; this unit makes it possible to situate significant events with a precision that makes sense for an individual (such as a wedding date, the date of the birth of a child etc.). On the scale of a life, one can have coarser granularity, such as the month or the year, to locate an event for which the precision in terms of the day is impossible (the precise date might be forgotten) or not necessarily required (for example, locating when the idea to move took hold). The model must, therefore, support different degrees of precision in dating.

---

[4] Nomenclature of socio-professional categories / CSP (https://www.insee.fr/fr/metadonnees/definition/c1758; English version available at: https://www.insee.fr/en/metadonnees/definition/c1758).

Similar reasoning is applied to determine the level of granularity when geographical information is considered. Unlike time, however, (abstract or geographical) space is a repository that can evolve over time. We do not redefine what a month is, for example, while a municipality can evolve (merge with another, split into two etc.), which makes it necessary to manage territorial changes over the long term (at the scale of a life, in this case). Here we will use our approach (Bernard et al., 2018) that allows the traceability of the changes that have an impact on territorial units (district, city, department etc.). At the same time, the impact of the spatial division used to account for the data, known as the modifiable areal unit problem (MAUP) (Openshaw and Taylor, 1979), is a second argument that leads us to suggest collecting spatial information that is as detailed as possible and consequently offers more latitude in choosing the levels at which spatial aggregations will be carried out in the study of lifelines.

11.3.5 Integrating Explanatory Factors

The notion of an *explanatory factor* is proposed to allow analyses of lifelines on which the individuals themselves can shed some light. For example, one of the motivations behind this work is a better understanding of the reasons for individuals' residential choices. To this end, collecting explanations directly from them seems relevant.[5] We propose to integrate explanatory factors into the model in order to translate these explanations. Of course, returning to our objective of a generic approach, it is necessary to be able to express an explanatory factor in connection with any topic. Moreover, we postulate that an explanatory factor can explain *another event* on the trajectory – one that is not necessarily attached to the same point of view. In our view, an event can be explained either:

- by other life events: for example, Thomas moves (*event explained*) because he received a promotion (*event that is an explanatory factor*). This example shows how a link is established between the residential trajectory and the career trajectory.
- by the characteristics of an episode: for example, Thomas moves (*event explained*) because the surface area of his previous apartment was too small (*episode that is an explanatory factor, in this case, because of the value of the descriptive attribute "surface area"*).
- or by combinations of events and/or episodes: for example, Thomas moves (*event explained*) because (1) he received a promotion (*event*

[5] This may be up for legitimate debate (potentially biased character of introspection, cognitive dissonance), which we will not address in this chapter.

that is an explanatory factor), (2) he had a child (*another event that is an explanatory factor*), and (3) his previous apartment was too small (*this episode is an explanatory factor because of an insufficient number of bedrooms, translated by the attribute "number of rooms = 1"*).

The last point shows how links of causality between events and episodes attached to different points of view of the same trajectory are established through explanatory factors. The expression of this type of relationship makes a complementary analysis of lifelines possible. While we can explore the trajectories by observing, for example, temporal successions (the individual lived here, then there) or spatial concomitances (the individual worked and lived in the same neighbourhood), our model also allows us to move towards some understanding of the reasons behind such observations. Thus, for a more detailed understanding, the explanatory factors are accompanied by a textual explanation provided by the individual and a weighting to relativise the weight of different factors in the occurrence of an explained event. We should recall that we are aiming here for an explanation provided by the individuals themselves regarding what played a role in some of their decisions. In the guidelines for the collection of data, the focus can then be on finding out about their quality of life and their well-being.

The explanatory factors may be internal or external, that is, they may either relate to the circumstances of the individual's life (as illustrated above with Thomas's case) or depend on circumstances that are not directly related. In fact, the lifeline's explanatory factors can also be found in terms of the quality of the (economic, social etc.) environment in which the individual evolves. These external explanatory factors are only represented to the extent that the individual feels impacted by them and expresses it as (a) reason(s) that has/have led to an event in *his/her* trajectory. In general, the fact that bank loan conditions are favourable can be decisive for a real estate purchase. While such external factors can be considered plausible explanations of an event, what interests us here is the fact that the individual mentions them explicitly as an explanatory factor at a specific moment. Here, too, the search for elements related to the quality of life and the well-being of individuals could be preferable.

11.4 MODELS, METHODOLOGY AND DEDICATED SOFTWARE SOLUTION

For the implementation of our proposal, we have defined models rooted in an ontology-based approach that are intended to be published according to the principles of the Semantic Web. Ontologies formally define concepts and their relationships (in this respect, they are a *model*) and are intended to be instantiated (in this respect, they convey *data* that conform to the model). We firmly place our ontologies in the Linked Open Data (LOD) web, especially to guarantee the interoperability of our works. This involves, for example, the exploitation of existing descriptions that have been proved and are available (for example, for spatial and temporal information), as well as the use of Semantic Web languages whose expressiveness for representation and querying allows for a rather detailed analysis of the data. We propose a software architecture (see Figure 11.2) that takes advantage of the Semantic Web throughout the process presented below. This architecture is composed of four modules offering features that can be called upon via the APIs (Application Programming Interfaces). These features support an approach that includes four steps illustrated by the bullets numbered 1 to 4 in Figure 11.2: (1) modelling of the trajectory by an expert from the target application domain using the Ontology Manager module; (2) acquiring the data that will feed the model through the Collect Manager module; (3) enriching the information collected through the Triple Store Manager and (4) exploiting the data by experts for analysis purposes through the Exploitation Manager module. We present each of these steps below, detailing the first two in particular, which have been the subject of developments made to date.

11.4.1 Modelling a Lifeline: an Approach based on Ontology Patterns

Ultimately, the lifeline model depends heavily on the target application domain. Our architecture's first *Ontology Manager* module (see Figure 11.2) allows an expert to easily model a multi-dimensional lifeline in relation to his area of expertise. For this phase, generic design patterns, which we have defined, as well as an approach to exploit these patterns, are made available. An ontology pattern is a high-level model that is applied to create an ontology (in the sense of a model intended to host data). The main pattern essentially describes and organises the concepts of trajectory, episode and event. It will be used to define *one part of the ontology* adapted to represent *a thematic trajectory*. The second pattern is used to characterise the concept of an explanatory factor by establishing *ad hoc* links with the episode and event concepts described with the help of the first pattern. This makes it possible to endow any event associated with a thematic trajectory with the capacity to be used as an explanatory factor in the ontology.

During the model creation phase, an expert wishing to model a lifeline

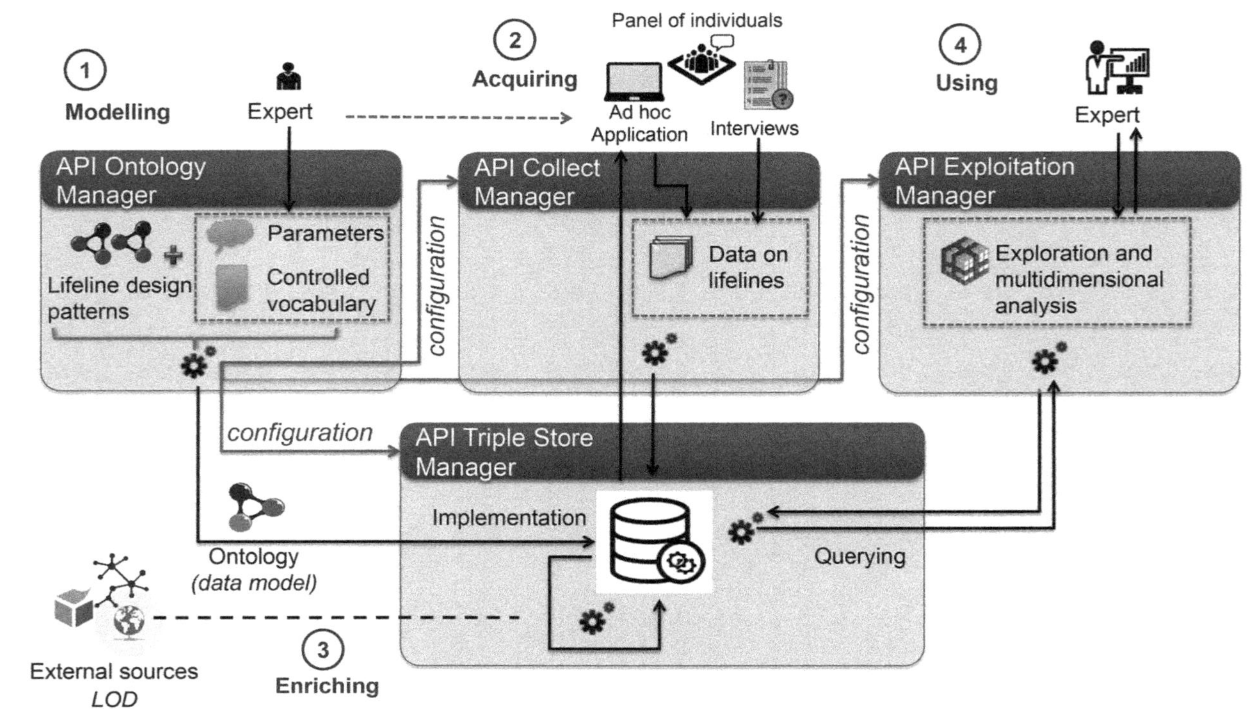

Source: Villanova-Oliver (2018).

Figure 11.2 Architecture for the collection and analysis of lifelines

for a particular application domain uses the *Ontology Manager* module. This software component offers automated procedures (Noël et al., 2017) that produce, on the basis of the patterns, the ontology (the model) to acquire, enrich and exploit the data. Figure 11.3 illustrates the modelling process that requires the expert to provide the parameters necessary to create the ontology.

The configuration of attributes to represent a lifeline's "owner" is initiated (step 1). The elements are provided that will be used to describe the individuals for whom the ontology is created: at a minimum, a code, which remains constant over time and cannot be traced, if there is a desire for anonymity, will be used. Of course, other attributes (allowing socio-demographic analyses, for example) can be provided, but it must be information that doesn't change (a year of birth, for example).

The first thematic trajectory is then configured (step 2). The expert gives: a name (used to generate the classes of trajectory ontology for the created theme – for example, residential in Figure 11.3), its type (non-geographical or geographical; depending on this particular type, the pattern does not produce quite the same ontology), the list of the different descriptive attributes that will pertain to the definition of the episodes of this theme. The expert gives a name and type to each attribute. For the latter, we can use a controlled vocabulary. This will be the case, in particular, for geographical attributes (to name a city of residence, for example, we will use reference ontologies) and, thus, to benefit implicitly and automatically from knowing the hierarchical administrative structure of the territory's organisation during the analyses. The configuration also includes providing the elements to describe the events. In particular, typologies of events relevant to a theme can be provided (for example, for the residential theme, we will certainly be dealing with *removal*, *purchasing of goods*, *work*, etc.).

From these parameters and the design pattern, the first part of the lifeline ontology is automatically created thanks to dedicated programmes (step 3). The controlled vocabulary is also automatically stored to be used later during the data collection and exploitation phases.

Steps 2a and 3a indicate that the expert will be able to reapply the configuration and generation process as many times as necessary (i.e. as many as there are thematic trajectories to the ontology that need to be created for the study). In Figure 11.3, we create a second thematic (namely, professional) trajectory, which is automatically linked to the previously created part of the ontology. In the end, the ontology produced by the module is a data model capable of storing data on lifelines that (1) are observable from different points of view (i.e. the different thematic trajectories that have been defined) and (2) include an explanatory dimension through the notion of explanatory factors.

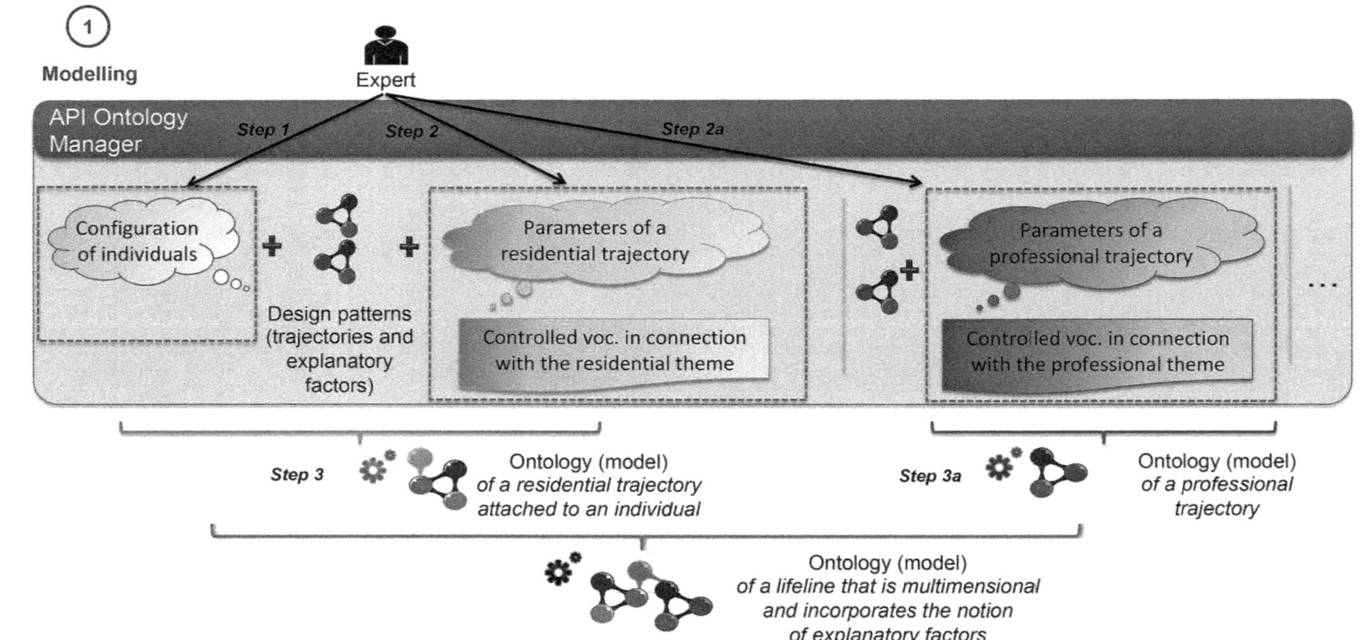

Source: Villanova-Oliver (2018).

Figure 11.3 Illustration of the steps in the modelling process

At the end of the modelling process described above, the Ontology Manager module sends the model to the Triplestore Manager module, which completes the implementation of the ontology in a dedicated storage structure[6] (see Figure 11.2). The Ontology Manager module also helps to configure the API code of the other modules in order to make them compatible with the created lifeline ontology (see Figure 11.2). Thus, for example, the Collect Manager module is offered in a completely adapted version that allows for the acquisition of data to feed the model.

11.4.2 Acquiring the Data

Once the lifeline ontology has been created according to the needs of the case study, we propose to facilitate the collection of lifeline data by providing a set of data recording programmes automatically set to populate the model developed in the previous step. These programmes can be used to process data sources such as files built to collect interviews with a panel of individuals or those gathered by harvesting social networks. The API of the Collect Manager module can also be exploited by a dedicated application for end users. In this case, there will have to be *ad hoc* developments before proposing adapted user interfaces. Figure 11.4 illustrates a proposed form developed as part of our first tests. This is to collect information relating to individuals' residential trajectory. The upper part of the figure shows the different attributes that must be completed to describe a residential episode. Fields such as *Moving date* or *Number of parts* are among the attributes that were used to set up the process for generating the residential path ontology described in the previous section. The figure also illustrates the possibility of choosing the granularity (see section 11.3.4) given to the date of moving in (here, the month). The controlled vocabulary (from the INSEE) is used for the *Residential situation* attribute.

The place of residence can be geographically localised by means of a map equipped with a text search functionality to facilitate the capture: for example, when the name of a district is given (here, "Green Island"), the map centres on the corresponding polygon; if needed, there is an option to zoom in to receive more exact information (place, street etc.). Finally, the lower part of Figure 11.4 shows how the user can enter explanatory factors related to the move (event) that marks the beginning of the episode

---

[6] The storage structure is a triplestore GraphDB (http://graphdb.ontotext.com), a database designed to store and retrieve a vast amount of data in the Resource Description Framework (RDF) format (http://www.w3.org/RDF).

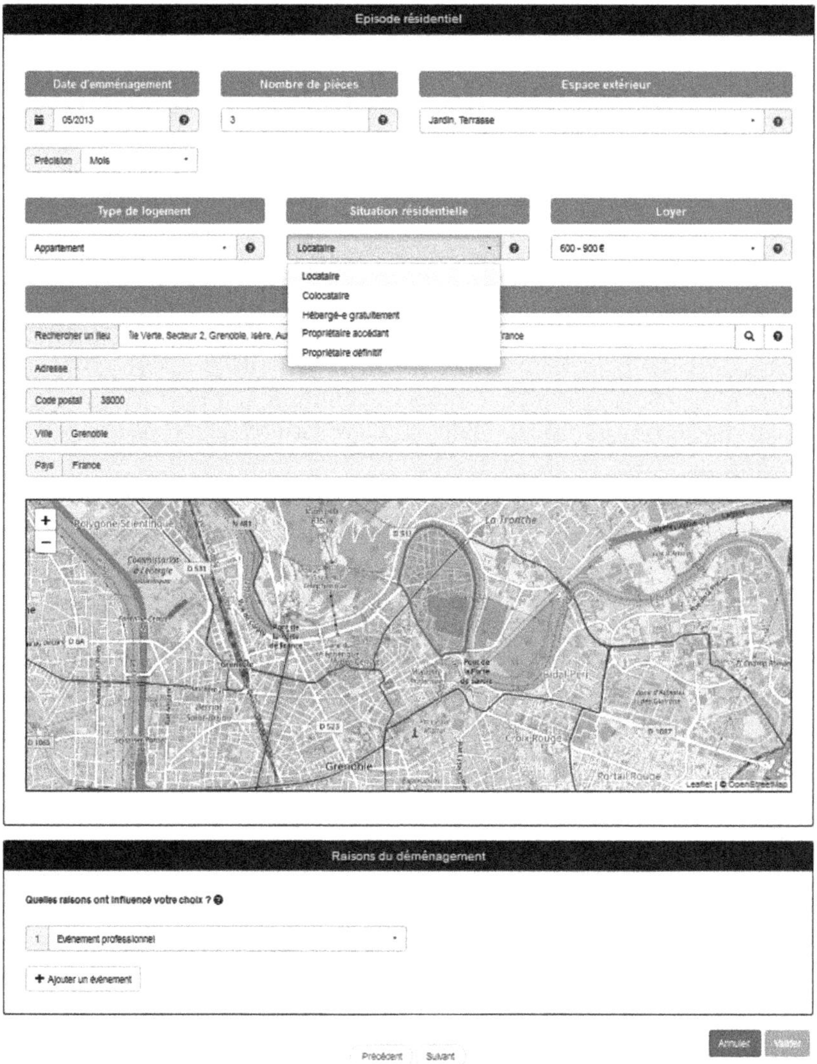

Figure 11.4 *Example of interface developed for the collection of residential trajectory data*

that is described: he/she can choose an event type from the list (here, only an event of the professional theme is visible, but it could also be a family-related event for instance) and fill in the connected fields that will then become accessible.

11.4.3 Enriching the Collecting Data

During this phase, in order to facilitate and increase the possibilities of analysing the trajectories, external resources are used to enrich the data. For example, data on territorial divisions can be connected to the collected data in order to allow analyses at various spatial scales or with different study approaches. Thus, if we have places of residence, such as cities, explicitly mentioned in the collection, we can automatically report the data to another administrative level of the territorial division (using administrative nomenclatures) and also by projecting them onto a completely different thematic network, like the one concerning employment areas. The work that we are conducting elsewhere (Bernard et al., 2018) on the management of territorial evolutions and the traceability of change also opens up the possibility of considering lifeline analyses while avoiding the issues raised by the MAUP (see section 11.3.4) that could compromise interpretations of routes – particularly those whose locations have undergone modifications of names or borders. Similarly, the opening of the Linked Open Data, LOD, makes it possible to contextualise (sociologically, politically, economically etc.) information about the trajectory. Thus, by exploiting the huge distributed database of LODs on the Web and by searching for other resources that provide additional useful information for analysis, descriptions of certain elements of our trajectory ontology can be enriched.

11.4.4 Making use of the Trajectory Data

Features that can be used to explore and analyse lifeline data are pre-programmed to search through the data. These features, which are accessible via the Exploitation Manager module, take the form of configured queries that make it possible to obtain results complying with spatial, temporal and/or thematic criteria tapping the lifeline ontology. Appropriate rendering and visual exploration interfaces (including cards, graphics, space–time cube etc., possibly combined and synchronised) can be developed by using these features (via the API). Below are some examples of what can be achieved.

With regard to the temporal dimension, the queries make it possible, among others, to know the situation of one (or more) individual(s) at a moment t or during a time interval $[t_1, t_2]$. Here, "situation" means reconstructing episodes and events observed at time t or during $[t_1, t_2]$.

On the spatial level, it is possible to know which places (on the basis of the granularity chosen for the model's spatial attributes) are part of the individuals' trajectory. Such queries can aim to compare individuals' locations of residence (residential trajectory) and of work (professional trajectory) to analyse their geographical proximities.

The model also makes it possible to know the explanatory factors reported by individuals to shed light on their trajectories. For example, one can look at a specific event in the trajectory and investigate its causes by skimming the model.

Naturally, queries combining temporal, spatial and thematic dimensions, including criteria relating to explanatory factors, are possible. In view of the goal of observing both urban migration and decision aids in the fields of urban planning and regional/territorial planning, such application possibilities will allow the verification of hypotheses that should be formulated in collaboration with specialists on these issues.

11.5 CONCLUSION AND DISCUSSION

In this chapter, we have presented a generic approach for modelling multi-dimensional lifelines that make it possible to observe individuals according to different spatial, temporal and thematic points of view (professional, family, residential, etc.). The other major feature of the approach is that it integrates an ability to explain the reasons that motivated or led to the choices. We have shown how this approach, which is anchored in the Semantic Web whose expressive capacities it utilises, is equipped from a methodological and a software point of view, guaranteeing its implementation with relative ease. We have indicated how data collection can be used to feed the ontology of lifelines and, hence, allow them to be analysed. One of the desired applications is to contribute to a better understanding of the factors that assist in defining the quality of life and the well-being of individuals during their life. Thus, through spatio-temporal and multi-thematic analyses, elements relating to the living environment, the landscape, the proximity of services and shops, the tranquillity of the neighbourhood and so forth could emerge as determining factors at certain periods in life but not at others, for some types of households but not for others and so on.

The model's complexity, which is easy to reach (the result of multiplying the themes, their descriptive attributes etc.), must not be a brake on the contributors' participation. It is therefore important to focus on ways to ensure that the model is fed with data. Two tracks can be followed here concerning the design and development of adapted, simple and usable tools that will have to be made available to contributors. Beyond a consideration of the good properties of the proposed interfaces (intuitive, efficient etc.), a first track involves highlighting the parameters that will encourage contributors to participate. In other words, what should be brought or offered to the individual to get him/her to participate? While for some user-contributors, science is sufficient to motivate participation, it is clear that others will only be encouraged by a more personal interest before agreeing to participate in the project. As a result, exploratory work will soon be carried out in this regard in order to draw up a typology of expectations according to inhabitant profiles that will serve as a guide to adapt the tools to the different populations that were approached during survey campaigns. A second track involves interoperability with social networks (*Facebook*, *LinkedIn* etc.) because they cover factual fields relevant to the lifeline. The hypothesis formulated here is that automatically extracting and formatting trajectory elements contained in social networks to make them compatible with our model greatly reduces the burden on a contributor. It is clear, however, that privacy issues cannot be ignored. To date, there has not been a tool that residents can use to collect, in the participatory mode, data relating to their lifelines, nor is there any advanced exploration tool for sociologists, urban planners and land-use planners to visualise and analyse these data on residential trajectories according to different (personal, professional, socio-cultural etc.) dimensions. Finding an easy way to combine the inhabitants' contribution with the analysis of experts in the field of urban migration is one of the challenges addressed by the approach that we have presented here.

ACKNOWLEDGEMENTS

We would like to extend our thanks to the Auvergne-Rhône-Alpes region for the support it provided for this work through the doctoral research grant awarded to David Noël under the "Communautés de Recherche Académique" framework (especially l'ARC 7: Innovations, mobilités, territoires et dynamiques urbaines), as well as the *Territoires en Réseaux* Federative Research Structure (SFR) for funding the internship and missions connected to this research.

REFERENCES

Abler, R., Adams, J.S. and Gould, P. (1971), *Spatial organization: the geographer's view of the world*, Englewood Cliffs, NJ: Prentice-Hall.

Alvares, L.O., Bogorny, V., Palma, A.T., Kuijpers, B., Moelans, B. and de Macelo, J.A.F. (2007), "Towards semantic trajectory knowledge discovery", in Technical Report, Hasselt University, Belgium, October.

Authier, J.Y., Bidet, J., Collet, A., Gilbert, P. and Steinmetz, H. (2010), "État des lieux sur les trajectoires résidentielles", Paris: Rapport pour le PUCA, Ministère de l'Ecologie, de l'Energie, du Développement Durable et de la Mer.

Beauchard, J. (1985), *La puissance des foules*, Paris: PUF.

Bernard, C., Villanova-Oliver, M., Gensel, J. and Dao, H. (2018), "Modeling changes in territorial partitions over time: ontologies TSN and TSN-Change", paper presented at Proceedings of ACM SAC Conference, Pau, France, April 9–13.

Bonvalet, C. and Bringé, A. (2012), "Les trajectoires géographiques des Franciliens depuis leur départ de chez les parents", in Bonvalet, C. and Lelièvre, E. (eds), *De la famille à l'entourage*, Paris: Ined, pp. 177–202.

Christophe, S., Davoine, P.-A., Jambon, F., André-Poyaud, I., Chardonnel, S., Lutoff, C. and Lbath, A. (2010), "Acquisition de connaissances sur les déplacements quotidiens des individus dans un contexte de risques naturels: protocoles d'enquête à l'aide de technologies mobiles, SAGEO 2010", paper presented at Colloque International en Géomatique et Analyse Spatiale, Toulouse, November.

Clark, W. and Whiters, S. (2008), "Family migration and mobility sequences in the United States: spatial mobility in the context of the life course", *Demographic Research*, **17** (20), 591–622.

Coulter, R. and Van Ham, M. (2013), "Following people through time: an analysis of individual residential mobility biographies", *Housing Studies*, **28** (7), 1037–55.

De Certeau, M. (1980), *L'invention du quotidien*, Paris: UGE.

Duvignaud, J. (1977), *Lieux et non-lieux*, Paris: Galilée.

Fournier, S., Claramunt, C. and Devogele, T. (2007), "Un modèle de raisonnement spatial contextuel pour la navigation maritime", *Revue Internationale de Géomatique*, **17** (1), 63–89.

Grafmeyer, Y. and Authier, J.Y. (2011), *Sociologie urbaine*, Paris: Armand Colin.

Güting, R.H. and Schneider, M. (2005), *Moving objects databases*, Burlington, VT: Morgan Kaufmann Publishers.

Hägerstrand, T. (1970), "What about people in regional science?", *Papers of the Regional Science Association*, **24** (1), 6–21.

Halbwachs, M. (1994), *Les cadres sociaux de la mémoire*, Paris: Albin Michel.

Haumont, B. and Morel, A. (2005), *La société des voisins*, Paris: Editions de la MSH.

Hornsby, K. and Egenhofer, M.J. (2002), "Modeling moving objects over multiple granularities", *Annals of Mathematics and Artificial Intelligence*, **36** (1), 177–94.

Hu, Y., Janowicz, K., Carral, D., Scheider, S., Kuhn, W., Berg-Cross, G., Hitzler, P. et al. (2013), "A geo-ontology design pattern for semantic trajectories", in Tenbrink, T., Stell, J., Galton, A. and Wood, Z. (eds), "Spatial information theory. COSIT 2013, Lecture Notes", *Computer Science*, **8116**, 438–56.

Jensen, C.S. et al. (1998), "The consensus glossary of temporal database concepts", in Etzion, O., Jajodia, S. and Sripada, S. (eds), "Temporal databases: research and practice. Lecture notes", *Computer Science*, **1399**, 367–405.

Joseph, I. (1984), *Le passant considérable*, Paris: Le Méridien.

Krisnadhi, A.A. and Hitzler, P. (2016), "A core pattern for events", paper presented at Workshop on Ontology and Semantic Web Patterns (7th edn), WOP 2016, Kobe, Japan, 18 October.

Laube, P. and Purves, R. (2006), "An approach to evaluating motion pattern detection techniques in spatio-temporal data", *Computers, Environment and Urban Systems*, **30** (3), 347–74.

Lelévrier, C. (2007), *Mobilités et trajectoires résidentielles des ménages dans trois*

opérations de rénovation urbaine en Île-de-France, Rapport final de recherche, Paris: Research report PUCA.
Mulder, C.H. and Hooimeijer, P. (1999), "Residential relocations in the life course", in van Wissen, L.J.G. and Dykstra, P.A. (eds), *Population issues. The plenum series on demographic methods and population analysis*, Dordrecht: Springer, pp. 159–86.
Mulder, C.H. and Wagner, M. (1993), "Migration and marriage in the life course: a method for studying synchronized events", *European Journal of Population/ Revue Européenne de Démographie*, **9** (1), 55–76.
Noël, D., Villanova-Oliver, M., Gensel, J. and Le Quéau, P. (2017), "Modélisation de trajectoires sémantiques intégrant perspectives multiples et facteurs explicatifs: application aux trajectoires de vie", *Revue Internationale de Géomatique*, **26** (4), 491–510.
Openshaw, S. and Taylor, P.J. (1979), "A million or so correlation coefficients: three experiments on the modifiable areal unit problem", *Statistical Applications in the Spatial Sciences*, **21**, 127–44.
Park, R.E. (1990), "La ville", in Grafmeyer, Y. and Joseph, I. (eds), *L'école de Chicago*, Paris: Aubier.
Sansot, P. (1984), *Poétique de la ville*, Paris: Méridiens-Klincksieck.
Simmel, G. (1989), *Philosophie de la modernité*, Paris: Payot.
Spaccapietra, S., Parent, C., Damiani, M.L., de Macedo, J.A., Porto, F. and Vangenot, C. (2008), "A conceptual view on trajectories", *Data & Knowledge Engineering*, **65** (1), 126–46.
Thériault, M., Claramunt, C., Séguin, A.-M. and Villeneuve, P. (2002), "Temporal GIS and statistical modelling of personal lifelines", in Richardson, D.E. and van Oosterom, P. (eds), *Advances in Spatial Data Handling*, Heidelberg: Springer, pp. 433–49.
Thériault, M., Séguin, A.M., Aubé, Y. and Villeneuve, P.Y. (1999), "A spatio-temporal data model for analysing personal biographies", paper presented at Proceedings of Tenth International Workshop, Database and Expert Systems Applications, IEEE, pp. 410–18.
Vandersmissen, M.H., Séguin, A.M., Thériault, M. and Claramunt, C. (2009), "Modeling propensity to move after job change using event history analysis and temporal GIS", *Journal of Geographical Systems*, **11** (1), 37–65.
Villanova-Oliver, M. (2018), "Représentations de connaissances spatiales évolutives: des ontologies aux géovisualisations", Habilitation à Diriger des Recherches, Communauté Université Grenoble Alpes.
Weber, M. (1982), *La ville*, Paris: Aubier-Montaigne.
Willekens, F.J. (1991), "Understanding the interdependence between parallel careers", in Siegers, J.J., de Jong-Gierveld, J. and van Imhoff, E. (eds), *Female Labour Market Behaviour and Fertility*, Berlin and Heidelberg: Springer, pp. 11–31.
Wirth, L. (1980), *Le Ghetto*, Grenoble: PUG.
Zheni, D., Frihida, A., Ghezala, H.B. and Claramunt, C. (2009), "A semantic approach for the modeling of trajectories in space and time", in Heuser, C.A. and Pernul, G. (eds), "Advances in conceptual modeling – challenging perspectives. ER 2009. Lecture Notes", *Computer Science*, **5833**, 347–56.

12. Natural amenities and social justice

Jean-Christophe Dissart, David W. Marcouiller and Yves Schaeffer

12.1 INTRODUCTION

Natural amenities are place-based natural attributes that provide local benefits to people or firms (Schaeffer and Dissart, 2018). As such, natural amenities are often central to quality of life and regional development debates. This has been true for several decades, but the interest in their connection with social justice is rather recent. As access to amenities – and thus, to an enhanced quality of life – may be unequal among various socio-economic groups and across space, this chapter addresses the following question: to what extent are natural amenities and social justice related?

This introductory section addresses quality of life, amenities and social justice issues in turn before assessing the connection between the three notions.

12.1.1 Quality of Life

First, although it has common sense appeal and meaning, the term "quality of life" does not have a generally accepted definition, nor does it have a clear origin (Szalai, 1980). It broadly refers to the more or less satisfactory, or good, character of a person's life (Szalai, 1980). The lack of a universally accepted definition of quality of life has led to its being used interchangeably with other terms such as well-being, welfare, happiness and life satisfaction.

Reasons for the absence of a common definition include the diversity of conceptual filters and languages to interpret psychological processes relevant to quality-of-life experiences, the collective and individual values tied to the notion of quality of life, and the complexity of understanding the various factors that have an impact on human growth and developmental processes (Romney et al., 1994).

Not surprisingly, these definitional issues have saturated measurement debates. There is a classic dichotomy, which most analysts acknowledge, between the exogenous (objective) facts of an individual's life and the endogenous (subjective) perception he/she has of these facts and of him- or herself.

Thus, research on quality of life attempts to measure the effect of these objective and subjective factors on well-being. "Objective measures, or social indicators, represent in a broad sense the individual's standard of living represented by verifiable conditions inherent in the given cultural unit" (Evans, 1994: 53). By contrast, subjective quality of life has been defined as "the degree to which the individual's life is perceived to match some implicit or explicit internal standard or referent" (Evans, 1994: 53).

An illustration of a combined approach is the OECD's better life index (OECD 2017), which is based on both objectively observable facts (e.g., "employment rate" on the "jobs" dimension) and people's own subjective assessment of their life (e.g., "quality of support network" on the "community" dimension). Quality-of-life measurement, especially when based on several indicators, is subject to debates regarding the choice of indicators, substitutability among variables, weighting and aggregation issues, among others.

12.1.2 Natural Amenities

Quality of life, especially as it relates to places, leads to an interest in the concept of amenities. Although there is no unique definition of amenities, it is commonly agreed they present two main features: they are site-specific, and they enhance local attractiveness (Dissart, 2007). Therefore, amenities contribute to quality of life – at least, for some people – and place differentiation. Given such broad characteristics, the nature of amenities is diverse, including landscapes (e.g., vineyards), climate (e.g., sunny days), social characteristics (e.g., crime rate), environmental quality (e.g., air pollution) and the built environment (e.g., architectural heritage). The focus of this chapter is on natural amenities.

Amenities provide benefits to people through the direct consumption of specific aspects of land, natural resources and human activity (OECD, 1994). However, enjoyment of these benefits varies according to the public-to-private, non-marketed-to-marketed nature of the services delivered by amenities. Consequently, amenity valuation is complex. Valuation is easier when actual payment is needed to access the amenity (e.g., a parking space or a fishing permit). When access to the amenity is not limited, valuation is more difficult, which leads to use-revealed preference (hedonic pricing, travel cost) or stated preference (contingent valuation, choice experiment) methods.

This is the reason why Rosen (1979) and Roback (1982) used hedonic pricing to establish implicit prices (in both the labour and housing markets) for amenities that reflected the quality of life in a given location (in Roback: population density, heating degree days, total snowfall, cloudy days, clear days). Their seminal work explained why people were willing to migrate to locations where they would earn lower wages: because they received compensation by a wider range of amenities in those locations. This approach has been used extensively to calculate indices of quality of life and produce rankings of places (e.g., Blomquist et al., 1988). In another classic study about amenities and migration, McGranahan (1999), using a natural amenity index based on climate, topography and water area indicators, found that natural amenities were highly related to rural county population change over the 1970–96 period.

Amenity and quality-of-life issues also impact firm location. Given the shift toward services, as well as technological improvements and the critical role of skilled labour, studies suggest that firms are shifting their location decision criteria from cost minimisation to quality of life. According to Blair and Premus (1987), there is an indication that economic factors of location, such as market or labour force, play a greater role than quality-of-life factors but increasingly less so.

Finally, many studies have shown the impact of amenities on regional growth. For example, in their classic article, Carlino and Mills (1987) analysed the impact of economic, demographic and climatic variables on county growth; their results showed that amenities influence population and employment levels. Deller et al. (2001) showed positive relationships between amenities (land, water, winter, climate, and developed recreational infrastructure) and local economic performance, as indicated by changes in population, employment and per capita income. And in their review of migration, regional economic and hedonic pricing studies, Waltert and Schläpfer (2010) reported that studies at larger geographic scales and studies involving urban areas were more likely to identify significant amenity effects.

12.1.3 Social Justice

Social justice is about the principles that govern the definition and fair distribution of rights and duties between members of society; it focuses on social institutions (rather than individual behaviour), and more specifically on the "just" character of these institutions (Arnsperger and Van Parijs, 2003). In this perspective, what matters is that the institutional constraints that bound individual or organisational behaviour need to be perceived as just or fair (lest they not be accepted). Since it is reasonable to think that people have different ideas about what doing "good" means, it is difficult to think about the principles that characterise "just" institutions without acknowledging the existence of different visions of the "good" society.

Therefore, different approaches may be used to evaluate or make judgments about policy choices. Arnsperger and Van Parijs (2003) explain four main contemporary approaches to social justice: (1) utilitarianism is based on the simple yet powerful idea that a just society is a happy society and is characterised by the pursuit of the greatest happiness for the greatest number of individuals; (2) libertarianism is founded on liberty as a core principle, emphasising freedom of choice and individual rights so that a just society is first and foremost a free society; (3) in Marxism, equality of individuals is key; and (4) liberal egalitarianism combines ideals of liberty and equality so that, in a just society, institutions distribute primary social goods (such as civil rights or access to wealth) in a fair manner among its members by acknowledging that individuals differ in terms of primary natural goods (such as intelligence or health). Liberal egalitarianism is relatively recent (Rawls's seminal book, *A Theory of Justice*, was published in 1971) and has spawned further developments, including Sen's capability approach (Sen, 1979).

How do social justice issues connect with space? Casual observation indicates that resources (in the broadest sense: from natural resource endowments to social ties) are unevenly distributed across space and that people living in different places enjoy different levels of quality of life (e.g., crime, pollution, or access to health services). Therefore, from neighbourhoods to regions, inequality among places translates into inequality among individuals and vice versa.

Spatial justice seems to have become a central issue in designing urban and regional planning policies in France (Fol, 2016). Policies that are place-specific (*territorialisées*) are aimed at reducing inequalities and redistributing resources among places to ensure access to those resources for everyone. However, such policies seem to aim less at reducing structural inequalities than correcting the most obvious disparities, with inconclusive results regarding education or employment, for example (Fol, 2016).

Depending on the social justice approach chosen to make policy decisions, a case can be made that everyone should have equal access to the same amenities (Marxism), that access to amenities should be procured primarily for those who enjoy them most (utilitarianism), that the rights of the individuals who have access to amenities should be protected (libertarianism), or that socially disadvantaged individuals should have fair access to amenities (liberal egalitarianism).

Therefore, a connection may be made between amenities and social justice by considering, through the lenses of the normative principles offered by a social justice approach, who does or does not benefit from them. To move beyond this somewhat theoretical connection, the rest of this chapter empirically addresses the amenity–justice relation by focusing on the cases of rural lakefront property in Lake States in the USA and amenity-driven migration in the metropolitan areas of Marseille and Grenoble in France.

The methodological approach differs depending on the case. In the US case, qualitative experience-based and interview methods triangulated with parcel-level tax record information are discussed in light of the socioeconomic differences between local and non-local owners of town land-based property with significant proportions of high amenity waterfront property. In the French case, a statistical analysis of individual migration data is used in combination with simulations to show the amenity preferences of household types, which impact spatial segregation as they move. As the natural settings and institutional contexts of the two cases are different, as are the methods to investigate them, our objective here is not to establish a strict comparison between them. Rather, our goal is to provide an empirical basis to show that, even with strikingly different cases, connections between amenities and social justice issues do exist.

12.2 US CASE: RURAL LAKEFRONT PROPERTY IN THE LAKE STATES

12.2.1 The Importance of Natural Amenities in the USA

Amenities play an increasingly important role in post-industrial American economic change. Despite their latency, they serve as a key factor resource in the production of firm output. It is important to note that America is an increasingly consumer-driven economy, with retail and service sectors becoming ever more prominent as a contributor to economic growth. Amenities writ large serve as the basis for creative class demands, economic diversity, small business and entrepreneurial vibrancy, tourism attraction and local quality of life. Spatial heterogeneity is evident with respect to the importance of differing amenity types. Urban amenities are often represented by arts, culture, civilised nature, urban edifice and built environment, while rural amenities tend more toward the natural and wild, as represented by bucolic landscapes, mountains, forests and water resources. It is these rural amenities (in particular, water) that serve as the basis for this case study. Consumerism and the specific attributes of location of consumer origin provide our focus on social justice.

It is important to note that in the United States there are several broad regions in which natural amenities play a significant role in community development. The first includes most lands found along oceanic coastal regions. These comprise the western parts of Washington, Oregon and California, the southern parts of states along the Gulf Coast and the eastern parts of states along the Atlantic Coast, from Florida to Maine. Coastal areas are attractive due to their high levels of natural amenities and more temperate climates. Natural amenities provide an important driver for residential decision making. Broadly representative of this fact, it is estimated that roughly one half of the US population lives on coasts that comprise about 17 per cent of the total land area (Brody, 2012).

Moving inland, water also plays a significant role as a natural amenity asset and serves as a migratory attractant. For instance, the Great Lakes from Lake Superior in the Midwest to Lake Ontario and the St Lawrence Seaway in the east have transitioned from an industrial and transportation asset to an amenity asset over the past 50 years or so. With respect to this section, a portion of this inland region serves to illustrate social justice issues that arise from natural amenities.

12.2.2 The Case of Rural Lakefront Property in the Lake States

Water in its many forms (rivers, lakes and oceans) serves as an important and interesting natural amenity to represent several key social justice attributes. The Lake States of Minnesota, Wisconsin and Michigan are home to three of the Great Lakes (Superior, Michigan and Huron) plus over 30 000 smaller inland lakes and a large variety of rivers. Indeed, water accounts for roughly 24 per cent of the total area of these three states (USDI 2017), and the bodies comprise well over 60 000 miles of developable water frontage (Marcouiller, 2015).

This latter statistic is important. Water frontage serves as the primary location for an abundance of amenity seekers. Mostly owned by non-local urban professionals with higher incomes, almost 600 000 residential parcels are classified as Seasonal, Recreational and Occasional Use (SROU) housing units by the US Census Bureau in these three Lake States (Marcouiller, 2015). These second (and sometimes third or fourth) homes are owned and occupied as private residences by an increasingly wealthy cohort of citizens.

Historically based in a more rustic backwoods culture (Stevens, 2013), early lakefront developments from the post-war era are in a continuing transition from uninsulated three-season cabins to full-sized four-season luxury residences. Indeed, some have equated these luxury leisure-based residences with Veblen goods (Rudzitis et al., 2011). Their property titles have likewise transitioned from being primarily locally owned to being predominantly non-locally owned.

This brings us to a discussion of social justice. Several attributes of the second-home phenomenon warrant discussion with respect to this topic. To begin with, an obvious demographic distinction needs to be made between amenity-seeking second homeowners and those who do not live on lakes but reside in these lake regions. With a few minor exceptions, contemporary rural waterfront development in the Lake States is chiefly the domain of non-local residents. Local residents who live within surrounding gateway communities tend to have been priced out of waterfront real estate, in particular over the past 25 years. Keeping pace with sharply rising purchase prices, annual property taxes based on value have increased commensurately. Ability-to-pay has guided locational choice in residential settings. Most local residents are not nearly as wealthy as their lakefront neighbours, which leads to significant spatial dislocation over time and local segregation based on household affluence.

To substantiate the dominance of non-locals to ownership of water frontage, we have examined several rural micro-regions across the Lake States during the past six years. To provide a method of identifying micro-regions, one key metric used involves the percentage of total housing units in a county that are classified as SROU. This serves as a proxy for waterfront homes as they exist as predominantly non-primary residences used for leisure purposes. In Wisconsin, Vilas County stands out: of the 3144 county geographies in the United States, it ranks 10th in the percentage of total housing units classified as SROU (Winkler et al., 2015). With 57 per cent of all housing units in the county classified as SROU, this location is rife with local–non-local social justice issues.

It is important to note that geographic scale matters to the identification and isolation of social disparity. As scale becomes more finely grained, household income levels become more distinct. As an example of this, waterfront properties in rural regions are found typically ringed one household deep on 50- to 100-foot lot widths with acreage just behind these residences mostly used for hunting game species of wildlife and producing forest products and/or agricultural commodities. Household income levels and the manner in which occupants interact socially within the local region are strongly dictated by proximity of residence to the waterfront. When examining regions at the broader level, social and economic disparities tend to be "washed out" and are more transparent.

To illustrate this finely textured geographic scale, we focus our attention on the town of Presque Isle in Vilas County, Wisconsin. Presque Isle has the highest percentage of SROU housing units in the county (more than 78 per cent of all housing units). The town has 65 named and 159 un-named lakes, many of which are ringed one-deep with leisure homes. Seventy-one per cent of the roughly 603 parcels are owned by individuals and families that have non-local primary residences for property tax communication purposes. While there could be locals with non-local tax addresses, it is much more realistic and likely to associate these parcel owners with non-local primary residence owners. Whereas the nearby Fox River Valley (roughly 200 miles away) is a common origin for these homeowners, the majority come from farther afield, including elsewhere in Wisconsin (Milwaukee and Madison) or neighbouring Illinois (Chicago), some 400 miles away, as shown in Figure 12.1. Note from this figure that there is a strongly urban character to these rural parcel owners.

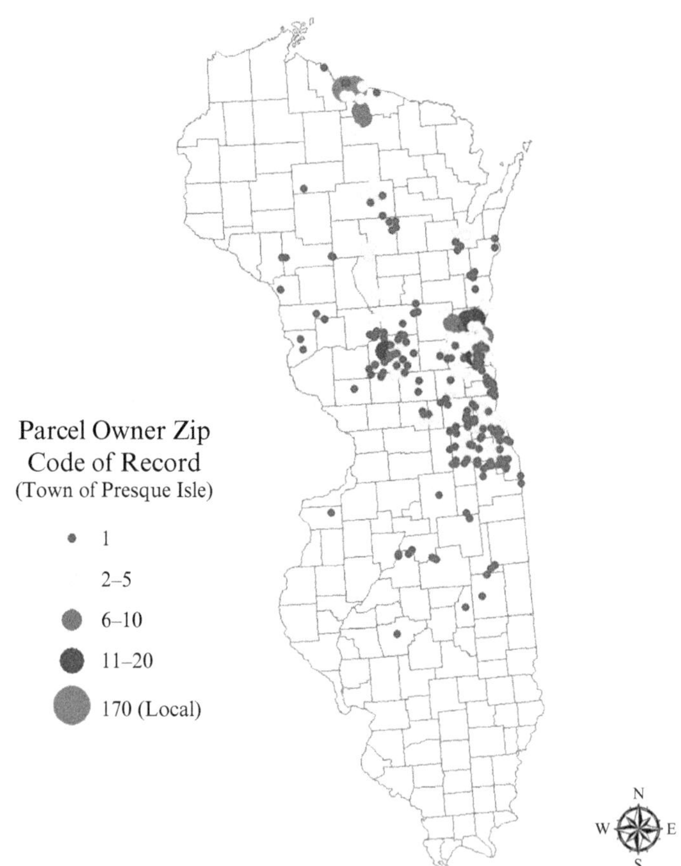

Source: Local parcel-level property tax records, Vilas County – obtained in 2011.

Figure 12.1 Wisconsin and Illinois residents owning property in the town of Presque Isle, WI

Looking more broadly, it is perhaps not surprising that many of Presque Isle's parcel owners originate from states as far away as California and Florida, as shown in Figure 12.2. While this reflects a distinctly non-local character, it is plausible that owners hailing from far away could be local "snowbirds" who split their time seasonally with the southwestern and southern states, which experience milder winter temperatures.

Relationships between local residents and non-local waterfront property owners are important to understanding the context of social justice. It is fair to say that those local residents most closely allied with non-local second homeowners on nearby lakes have economic relationships within service and retail settings.

First and foremost are local real estate, finance and insurance professionals who benefit from the hedonic premiums associated with lakefront properties driven by non-local demands. Furthermore, construction and remodelling occupations, including plumbers, electricians, carpenters and contractors, respond to local demands from non-local second homeowners. Also, local professional service occupations in the health and recreation services fields are linked to non-local second homeowners for their livelihoods. Local retail in the form of grocery, hardware and gift/craft stores rely on non-local second homeowners for a significant portion of their receipts. In addition, locally owned recreational equipment dealers who peddle docks, lifts, boats, tractors and all-terrain vehicles rely on waterfront property owners for their livelihoods. Finally, local restaurants, particularly during the busy summer season, rely on non-local customers as a demand source.

Thus, social justice issues remain tempered by the server–client (or servant–master) relationship. Empirical evidence of these relationships and the distinctions in social justice attributes has been the focus of previous research (Winkler, 2013).

Much like the hedonic premiums that accrue to lakefront properties, there are other issues associated with inflationary results of increased local demands. Non-local second homeowners place increased seasonal demands on locally available goods and services. This can and often does create seasonal price inflation on goods and services across the board. While those local residents who serve or sell items to non-local second homeowners can reap significant profits from these transactions, local residents not directly connected to second homeowners face the burden of higher local prices.

Local and state governments are affected by waterfront property owners. It is fair to say that non-local waterfront property owners, while paying substantial annual payments in the form of property and sales taxes, do not present a corresponding and commensurate demand

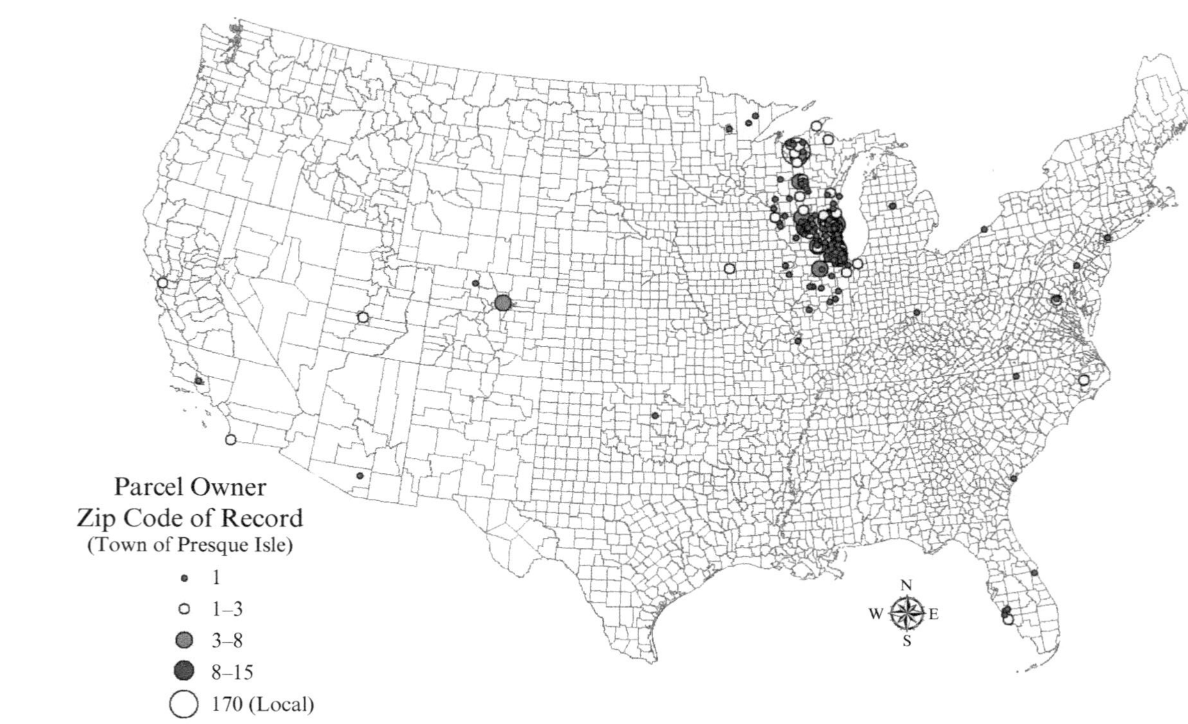

Source: Local parcel-level property tax records, Vilas County – obtained in 2011.

Figure 12.2 Location of primary residence (zip code) for parcel owners in the town of Presque Isle, WI

for public service goods provided in and around their waterfront properties.

The most obvious local publicly provided good and/or service not demanded by waterfront property owners is education. Local public schools in lake regions do not generally educate the children of non-local waterfront property owners since the non-locals tend either to send their family members to schools close to their distant primary residence or to be mature (often retired) adults without children living at home. Likewise, many second homes are located in very rural places where roads are better characterised as cart tracks that exist as minimum maintenance local thoroughfares. Like most rural areas, these residential areas rarely have curbs, gutters or pavements. Furthermore, they do not typically have publicly provided sanitary infrastructure like sewage disposal or water provision but rely on septic systems and drinking water wells paid for and maintained by the private homeowner.

Another aspect of social justice in amenity-rich rural regions of the US Lake States is tied to environmental access. Often characterised as an environmental justice issue, access to underlying natural amenities and the dislocation of local residents poses the potential for conflict. Lakefront property owners store their boats next to their docks (or private piers) for most of the warm season and use public access points only twice a year (to put in at the beginning of the season and take out at the end of the warm season).

This is distinctly different from the experience of locals who own watercraft. To access fishing and water-based recreation, locals need to put in and take out every day, as inland marinas are rare. Locals may use various public access points from 50 to 100 times a year to park their vehicle and boat trailer at the landing while out on the lake. The winter is a different story, as ice covers these inland lakes and allows locals and non-locals alike broad access to frozen water bodies to use the lake for ice fishing and other forms of winter recreation.

Also, because of the riparian doctrine of water rights, water bodies in the Lake States are publicly owned common pool resources. Riparian water rights give the owners of private land proximate to a water body ownership rights only down to the ordinary high-water mark of the water body. Nonetheless, most waterfront properties have docks and boat storage equipment that extend well into and over public waters. Furthermore, many consider the entire riparian zone and nearby water as a private good.

By contrast, locals and people who bring in boating equipment are chiefly responsible for introducing invasive aquatic species like the Eurasian watermilfoil, the zebra mussel and other introduced species deemed invasives. This has become an epidemic throughout the Lake

States and has broad implications for water quality, fisheries and the functioning of the ecosystem.

In this brief overview of one specific case study in the US Lake States, several social justice issues have been examined. To be sure, there are income disparities and income inequalities in rural lakes regions; however, the focus of this case study is on broader social justice issues. These involve local and non-local residents co-existing in rural America and the differences in public service needs, taxation mechanisms, servant/client contexts and environmental justice. The server–client (or servant–master) relationship is important for an understanding of the social justice context. Through experiential methods and in-depth interviews triangulated with available data on housing and property tax records, social justice elements can be inferred.

12.3 FRENCH CASE: MIGRATION IN THE MARSEILLE AND GRENOBLE METROPOLITAN AREAS

12.3.1 The Importance of Natural Amenities in Europe

The North American regional science literature has increasingly focused on the role of natural amenities in individual quality of life and migration decisions. To what extent has this role also been investigated in a European context? Studies conducted on a Europe-wide scale are scarce. Two exceptions are Rodríguez-Pose and Ketterer (2012) and Kopmann and Rehdanz (2013). The first two authors assess the impact of amenities on regional migration patterns in the EU, while the other two evaluate the economic value of European landscape amenities.

Rodríguez-Pose and Ketterer (2012) analysed aggregated migration data for 133 European regions (12 countries) over 17 years (1990–2006). They wanted to test the hypothesis that non-economic place-specific attributes – especially natural amenities – play a less important role for migration in Europe than in the USA (Faggian et al., 2012). Several European studies have shown that natural amenities matter for short-distance or within-country moves (Faggian and Royuela 2010; Biagi et al. 2011). But the only previous EU-wide study, which focuses on differences in population growth rates across European Functional Urban Regions (FURs), found them to be irrelevant at the cross-regional scale (Cheshire and Magrini, 2006). Using regions rather than FURs to better capture the impact of non-urban land cover variables, as well as more sophisticated econometric techniques, Rodríguez-Pose and Ketterer (2012) found that places with better natural amenities had greater attractiveness: higher January temperatures and fewer clouds, recreation-supporting or scenic landscapes, or ecosystem-related factors of aesthetic value. They stressed the importance of natural amenities not only on a national or intra-regional scale but also on a cross-regional European level. Migrants in Europe may thus respond to the same territorial factors as migrants in North America.

Kopmann and Rehdanz (2013) analysed data of the European Quality of Life Survey (EQLS) from 2007, which provides information for 35634 people living in 292 European regions (31 European countries). Their objective was to provide a comprehensive assessment of the economic values of European landscape amenities with the help of an econometric method exploring the impact of natural amenities on people's quality of life: the subjective well-being method. The subjective life satisfaction stated in the EQLS is estimated as a function of personal incomes, other personal characteristics (age, employed. . .) and regional factors such as natural amenities. If natural amenities contribute to people's quality of life, then the estimated function makes it possible to derive an implicit marginal willingness to pay for each considered natural amenity. Kopmann and Rehdanz (2013) focused on natural land covers and included climate variables. They found that natural amenities had an effect on the well-being of people living in Europe, regardless of region, and that people prefer "balanced" over "extreme" allocations of land cover (i.e., they prefer having more of the scarcer natural amenities).

In summary, these European studies suggest that, as in North America, people value natural amenities for their influence on the quality of life, and natural amenities contribute to driving both short-distance and long-distance migrations across Europe.

12.3.2 French Case Studies

We now consider two case studies conducted in the metropolitan areas of Grenoble and Marseille, both located in the south-eastern part of France (see Schaeffer et al., 2016 for a more extensive presentation of these cases and related results). A common methodology, based on discrete choice modelling of household data, was applied in both metro areas to investigate the impact of natural amenities on intermunicipal migration.

Our first objective (O1) was to check whether natural amenities are among the factors driving short-distance migration and to reveal differences in preferences for natural amenities between different social groups. Our second and primary goal (O2) was to explore whether this between-group heterogeneity in preferences for natural amenities was, in turn, a driver of social segregation dynamics or, put differently, to look for "natural amenity-driven segregation" processes. Data and methods are presented next, followed by the results regarding O1 and O2.

12.3.2.1 Study zones, data and methods

The Grenoble and Marseille metropolitan areas, located in a mountainous and a coastal environment, respectively, both have many natural amenities. The Grenoble metropolitan area is regarded as the capital of the French Alps. It consists of a dynamic, medium-sized city of around 500000 inhabitants and a mountainous hinterland accommodating some 170000 inhabitants. The Marseille metropolitan area is a major polycentric metropolitan area with nearly 2.5 million inhabitants that lies on the Mediterranean coast. It is organised around the city of Marseille, which has more than 850000 inhabitants, and the smaller municipalities of Aix-en-Provence and Toulon, each with around 150000 inhabitants and hilly Provence landscape hinterlands.

In a departure from classic migration studies (e.g., Rodríguez-Pose and Ketterer, 2012), we work not with migration data aggregated at a given regional level but directly with household data. The dataset is based on the 2008 French population census (INSEE) and contains information on each household with regard to the current and previous municipality of residence and various socio-demographic characteristics. In line with previous similar studies (e.g., Goffette-Nagot and Schaeffer, 2013), we focus on recent movers, that is, those moving house in a given municipality in 2003–2008, rather than on the household population at large.

The methodology is based on a two-step approach implemented independently for each metro area. In the first step, we estimate a Mixed Logit (ML) model of household location choice. Explanatory variables include natural amenities and other factors serving as control variables, such as accessibility to job and service centres, local incomes and housing forms and prices. To analyse cross-group heterogeneity in tastes, all natural amenity variables are interacted with household socio-demographic dummies. This step addresses O1. The second step is the segregation analysis, which addresses O2: the model estimated in step 1 allows for simulating location choices and resulting residential patterns. Consequently, we can compare the social segregation indices (Duncan and Duncan, 1955) corresponding to observed residential patterns and a counterfactual in which natural amenities have no influence on location choices.

12.3.2.2 The impact of natural amenities on short-distance migrations

Estimation results for natural amenity variables are presented in Table 12.1. The many statistically significant coefficients clearly show that

Table 12.1 Estimation results (natural amenity variables)

	ML – Marseille	ML – Grenoble
	Mean	Mean
% Forest	ns	* +
x executive	** –	*** –
x retiree	*** +	* +
x 1-person	ns	ns
x 3-person	*** +	*** +
% Open space	* +	** +
x executive	* –	** –
x retiree	* –	* +
x 1-person	ns	ns
x 3-person	ns	ns
Water	*** +	° +
x executive	ns	ns
x retiree	ns	*** –
x 1-person	ns	* +
x 3-person	ns	ns
Elevation	*** +	ns
x executive	*** +	ns
x retiree	* –	*** –
x 1-person	ns	° +
x 3-person	ns	*** –
Coast	*** –	
x executive	** +	
x retiree	*** +	
x 1-person	° –	
x 3-person	ns	
Control variables	yes	yes
# Observations (weighted)	248 203	60 050
# Observations (unweighted)	98 048	21 074
Alternatives	112	79
logLikelihood	−208 135	−48 022
McFadden R^2 (adj.)	0.550	0.477

Note: *** p-value < 0.001; ** p < 0.01; * p < 0.05; ° p < 0.1; ns: non-significant (p > = 0.1).

Source: Schaeffer et al. (2016).

natural amenities are significant drivers of residential location choices in both metropolitan areas. In addition, many interaction terms are significant, which shows that preferences for natural amenity systematically differ according to household socio-demographic characteristics.

In the models, the reference category is a two-person household headed by neither an executive nor a retiree. These households seem to be attracted by natural landscapes: they present a higher probability, *ceteris paribus*, of choosing a municipality endowed with a river or a lake or a higher share of open space (or forest, in the case of Grenoble). In Marseille, municipalities at higher altitudes – probably offering a greater scenic view over the sea and/or the hinterland – are also more attractive. Surprisingly, however, coastal municipalities are less appealing to them. The major road congestion along the coast, especially during the tourist season (which cannot be controlled for), might explain this result.

Compared with the reference households, executives differ in their preferences for natural amenities. The most striking difference is that a higher share of open space or forest is clearly associated with a lower probability of choice for them. An explanation here could be the "substitution effect" shown by Tu et al. (2016) in a choice experiment conducted in the French city of Nancy: wealthier families may substitute private gardens for accessibility to public green spaces. In a household location choice study that is similar to ours and was carried out in the Netherlands, van Duijn and Rouwendal (2013) consistently show that highly educated households put greater value on historical amenities than on natural ones.

Retirees also exhibit specific preferences for natural amenities. Forests exert a strong appeal on them (and open space in Grenoble). In Marseille, they have a strong preference for coastal municipalities. Retirees are less constrained by road congestion than economically active households, and they have more idle time to benefit from coastal amenities, so a higher tendency to locate near the coast was expected. The appeal of green amenities was also expected and is consistent with what van Duijn and Rouwendal (2013) observed for the elderly. Perhaps more surprisingly, in Grenoble retirees show a marked tendency to avoid higher altitudes. However, elevation is associated with mountain roads that complicate access to various services, notably health services, and, in this region of the Northern Alps, it is also associated with a harsh climate in the winter. Living in the valleys around Grenoble makes it possible to enjoy mountainous scenic landscapes without having to endure these disadvantages. In Grenoble, retirees tend to avoid rivers and lakes, a result that we find more difficult to explain but is consistent, again, with the findings of van Duijn and Rouwendal (2013).

Finally, preferences for natural amenities also differ according to household size. Everything else equal, a large household (i.e., three or more people) is associated with a higher probability of choosing a forested municipality. Van Duijn and Rouwendal (2013) consistently found that green amenities are attractive to large households. And in a location choice study in the Paris region, de Palma et al. (2007) showed that households with children seek the vicinity of parks and forests. In Grenoble, large households have a lower probability of choosing higher altitude municipalities. By contrast, one-person households look for elevation and the presence of lakes or rivers. This last result may reflect the specific appeal of mountain recreational amenities to younger people (consistent with one-person households), in line with the reputation of the Grenoble metropolitan area as being attractive to them thanks to its Alpine location and keen orientation toward outdoor activities.

The Grenoble results can be discussed in the context of a qualitative study about a peri-urban community on the slopes of the Vercors mountain range (Bachimon et al., 2014). This study shows that the natural landscape is one of the main factors put forward by newcomers of this community to explain their choice of residence, even if, paradoxically, their actual recreational use of natural areas is quite low. Seemingly less in line with our results, altitude is viewed as another attractive aspect of the place; it is associated with lower air pollution and more freshness in the summer, and among the newcomers there are many well-off people with children. Such local results do not contradict the quantitative results obtained for the whole metro area. Indeed, even if mean locational preferences are not significantly or even negatively affected by the community's altitude for most groups (with the exception of one-person households), our econometric estimation also reveals a significant and strong intra-group heterogeneity of preferences for this locational attribute (see Schaeffer et al., 2016 for details). Therefore, the newcomers surveyed in high-altitude communities are precisely those who prefer to live at higher altitudes. Whether they represent a majority is another issue.

12.3.2.3 Natural amenity-driven segregation

The second goal of our analysis was to explore the implications of these differences in preference for natural amenities on social segregation processes with respect to socio-professional status and household size.

The main results of this segregation analysis are presented in Table 12.2. This table shows the values of estimated and counterfactual segregation indices[7] that relate to the spatial distribution of households simulated

---

[7] The S-index (Duncan and Duncan, 1955) measures the departure from the "even" distribution for a given group, where the distribution of this group among spatial units would

Table 12.2 Results for simulated Duncan segregation indices (S-indices)

	Category	Simulated S-index		
		{1} with natural amenities	{2} without natural amenities	Difference (%)[a]
Grenoble	One-person	0.179	0.120	***49.0
	Two-person	0.061	0.060	ns
	3-or-more-person	0.188	0.130	***44.8
	Executive	0.165	0.170	***−3.1
	Retiree	0.100	0.123	***−18.8
	Reference	0.124	0.111	***11.6
Marseille	One-person	0.153	0.154	*−0.6
	Two-person	0.039	0.039	ns
	3-or-more-person	0.147	0.145	***1.1
	Executive	0.197	0.192	***2.4
	Retiree	0.120	0.090	***32.7
	Reference	0.126	0.119	***5.5

Notes: [a] Calculated as ({1}−{2})/{2}*100, with non-rounded values; *** p-value < 0.001; ** p < 0.01; * p < 0.05; ° p < 0.1; ns: non-significant (p > =0.1).

Source: Schaeffer et al. (2016).

"with" or "without" preferences for natural amenities. If there is no significant difference between these values, it means that, although preferences for natural amenities differ systematically according to household size and socio-professional status, the impact of heterogeneous preferences on segregation dynamics is negligible. Table 12.2 shows that most of the differences between estimated and counterfactual segregation indices are significant, and in most cases they are positive, which indicates that heterogeneous preferences for natural amenities often contribute to stronger segregation dynamics. Nevertheless, a few differences are significant and negative, meaning that natural amenities can also mitigate segregation dynamics.

On the one hand, natural amenities have a strong positive impact on the segregation dynamics of retirees in Marseille: the segregation index

---

be proportional to the distribution of the whole population. It varies between 0 and 1 and can be interpreted as the share of the group's population that would have to change its residential location to achieve the even distribution.

in the realistic scenario is 32.7 per cent higher than in the counterfactual scenario in which the impact of natural amenities is controlled for. The location factors driving this increase are, in all likelihood, forest and coastal amenities. Increases in segregation indices are even greater for one-person and large households in Grenoble (49 per cent and 44.8 per cent, respectively). Their opposite preferences regarding location at higher altitudes and the strong interest of large households in forest amenities are certainly behind these values. Lastly, lower but still highly significant increases concern reference households in Marseille and Grenoble (11.6 per cent and 5.5 per cent) and executives in Marseille (2.4 per cent).

On the other hand, natural amenities have a highly significant negative impact on the segregation dynamics of retirees and executives in Grenoble: segregation indices for the two cohorts are 18.8 per cent and 3.1 per cent lower, respectively, in the realistic scenario than in the counterfactual one. These results might seem surprising: executives tend to avoid forests and open space, while retirees actively seek them out, and retirees dislike higher altitudes and water bodies.

These (perhaps) counterintuitive results highlight a key issue: the interplay between preferences for natural amenities and preferences for other location factors (e.g., access to jobs, facilities, social interactions) is important to segregation dynamics. The fact that a social group exhibits specific preferences for natural amenities is not sufficient to infer that its level of segregation will increase as a result, since this group may also present specific preferences for other location factors. The two sets of preferences may be mutually reinforcing (i.e., both natural amenities and other location factors may drive a given group in similar locations) or working against each other (i.e., natural amenities may drive that group in locations that are not attractive with respect to other location factors, or vice versa). Thus, preferences for natural amenities may help counteract other segregation processes, as is apparent in the results obtained for retirees and executives in Grenoble.

This interplay between what might be called the "natural amenity-driven" segregation channel and the many other segregation channels is, without a doubt, highly complex. This is why we should expect place-specific outcomes. Indeed, we observe that, overall, segregation analysis results differ strongly between the two study zones.

12.4 CONCLUSION

By definition, natural amenities, as location-specific features that enhance the attractiveness of a given locale, contribute to the quality of life of individuals (or groups of people, depending upon individual preferences). It is possible to investigate which and how benefits are brought about by amenities and who benefits from them (e.g., providing recreation opportunities for mobile vs. disabled people).

The study of the relation between natural amenities and local quality of life may be theoretical or empirical but does not involve a judgement of justice *per se*. However, a connection can be made with justice issues when these benefits are reconsidered through the lenses of a given social justice approach's normative principles. For instance, the difference principle stated by Rawls only admits social inequalities that improve (in a long-run perspective) resource access for the most disadvantaged group in society. Thus, amenities may be connected with environmental injustice when disadvantaged social groups have a sustained and non-compensated lower level of access to natural amenities (and consequently, also to the benefits they provide, e.g., health-related) as a result of, for example, socio-spatial segregation processes or limited mobility options.

The two cases we studied in this chapter illustrate inequalities associated with natural amenities. The case of rural lakefront properties in the US Lake States shows how the presence of a natural amenity (a body of water, such as a lake) furthers inequality between long-time residents of the area and relative newcomers in terms of access to the amenity; in an extreme situation, long-time residents are priced out of the areas that comprise the highest amenity values. It also shows how amenities influence local development dynamics as some sectors benefit from the body of water while others do not. The case of household migration in the French metropolitan areas of Marseille and Grenoble demonstrates the heterogeneity of preferences between social groups for different amenities. These different preferences translate into different location choices (short-distance migration) that have an impact on the distribution of different social groups across space, which has a bearing on residential segregation dynamics.

Overall, this means that natural amenities are both theoretically and empirically associated with economic inequalities, environmental gentrification and socio-spatial segregation processes, that is, social justice issues. Regarding economic inequalities, the connection with justice issues is obvious. But environmental gentrification and socio-spatial segregation are also generally considered problematic for social equity and social cohesion. They are likely to bring additional economic disadvantages to the most disadvantaged groups, reducing their present and future economic prospects (e.g., Hedman et al., 2015), therefore their quality of life. In addition to economic segregation, residential segregation by age – as well as between retirees and economically active households – may also be an issue with respect to intergenerational dialogue and solidarity (Hagestad and Uhlenberg, 2006). And in the Alpine context, the link between amenity migration and gentrification raises issues regarding the embeddedness and loyalty of the newcomers (Perlik, 2011).

In this chapter, we do not purport to suggest which social justice approach should be chosen – that is, which normative lenses should be worn – to evaluate public policies or to enhance the quality of life of specific groups. Our findings suggest the need for a greater consideration of the natural environment in justice and cohesion policies aimed at reducing economic inequalities or mitigating gentrification and segregation. From an urban and regional planning perspective, this could be done at both the diagnostic (survey) and the project (plan) levels.

First, surveys, in preparation of plans, could have a specific focus on the location of disadvantaged households with respect to "natural" amenities, from urban parks to riverways to peri-urban outdoor recreation sites. Thus, when devising plans, planners would have the necessary information to take into account access to amenities for different household types. Also, findings from empirical research that tracks the economic and social inequalities associated with the combination of increasingly affluent newcomers to amenity-rich areas and their trickle-down impact on the local provision of goods and services would provide prospective insights into future local dynamics.

Second, at the project level, plans could more systematically ensure that the worst-off have fair access to natural amenities: for example, planning bus or train lines to connect disadvantaged neighbourhoods to (urban or regional) parks, beaches, or mountain sites, depending on the local physical environment, or making sure a share of newly built housing units close to parks are rent-controlled, or maintaining public access to waterways or water bodies in danger of becoming privately enclosed. Given the increased interest in natural amenities across the population, there is a need to better understand and develop policy responses that manage the spectrum of use compatibilities needed to maintain and improve the quality of important amenity resources. Indeed, national and local authorities act as both providers of public services and regulators of access to natural amenities.

There is a host of potential solutions to mitigate environmental gentrification and socio-spatial segregation processes, thereby promoting the social fabric of communities and enhancing the local quality of life for a diversity of households.

REFERENCES

Arnsperger, C. and Van Parijs, P. (2003), *Ethique économique et sociale*, Paris: La Découverte.

Bachimon, P., Bourdeau, P., Corneloup, J. and Bessy, O. (2014), "Du tourisme à l'après-tourisme, le tournant d'une station de moyenne montagne: St-Nizier-du-Moucherotte, Isère", *Géoconfluences*, accessed 17 June at https://journals.openedition.org/viatourism/1936?lang=de.

Biagi, B., Faggian, A. and McCann, P. (2011), "Long and short distance migration in Italy: the role of economic, social and environmental characteristics", *Spatial Economic Analysis*, **6** (1), 111–31.

Blair, J.P. and Premus, R. (1987), "Major factors in industrial location: a review", *Economic Development Quarterly*, **1** (1), 72–85.

Blomquist, G.C., Berger, M.C. and Hoehn, J.P. (1988), "New estimates of quality of life in urban areas", *American Economic Review*, **78** (1), 89–107.

Brody, S.D. (2012), "Land-use change and increased vulnerability", in Bedient, P.B. (ed.), *Lessons from Hurricane Ike*, College Station, TX: Texas A&M University Press, pp. 138–55.

Carlino, G.A. and Mills, E.S. (1987), "The determinants of county growth", *Journal of Regional Science*, **27** (1), 39–54.

Cheshire, P. and Magrini, S. (2006), "Population growth in European cities: weather matters – but only nationally", *Regional Studies*, **40** (1), 23–37.

De Palma, A., Motamedi, K., Picard, N. and Waddell, P. (2007), "Accessibility and environmental quality: inequality in the Paris housing market", *European Transport*, **36** (7), 47–74.

Deller, S.C., Tsai, T.S.H., Marcouiller, D.W. and English, D.B.K. (2001), "The role of amenities and quality of life in rural economic growth", *American Journal of Agricultural Economics*, **83** (2), 352–65.

Dissart, J.-C. (2007), "Landscapes and regional development: what are the links?", *Cahiers d'Economie et Sociologie Rurales*, **84–85**, 61–91.

Duncan, O.D. and Duncan, B. (1955), "A methodological analysis of segregation indexes", *American Sociological Review*, **20**, 210–17.

Evans, D.R. (1994), "Enhancing quality of life in the population at large", *Social Indicators Research*, **33**, 47–88.

Faggian, A. and Royuela, V. (2010), "Migration flows and quality of life in a metropolitan area: the case of Barcelona-Spain", *Applied Research in Quality of Life*, **5**, 241–59.

Faggian, A., Olfert, M.R. and Partridge, M.D. (2012), "Inferring regional well-being from individual revealed preferences: the 'voting with your feet' approach", *Cambridge Journal of Regions, Economy and Society*, **5**, 163–80.

Fol, S. (2016), "Résoudre la question sociale par l'action territoriale?", in Desjardins, X. and Géneau de Lamarlière, I. (eds), *L'aménagement du territoire en France*, 2nd edn, Paris: La Documentation Française, pp. 95–113.

Goffette-Nagot, F. and Schaeffer, Y. (2013), "Accessibilité ou voisinage? Une analyse des sources de la ségrégation résidentielle au sein des aires urbaines françaises", *Revue Economique*, **64**, 857–82.

Hagestad, G.O. and Uhlenberg, P. (2006), "Should we be concerned about age segregation? Some theoretical and empirical explorations", *Research on Aging*, **28**, 638–53.

Hedman, L., Manley, D., van Ham, M. and Osth, J. (2015), "Cumulative exposure to disadvantage and the intergenerational transmission of neighbourhood", *Journal of Economic Geography*, **15**, 195–215.

Kopmann, A. and Rehdanz, K. (2013), "A human well-being approach for assessing the value of natural land areas", *Ecological Economics*, **93**, 20–33.

Marcouiller, D.W. (2015), "North American perspectives on tourism and outdoor recreation", in Dissart, J.-C., Dehez, J. and Marsat, J.-B. (eds), *Tourism, recreation, and regional development: perspectives from France and abroad*, Farnham: Ashgate Publishing, pp. 209–24.

McGranahan, D.A. (1999), "Natural amenities drive rural population change", Agricultural Economic Report no. 781, Washington, DC: Economic Research Service, US Department of Agriculture.

OECD (1994), *The contribution of amenities to rural development*, Paris: OECD Publishing.

OECD (2017), OECD better life index, accessed 21 June 2017 at http://www.oecdbetterlifeindex.org/.

Perlik, M. (2011), "Alpine gentrification: the mountain village as a metropolitan neighbourhood", *Journal of Alpine Research*, **99** (1), accessed 17 June 2019 at http://journals.openedition.org/rga/1370.

Rodríguez-Pose, A. and Ketterer, T.D. (2012), "Do local amenities affect the appeal of regions in Europe for migrants?", *Journal of Regional Science*, **52** (4), 535–61.

Roback, J. (1982), "Wages, rents, and the quality of life", *Journal of Political Economy*, **90** (6), 1257–77.

Romney, D.M., Brown, R.I. and Fry P.S. (1994), "Improving the quality of life: prescriptions for change", *Social Indicators Research*, **33**, 237–72.

Rosen, S. (1979), "Wage-based indexes of urban quality of life", in Mieszkowski, P. and Straszheim, M. (eds), *Current issues in urban economics*, Baltimore, MD: Johns Hopkins University Press, pp. 74–104.

Rudzitis, G., Marcouiller, D.W. and Lorah, P. (2011), "The rural rich and their housing: spatially addressing the 'Haves'", in Marcouiller, D.W., Lapping, M.L. and Furuseth, O. (eds), *Rural housing, exurbanization, and amenity-driven development: contrasting the "haves" and the "have nots"*, Farnham: Ashgate Publishing, pp. 129–56.

Schaeffer, Y. and Dissart, J.-C. (2018), "Natural and environmental amenities: a review of definitions, measures and issues", *Ecological Economics*, **146**, 475–96.

Schaeffer, Y., Cremer-Schulte, D., Tartiu, C. and Tivadar, M. (2016), "Natural amenity-driven segregation: evidence from location choices in French metropolitan areas", *Ecological Economics*, **130**, 37–52.

Sen, A. (1979), "Equality of what? The Tanner lecture on human values", paper delivered at Stanford University, 22 May.

Stevens, P. (2013), "Roughing it in comfort: family cottaging and consumer culture in postwar Ontario", *The Canadian Historical Review*, **94** (2), 234–65.

Szalai, A. (1980), "The meaning of comparative research on the quality of life", in Szalai, A. and Andrews, F.M. (eds), *The quality of life: comparative studies*, London: Sage.

Tu, G., Abildtrup, J. and Garcia, S. (2016), "Preferences for urban green spaces and peri-urban forests: an analysis of stated residential choices", *Landscape and Urban Planning*, **148**, 120–31.

USDI (2017), "How much of your state is wet?", US Geological Survey, accessed 17 June 2017 at http://water.usgs.gov/edu/wetstates.html.

Van Duijn, M. and Rouwendal, J. (2013), "Cultural heritage and the location choice of Dutch households in a residential sorting model", *Journal of Economic Geography*, **13** (3), 473–500.

Waltert, F. and Schläpfer, F. (2010), "Landscape amenities and local development: a review of migration, regional economic and hedonic pricing studies", *Ecological Economics*, **70**, 141–52.

Winkler, R. (2013), "Living on lakes: segregated communities and social exclusion in a natural amenity destination", *The Sociological Quarterly*, **54** (1), 105–29.

Winkler, R., Deller, S.C. and Marcouiller, D.W. (2015), "Recreational housing and community economic development: a triple bottom line approach", *Growth and Change*, **46** (3), 481–500.

13. Conclusion: renewal of methods and multidisciplinary curiosity

Natacha Seigneuret and Jean-Christophe Dissart

13.1 A BOOK TO STIMULATE MULTIDISCIPLINARY CURIOSITY

This book emphasises the importance of a multidisciplinary approach to understand the links between territorial actors, territorial resources and well-being. Given the complexity of the questions raised by the territorial nebulae described by Ascher (1995), the research has to be multidisciplinary, even at the risk of producing a complex sequence of chapters, because there is an opportunity to enrich the readers and their understanding of the issues.

Throughout this book, the chapters seek to help readers develop a stimulating multidisciplinary curiosity. At the request of the Territories federative research structure (SFR), the authors agreed to experiment with a new form of collective exercise. They faced the challenge of highlighting the relevance of their own disciplines while simultaneously engaging in a constructive dialogue between different disciplinary fields to ask, in Part I, in what regard a resource is a resource and, in Part II, what contributes to well-being.

13.2 TO OBSERVE NEW MODELS OF COLLECTIVE INTELLIGENCE AND RESOURCE MANAGEMENT

In Part I, after an introductory chapter that presents the relationships between the mobilisation of territorial resources and the concepts of proximity and territorial coordination, the researchers turned to resources that are not commonly identified as such: the ground, with a new definition of land in shrinking cities, and the past, as a reservoir that can benefit fragile rural territories and assist in creating fruitful relationships between the territory and heritage sites. Finally, given France's ecological and inclusive transition, the topics of snow and energy are addressed – in particular, for the former, its varying value in the mountain tourist regions and, for the latter, the new iterative modalities of coordinating the actors.

At the end of this part, all the researchers observe that, whatever their nature (whether land, heritage, tourism or energy), territorial resources force the actors to work towards new standards and to develop an endogenous collective intelligence to take into account exogenous changes to their territories: the slowdown in economic activity, the crisis of the welfare state and climate change.

The fragmented contemporary territories identified by Secchi and Viganò (2012) do not necessarily imply the loss of a sense of territorial belonging, regardless of the geographical scale that is taken into account (Bourdin, 1998).

Furthermore, the contemporary strategic orientations are based on new models of cooperation between *territoriants*, who are actors attached to their territories (Muñoz, 2004), as well as the harnessing of local economic resources and the creation of immaterial resources to revive the local economy and work towards architectural and urban reclassifications.

According to Pecqueur and Koop, the use of the French concept of territory makes it possible to consider territory as the product of a particular form of coordination between different territorial actors: a non-static network of actors. They observe a flurry of initiatives and various projects regarding territories that, along with the analysis of territorial coordination, highlight the importance of proximities. Regarding territories that find themselves in perpetual economic uncertainty, their research discusses the process of revealing and constructing specific (whether existing or latent) resources that are yet to be revealed.

Sowa echoes these findings and suggests that the ground in the shrinking territories of declining cities be reconsidered. In the future, abandoned land in declining urban areas (e.g. Liverpool, Manchester, Essen, Leipzig, Pittsburgh, Detroit, Saint-Etienne and Roubaix) will be a potential resource. Her research proposes, on the one hand, thinking of the urban project as a tool to adapt to territories' urban cycles and, on the other hand, considering abandoned land no longer as mere land reserves but as a territorial resource with high social and ecological value.

Basset, Darroux and Judet also question the classical analysis of valorising the past. Here, the past as a reservoir for the benefit of a territory trying to overcome its fragilities is called into question. Thus, the collaboration of knowledge – scientific knowledge and collective social memory – in combination with a consideration of the ordinary perceptions of inhabitants and visitors constitutes a new local immaterial resource.

This idea is reinforced by the works of Ruault and Talandier, who suggest that the concept of a territorial asset be reconceived so that it can fit inside a more dynamic model. The priority is to (re)discover the economic, social and cultural activities that are often tied to the place's essence. The goal is to transform the territory into a resource for heritage sites – and vice versa – by finding a balance that benefits all.

As a result of the changes taking place because of climate change, the scarcity of natural resources and the transformation of lifestyles and social practices, territories are adapting and reinventing themselves. George and Achin observe that the transformations in tourism-oriented mountain areas concern new non-mountain-specific tourist developments. Their work proposes a follow-up of the new activities that are being promoted in order to evaluate the effects of these diversification processes on the sector's position in the context of international tourism and sustainability.

Novarina and Seigneuret note that the local communities in urbanised territories come up with territorial planning strategies, set up projects and seek new arrangements among actors from civil society to build a shared vision of what a post-carbon city could be. One of the most urgent issues to address is energy management to reduce the use of fossil fuels and promote local renewable resources. Their research shows that the differences between the chosen energy strategies are the result not simply of resource endowment but rather of the diversity of actors, their degree of mobilisation and the way in which they (do not) share the same vision of the qualities of the territory they inhabit and the possibilities of transforming it.

13.3 TO GRASP THE COMPLEXITIES OF PEOPLE'S WELL-BEING WITH NEW INTERDISCIPLINARY APPROACHES

The chapters in Part II focus on the relational resources that develop in the territories and contribute to people's well-being. This notion is tackled by using research topics that have previously been little exploited. Beyond the plurality of theoretical positions, all the researchers observe that, while social relationships are essential to people's well-being, their complexities require that analytical frameworks be renewed with interdisciplinary approaches.

Today, research and public policy programmes in several European countries encourage this diversity and multidisciplinarity to such a degree that they can lead to scientific creativity. Thus, the chapters in Part II attest to the richness of associations between disciplines to characterise and comprehend complex problems, such as the expression of sociabilities, accessibility for disabled and able-bodied persons, the integration of health in urban planning, the description of life trajectories, quality of life and the link between environmental amenities and social justice.

For Le Roy and Ottaviani, the IBEST experiment, taken as a whole, indicates that sociability cannot be summed up and understood by undertaking a conventional economic analysis. Fragility, in terms of people's income, obviously has an effect on their sociability and, more broadly, on their potential to flourish, but social ties and self-help practices are equally important. Their work shows the need to carefully consider the correlations between all the well-being indicators in order to identify the causalities between interpersonal sociability and institutional sociability.

Thomas calls into question the standardisation of modes of analysis and design rules with the goal of ensuring a place's accessibility. Whether for people with or for those without disabilities, the accessibility of a place should be the product as much of its ability to facilitate the physical movement of humans as of its ability to accommodate various modes of sharing and living in the space. This is why, in order to allow for an understanding of movement in the space, Thomas proposes comparing the usual data of analysis within a matrix augmented by sensory (visual, luminous, sound and tactile) data.

Sadoux and Di Marco examine the impact of urban design on lifestyles, health and well-being. A comparison of documents on territorial planning, architectural projects and social policies with each other makes it clear that the issue of health has returned to English urban planning with the Healthy New Towns programme.

Villanova-Oliver, Noël, Gensel and Le Quéau propose further multidisciplinary research that makes contributions in terms of methods and tools to model multidimensional life trajectories and understand metropolitan dynamics.

Lastly, Dissart, Marcouiller and Schaeffer strive for a better analysis of the impact of environmental amenities that make a place more attractive and contribute to individuals' quality of life. This is to avoid economic inequalities, processes of environmental gentrification and socio-spatial segregation and to take into account the link between amenities and social justice in urban and territorial planning.

13.4 A BOOK TO FACILITATE THE INTERFACE BETWEEN RESEARCH AND CURRENT SOCIETAL ISSUES

In conclusion, in the two wide-ranging parts of this book, the researchers encourage a renewal of methods and demonstrate a willingness to cross the boundaries between disciplines emanating from human and social sciences, as well as technical sciences, by using *in situ* analyses and conducting *in vivo* experiments.

Based on a rich array of research topics, this book makes it possible to capitalise on the knowledge that has been built up regarding territories and to disseminate it to various audiences and actors in the territory, such as tenants' associations, elected officials and technicians from local communities, as well as economic actors. This makes it possible to plan new experimental installations on the basis of knowledge and revisited concepts. It forms part of the implementation of an innovative conception in urban planning and development, as "an activity of expansive reasoning to change an existing territorial situation by imagining new decontextualised solutions and then re-contextualising them on this territory" (Scherrer et al., 2017, p. 20).

Finally, this book helps to strengthen the links between actors and researchers and to facilitate the interface between research and current societal issues, which is not always easy and has still not been adequately developed in academic circles.

REFERENCES

Ascher, F. (1995), *Métapolis ou l'avenir des villes*, Paris: Odile Jacob.

Bourdin, A. (1998), "Le gouvernement des villes institue autant qu'il coordonne, ou les limites de la gouvernance", in May, N., Veltz, P., Landrieu, J. and Spector, T. (eds), *La ville éclatée*, Paris: Editions de l'Aube.

Muñoz, F. (2004), "La ville multipliée, métropole des territoriants", in Chalas, Y. (ed.), *L'imaginaire aménageur en mutation*, Paris: L'Harmattan.

Scherrer, F., Lajoie, N., Abrassart, C. and Bastin, A. (2017), "La conception innovante en urbanisme: recherche-expérimentation pédagogique associée à l'atelier de maîtrise en urbanisme de l'Université de Montréal", RIURBA, no. 3.

Secchi, B. and Viganò, P. (2012), *La ville poreuse: un projet pour le Grand Paris et la métropole de l'après-Kyoto*, Paris: Métis Presses.

Index